D1387613

ASSASSIN!

ASSASSIN!

THE BLOODY HISTORY OF POLITICAL MURDER

Paul Elliott

BLANDFORD

A BLANDFORD BOOK

First published in the UK 1999 by Blandford

A Cassell Imprint

Cassell plc Wellington House 125 Strand London WC2R 0BB

www.cassell.co.uk

Distributed in the United States by Sterling Publishing Co., Inc.
387 Park Avenue South, New York, NY 10016–8810

A Cataloguing-in-Publication Data entry for this title is available and may be obtained from the British Library

ISBN 0-7137-2759-4

Printed and bound in Great Britain by MPG Books Ltd, Bodmin, Cornwall

Contents

Introduction

To get anywhere, you have to walk over corpses.

Carlos 'The Jackal'

Assassin! traces the sinister history of an ancient and deadly profession. The political killer has stalked the influential, the famous, the wealthy and the powerful. A brief moment of sudden and shocking violence can often produce momentous results. The act of assassination can shake empires and alter world history.

This book in no way attempts to enumerate the numerous assassinations that have been recorded by historians. That figure is incalculable. Simply listing the known assassinations since 1900 is a daunting task, for the total must run into the tens of thousands. In *Assassin!* we explore the often strange worlds of these killers, who are separated in time and space, yet linked by the same bloody baptism. From the bunkers of the Second World War to the ancient empires of the Ottomans and the Caesars, from the brutal world of organized crime to the unseen skirmishes of the Cold War, assassins have mercilessly plied their trade in human life. The following stories of cold-blooded murder and political intrigue have been chosen first, for their interest, second, for their importance, and third, for their infamy.

Exactly what constitutes assassination and what (if anything) differentiates it from murder or execution? Often the definitions blur. The terrorist might claim to have 'executed' a politician in the name of his party, while the media declare an 'assassination' to a shocked nation and the police begin an exhaustive 'murder' investigation to capture the terrorist. The term 'assassin' typically conjures up the image of a dedicated political killer, and movies in the last three decades have given us several variations on this theme. According to the movie-makers, assassins may be dedicated to the same murderous end but they are not necessarily all the same. Their motives are different and their methods often radically so – but they all murder people. The question has to be asked: aren't assassins simply murderers? Are murder and assassination separate and distinct crimes or just lifeless labels used to add colour to yet another grim news item?

Murder has always existed among human societies, and the killing of other humans has been perpetrated by many people for many different reasons. Murder is often the violent end result of an emotional outburst, an act of frustration. At other times the murderer coolly selects his victim and carries out his crime with a calm heart and an absence of conscience. A well-planned murder might even net the killer some reward or perhaps protection. No matter how bizarre, virtually every murder is inspired by some identifiable human motivation.

Assassination is political murder – for political gain. The definition of 'political' is a loose one – Collins *English Dictionary*, for example, defines politics as 'any activity concerned with the acquisition of power'. Not only does this include the political activity normally associated with the machinery of government and state but also the politics of religion, of the multinational corporations and of the powerful underworld crime syndicates. Wherever people compete with one another for power, over both individuals and groups, the use of violence can often be found as the contrivance of last resort.

Assassination defines the darkest side of human politics. Many individuals holding positions of great power, from American presidents to Mafia godfathers, understand all too well the place of assassination in the modern world. At any moment someone may try to have them murdered – to create a vacuum, to teach the world or the nation or the syndicate a lesson or to create a vacancy that may be filled by the individual or party for whom the assassin initially carried out his terrible crime. The reasons, as we shall discover in *Assassin!*, are many and varied, but two simple ingredients are part of every political assassination: first, the victim possesses some authority or significance, and second, the killer expects the victim's death to bring about some change, however small or seemingly inconsequential. Assassination is driven, not by mad passion and gut instinct, but by cause and effect.

Assassins fascinate us. We feel pity for the victim. We feel abhorrence at the crime. We are stunned by the ease with which one powerful man or woman is annihilated. The secure walls of power – bodyguards, armoured limousines, radio links, secret itineraries, wealth, influence, fame – can be totally extinguished by a man with a $50 revolver. Shock, revulsion, fascination. The most powerful men in history are as vulnerable as you or I, and any leader, whatever his status, can be permanently 'removed' by an individual as ordinary as you or I.

If there is just one lesson to be learned from the terrifying stories of assassins and their victims – and there are many possible lessons – it is that power, in whatever sphere, has a price. And occasionally that price is paid in blood.

Paul Elliott

1 The modern myth

The cool professional calmly assembles his high-powered rifle. As he reaches for the telescopic sight, the final piece of the deadly jigsaw, he gazes over the parapet of the skyscraper he has chosen as his position. Very soon the motorcade will pass this way and the gunman will be ready.

In the same city, decades earlier, a Model T Ford pulls up outside the most fashionable club in town. It closes within the hour, and when the owner emerges, the Model T's driver, one of the underworld's highest paid killers, will step out onto the sidewalk and gun him down with a terrible new invention, the Thompson sub-machinegun.

Four men, dedicated to the cause, whisper prayers to Allah. Their dark skins and jet black hair mark them as Arabs, their Russian-made Kalashnikovs mark them as killers of the first order. In the back of the Nissan van they load the guns and stuff live grenades into the pockets of their combat trousers. They oppose the imperialism of the West, and today their target is the prominent industrialist about to step into his chauffeur-driven limousine.

The feudal lord brushes away the serving girl and tastes the sumptuous banquet laid out before him. His hand reaches for the wine goblet placed nearby on the table. Only six chairs along, the lord's cousin watches intently. Soon the lord will be dead, dispatched by the agonies of poison, and the cousin, as the commander of the lord's garrison, will initiate the coup that topples what is left of the late lord's dynasty.

Fact or fiction? Myth or reality? The assassin is a familiar character in the stories told by authors, movie-makers and historians. The examples related here might be real, they might be fictional, but they should all strike a chord and do seem, however indistinct, to fit a certain stereotype. It often seems that the 'assassin' is a unique breed of killer – cold, ruthless, dedicated. Appearing as an unchanging stereotype in book, movie and popular thought, the assassin has attained almost mythical status among the general public. These fanatical killers are loners, moody and dangerous, isolated from society, yet forced to live within it to accomplish their evil ends. The assassin is one of us, until he commits that act that sets him apart. He is the hunter among a race of animals that gave up hunting for their existence almost 10,000 years ago.

As a figure within the history of dramatic literature, the assassin has a powerful presence. Shakespeare immortalized the medieval exploits of Macbeth, the son of Findleach and hereditary ruler of Moray. Complete with a modern-day actors' 'curse', the eerie play delves into the psyche of a dynastic assassin and then watches it slowly disintegrate. Shakespeare's masterly work depicts Macbeth as a military commander serving under Duncan, king of Scotland. When the king comes to visit Macbeth, his wife urges her husband to murder Duncan and take the throne for himself. Wracked by conscience, Macbeth cannot bring himself to carry out the ugly deed, but encouraged by Lady Macbeth he takes a dagger and assassinates the king. What follows is the depiction of a man's mind coming apart as he tries to come to terms with both the realities of the murder and the ghostly visions of Duncan that plague him. Even Lady Macbeth is driven mad by the recurring vision of blood on her own hand.

Predating Shakespeare's *Macbeth* by 2000 years but just as powerful and influential, is the ancient Greek play *Agamemnon*. The first in a trilogy dealing with the interwoven themes of murder, blood-guilt and vengeance, *Agamemnon* was written in 458 BC by the Athenian playwright Aeschylus. It tells the gripping story of King Agamemnon, the strong-headed leader of the Greek forces that have recently returned from the Trojan War. Ten years earlier, the king had sacrificed his own daughter to the gods to ensure victory at Troy. His wife, Clytemnestra, has never forgiven her husband for that outrage, and she now waits expectantly for his return. Waiting with Clytemnestra is her lover, Aegisthus. Agamemnon arrives at the palace, and the queen invites him to take a specially prepared bath. As he bathes, she throws a net over him and stabs him three times, killing him. She has paid Agamemnon back in blood for the crime he had committed against their daughter. But the blood-debt is carried by their son, Orestes, who, in the following play, is driven to murder his own mother in atonement. Both *Macbeth* and *Agamemnon* bear witness to the terrible repercussions of dynastic assassination. Both are potent and moving tragedies that stand as vivid landmarks within the history of Western literature.

Modern myth as propagated by the Hollywood movie industry has created an image of the assassin that has also transcended historical fact and that will likewise endure for decades to come. Our modern conception of this remarkable and wholly sinister occupation is often derived from the stories and images of the movie industry. And so the assassin, just like the estranged urban cop, the 'hooker with a heart', the feisty girl hero or the veteran army sergeant, has become just another story prop, an all-action hero with a dark and shadowy past – an archetype.

Two landmark movies have given us two separate, but distinct, archetypes that fuel our imaginations – and our fears. The plots of both movies, *The Day of the Jackal* and *Taxi Driver*, revolve around murder, but each movie has its own focus. In addition, both are intimately bound up with the events of a real-life assassination attempt. Yet these archetypes have recently been challenged by the emergence of an entirely new assassination genre, pioneered by directors like John Woo and Luc Besson.

THE DAY OF THE JACKAL

The horror of political murder has been depicted frequently in movies, perhaps because of the prevalence of this crime in human history. It is the all-or-nothing gambit represented by an assassination that often creates a dramatic hook for a story-line. Perhaps the quintessential movie depiction of an assassin came in 1973 with *The Day of the Jackal*. Almost a scene for scene remake of Frederick Forsyth's novel of the same name, it introduced the public to the machinations of the professional killer. An unnamed English assassin, a contract killer played by Edward Fox, accepts the offer of several million dollars to assassinate Charles de Gaulle, president of France. Although the assassination plot is wholly fictional, the movie is delivered documentary-style on two fronts: on one hand the Jackal (the assassin's code-name) follows a sophisticated plan of deception and preparation, while his opposite number, the French detective assigned to catch him, pursues his quarry with equal diligence. One hunter is set on the trail of another. Equally realistic is the background to the story. Charles de Gaulle survived thirty-one assassination attempts on his life during his long and tumultuous career, and Forsyth weaves his tale into this larger tapestry of violence.

In *The Day of the Jackal* the contract killer is hired by a cabal of desperate and embittered men, a group calling itself the Organisation de l'Armée Secrète (OAS). This group actually existed, and most of its members were later arrested for their complicity in various assassination attempts. De Gaulle had always been a powerful figure within post-war French politics, but even during the years of the Second World War he had been the subject of attacks by Frenchmen who opposed his anti-German stance. However, the most serious attacks on his life came after the Algerian War (1954–62). Algeria, as a French colony, had been a valuable part of the French system. But the anti-colonial movement marched ahead, across the globe. The time was right for Algerian self-determination – for independence – and this occurred under the presidency of Charles de Gaulle. The French military establishment had fought long and hard to retain Algeria as a French colony, however, and was not readily disposed to hand it over to the Algerians. Its loss, in the end, aroused bitter hatred among a right-wing alliance of military officers and refugee French Algerians. Although he was bowing to the international tide of self-determination that was sweeping colony after colony, many on the right held de Gaulle personally responsible for the Algerian 'disaster'.

The first major attempt by the OAS to kill de Gaulle came on 8 September 1961. As he was being driven with his wife, Yvonne, to their country house, an OAS device exploded on the roadside. Fifteen litres (almost 4 gallons) of napalm was instantly ignited by the blast caused by 50 kilograms (110lb) of plastic explosive. The fireball swept across the road and de Gaulle immediately insisted that his driver accelerate through the wall of flame, lest they be ambushed by armed men. Travelling at over 100 kilometres (62 miles) an hour, the car made it through the fire and to safety. The authorities could not trace those who were responsible for planting the bomb, but the finger of suspicion pointed at the OAS, already in existence at that time and violently opposed to de Gaulle's Algerian policies.

Almost exactly one year later, on 22 August 1962, the OAS struck against the president again, and this time OAS involvement would be proved without doubt. Once again de Gaulle and his wife were being driven home, this time in the company of several police motorcyclists and with a security car following behind. The speed with which the motorcade was travelling caught the OAS gunmen by surprise. But they reacted quickly. The fifteen-man hit squad was well armed with sub-machineguns, hand grenades and Molotov cocktails. When the Citroen swept past, the gunmen opened fire with the sub-machineguns and succeeded in blowing out one of the front tyres on de Gaulle's car and shattering its rear windscreen. The car skidded across the road, but the driver was able to regain control and get the president and his wife out of danger.

The investigation that followed the 22 August assassination attempt ended with the capture of several key OAS conspirators. It seemed that the threat to de Gaulle's life was about to be brought to an end. Fifteen defendants in the case were judged guilty by a military court which refuted the claim that they had only wanted to kidnap de Gaulle in order to put him on trial for supposed crimes. Some of the defendants were judged in their absence. All but one of those convicted were imprisoned. Lieutenant Colonel Jean-Marie Bastien-Thiry was given the death sentence, and a week later, on 11 March 1963, he was executed by military firing squad.

Frederick Forsyth sets his novel immediately after Bastien-Thiry's execution. The Jackal is a contract assassin with a reputation for excellence and professionalism. The surviving OAS members, desperate men on the run from the French authorities, insist on one more attempt to assassinate de Gaulle, and this man will carry out the murder for them. In meticulous detail we see the Jackal organize a system of communication between himself and the OAS that cannot be compromised. We see him arrange an array of false documents, from birth certificate to passport and driving licence. He has a custom-made gun prepared and modifies a car in which he smuggles the rifle into France. He is invisible to the French authorities. He has no criminal record and no ties to the OAS or the French military forces – he is not even French. He is one tourist out of thousands in Paris at that time. He is the perfect assassin. With de Gaulle refusing to change his timetable or take any of the necessary precautions, the Jackal has ample opportunity to kill the president. The public ceremony dedicated to members of the French resistance is to be attended by de Gaulle, and the Jackal arranges to be there, overlooking the proceedings from a perfect firing position. His disguises and false identities get the Jackal this far, but the detective charged with stopping him discovers the Jackal at the last second, and the assassin is killed in a hail of machinegun fire.

The Day of the Jackal is not a remarkable movie for its depth of characterization and its emotional appeal. The story centres on an assassin's attempt to assassinate the president of France and, although he is forced to murder innocent men and women to ensure his own survival, the character is undeniably the main focus of the story. We learn nothing of the Jackal's past or personality – it is the day of the *Jackal*. Of course, gangsters and criminals have been the anti-heroes of films throughout movie history. But, driven by passion, by motive, by an emotional reasoning with which the audience can identify (if not sympathize), these anti-heroes are human beings. Our assassin, the Jackal, is emotionless. He is driven only by the desire to collect the final payment for the murder and by his own cold and clinical professionalism. *The Day of the Jackal* is a landmark movie for its portrayal of the shadowy world of the contract killer. Its documentary style allows the audience to see in detail the extraordinary lengths to which an assassin must go to get the kill. Without emotional partisanship, it depicts not just a killer for hire but a man at work, stopped in his tracks by bad luck and the hard investigative work of the French authorities.

Later movies have covered this genre in more depth. The contract killer has featured in many, many movies, but Zinnemann's original stands out because it *is* the original. *The Mechanic*, another movie made later that decade, also explored the stark life of the professional contract assassin from the assassin's point of view. Michael Winner's little-known movie starred Charles Bronson and Jan Michael Vincent. Again the audience has little sympathy for the killer and learns nothing of his motives beyond his desire to carry out a clean and problem-free kill. The movie catalogues a series of disconnected assassinations. The audience is never told who these victims are or why they must die, giving the movie an eerie and fatalistic feel.

TAXI DRIVER

At the end of the 1970s one movie about a would-be assassin had more impact than any other, but in an unforeseen and unfortunate way. *Taxi Driver*, a landmark film for Martin Scorsese, was released in 1976, and its subject matter laid bare the sleazy underworld of New York for cinema audiences. Amid a media furore, it received mixed reviews. Some thought it grim and sick, others considered it a masterful insight into New York's darkest recesses and into the heart of one of cinema's strangest characters, Travis Bickle. Travis, played by an intense Robert de Niro, is a Marine veteran of the Vietnam War. Uneducated, jobless, bored and lonely, this anti-hero finds employment as a New York taxi driver. This job relieves the boredom of long sleepless nights, but Travis finds himself repelled by the disgusting and sleazy world of late-night life in Brooklyn and the Bronx.

Travis meets two women who profoundly affect him. The first is Betsy, a campaign worker for a fictional presidential candidate called Charles Palatine; the second is Iris, a twelve-year-old prostitute (played by Jodie Foster), who works for the street pimp called Sport. Pushed over the edge by his desire for Betsy and his desire to protect Iris, Travis becomes a lone assassin, trying first to assassinate Palatine and then turning on the pimp and his cronies in an orgy of killing. At the end of *Taxi Driver* Scorsese portrays Travis the killer and would-be political assassin as a hero, celebrated by the media. This did not impress some critics, who found the transformation of a psychotic loner and anti-hero into a bona fide hero a little hard to swallow.

The most unnerving aspect of *Taxi Driver* is that the screenwriter Paul Schrader admitted that the events in the movie were inspired by the real-life exploits of Arthur Bremer, who had tried to assassinate the Democratic politician George Wallace in 1972. Fiction has often mirrored fact, with real-life situations being adapted by enterprising writers to create interesting and entertaining stories. What distinguishes *Taxi Driver* from other movies, however, is the fact that it was not only inspired by an attempted political assassination but itself actually inspired an attempted political assassination. Fact mirrored fiction mirroring fact. The movie proved to be one link in a disturbing chain of disturbed personalities and, as yet, still unresolved motives.

In the movie Travis procures a small arsenal of handguns and spends time and effort concealing several weapons about his person. He practises drawing and redrawing these guns. He poses in front of the mirror, goading an invisible assailant. He imagines what it must be like to be a killer. Travis stalks Palatine, and his obsession with Betsy the campaign worker becomes an obsession with the powerful man she idolizes. When Palatine addresses a crowd in an attempt to win enough votes to propel himself to the presidency, Travis appears and attempts to draw and fire one of his handguns. Clad in combat jacket and sporting a distinctive mohican haircut, he is easily spotted by the Secret Service and is forced to flee into the city. It's at this point that Travis, the psychotic loner, turns on the pimp controlling Iris and becomes a vigilante killer.

Unlike Arthur Bremer, Travis fails to shoot at the politician. Instead he vents his anger and frustration on the street scum he has grown to abhor. Travis is a bitter loner, without any kind of voice or influence.

Paul Schrader envisaged the bloody ending of *Taxi Driver* as a catharsis, a psychological cleansing and an uplifting moment. Bremer turned his rage on Wallace and earned the scorn and derision of the nation. Travis turns his guns from Palatine at the last minute, and onto the ugly men who force twelve-year-old Iris to sell her body. Travis earns the gratitude of Iris's parents and the warm praise of the media, which, in one of the movie's final scenes, honour Travis as a good Samaritan.

Arthur Herman Bremer was a twenty-one-year-old janitor's assistant from Milwaukee, Wisconsin. For never-to-be-explained reasons, Bremer began stalking George Wallace (1919–98), the governor of Alabama, who was running for the Democratic presidential nomination. Bremer's hunt began on 1 March 1972. Only months before, the disaffected youth had been charged with the possession of a concealed handgun, but this charge was soon dropped in favour of the lesser offence of disorderly conduct. Although the weapon was confiscated, Bremer was quickly able to purchase two more guns. Throughout March he continued to shadow Wallace's campaign. For a short period, in April, he stalked President Nixon. At that time Nixon was on an official visit to Canada, and Bremer crossed the border to get to him. Unfortunately for his plans, the would-be assassin had foreseen neither the president's massive security screen nor the presence of an unwelcome and annoying crowd of anti-Nixon protesters. This large and vocal group followed the president everywhere he went and inadvertently prevented Bremer from getting sufficiently close to carry out his plan. He therefore turned his attentions to the less well-defended Wallace.

Wallace may have enjoyed less protection than the president, but he was not altogether ignorant of the possible dangers. When campaigning in Wheaton, Maryland, he had been ruthlessly heckled, and he began to express some fears about his safety. This healthy regard for self-protection manifested itself in an insistence that a bulletproof podium be available for his addresses, and he began to wear a bulletproof vest beneath his suit. On 15 May, at an open-air rally in the small Maryland town of Laurel, Wallace was forced to forego the bulletproof vest because of the intense heat and humidity of that Monday afternoon. His address proved popular that afternoon, and he descended from the podium to move freely among the crowd, shaking hands and chatting with people.

'Hey, George, over here,' a voice called. Again the same shout from the same direction. And again. Wallace drifted in the direction of the short-cropped, blond-haired young man who was shouting above the noise of the crowd. As Wallace neared him, Arthur Bremer drew a gun and began firing at almost point-blank range into the governor, who fell immediately to the floor. Four bullets hit Wallace and critically wounded him. The governor's security men pounced on Bremer, and as they lunged towards him, the youth emptied the magazine into the crowd, which had been pressing around on all sides. Three of these bystanders were wounded, none fatally.

The investigation began immediately. In fact, the authorities were able to discover so much so quickly that some suspected a conspiracy. It soon became clear that Bremer had spent thousands of dollars in his pursuit of Wallace, money that could not be accounted for. He had not earned it; he had not been given it by his parents. Where had the funds come from? He had spent over $5000 in just a few short months, yet his annual earnings amounted to barely a fifth of that. Rumours and allegations circulated, most of them hinting at some sort of Republican involvement. Watergate had only recently made the news, and Nixon was suspected of almost anything. But was he really involved in the attempted assassination of a possible presidential rival?

That murder attempt in May 1972 changed George Wallace's life in every way. First, and most importantly, the governor was permanently disabled. Despite winning the Maryland primaries, he was forced to abandon his attempt to become the Democratic candidate, and Senator George McGovern became the Democrats' hope for the presidency. In November 1972, however, Richard Nixon came out on top to win a second term. Wallace had previously been an outspoken supporter of Black segregation, and Alabama, the state he governed, had experienced the bus boycott staged by Martin Luther King in 1955. The segregationist stance that Wallace adopted had proved unpopular, and there was some speculation that Wallace had brought the shooting upon himself by supporting such discriminatory views. Although crippled by Bremer's bullets, Wallace was re-elected as governor of Alabama, this time with the support of many Black voters. He had been overcome by an unexpected crisis of conscience as he recuperated from the attempt on his life. He saw things differently from a wheelchair and turned away from the racist policies that had characterized his earlier political career.

In writing the screenplay for *Taxi Driver*, Paul Schrader was obviously only partly influenced by Arthur Bremer's assassination attempt. It is ironic and tragic that his fictional Bremer, Travis Bickle, inspired another dislocated young man to follow a similar path. This man was

John W. Hinckley Jr; his victim was the president, Ronald Reagan. Reagan had been addressing an audience at a hotel in Washington, D.C., on 30 March 1981 and was about to climb into a waiting limousine when Hinckley struck. The twenty-five-year-old had drawn a .22 revolver and fired point-blank at the president at least four times. Reagan was hit beneath the left armpit and the bullet ricocheted off a rib and tore through part of his left lung. The presidential bodyguard pounced on Hinckley the instant the shots were fired and disarmed him. Faltering momentarily from the shock, Reagan was pushed into the car, which sped away. Reagan was not critically wounded by the bullet that struck him, but according to those close to him, he was never the same again, and both his concentration and co-ordination were permanently affected.

The gunman, John Hinckley, turned out to be young drifter from Evergreen, Colorado, the son of a wealthy oil executive. He had been brought up in Dallas, surrounded by all the trappings of good living. As the investigation began, it became apparent that he inhabited his own strange fantasy world. The young man's motivation for trying to assassinate the president, it transpired, was to publicly proclaim his undying infatuation with Jodie Foster (as he had seen her in the movie *Taxi Driver*). At that time Foster was attending Yale University, and Hinckley had written several letters to her. Detectives discovered an unmailed letter dated 30 March that he had written barely two hours before the shooting. The letter read:

> Dear Jodie, There is a definite possibility that I will be killed in my attempt to get Reagan. It is for this very reason that I am writing to you now … although we talked on the phone a couple of times, I never had the nerve to simply approach you and introduce myself … Jodie, I would abandon this idea of getting Reagan in a second if I could only win your heart and live out the rest of my life with you, whether it be in total obscurity or whatever. I will admit to you that the reason I'm going ahead with this attempt now is because I just cannot wait any longer to impress you. I've got to do something now to make you understand in no uncertain terms that I am doing all this for your sake. By sacrificing my freedom and possibly my life, I hope to change your mind about me.

In an eerie re-make of Scorsese's movie, Hinckley had adopted the role of Travis, had sought the favour of Jodie Foster (or her character Iris)

19

and had purchased the guns with which he would vent his frustrations. President Reagan stood in for the fictional senator, Charles Palatine. Hinckley had been a member of the National Socialist Party (Nazi Party) of America since 1978, and he frequently travelled across the country. When his movements for the year before the shooting were plotted, they seemed to echo those of Arthur Bremer eight years earlier. Like Bremer, Hinckley had stalked another politician before settling on Reagan. When President Jimmy Carter visited Nashville, Tennessee, on 9 October 1980, John Hinckley had been hot on his trail. Unfortunately for him, airport security machines detected the portable armoury (three handguns with a store of appropriate ammunition) tucked away inside his luggage. Despite the presence of the president in town, Hinckley was not arrested and no attempt was made to keep him under surveillance. Instead, the guns were confiscated and he was fined a moderate sum for the transgression. Hinckley soon left the area and later returned to Dallas where he purchased two replacement firearms, one of which he used during the assassination attempt on Reagan.

While the CIA attempted to prove some sort of conspiratorial link with the Soviet Union, the FBI charged John Hinckley with trying to murder President Reagan and the case went to court. The jury, on hearing the evidence, found the gunman not guilty on the grounds of insanity, and Hinckley was committed to a mental institution. It was a verdict that stunned the nation, but one that obviously considered his obsession with both Foster and the mood and method of *Taxi Driver* to reflect the mind-set of a dreadfully unbalanced man.

More recent analysis of the Hinckley shooting has questioned some of the findings of the original investigation and promulgated a conspiracy theory that actually places the vice-president, George Bush, at its centre. Here we enter the murky world of assassination conspiracy, a world of 'patsies', of shadowy government agents, and of secrets, allegations, unconfirmed reports and establishment denials. The intimate link between cover-up and assassination has a history all its own, the fountain-head being the assassination of President John F. Kennedy. Several conspiracy theories are explored in Chapter 6. It is sufficient to note here that most provide only an alternative 'slant' on the motives of an assassin. Whether or not they represent the actual truth behind a tragic shooting, many of these theories continue to lack substantive real-world evidence and remain, for the time being at least, nothing more than intriguing and tantalizing possibilities.

ASSASSIN AS VICTIM

More recent celluloid depictions of the assassin and his or her distasteful work have added a new and flashy gloss to the movie archetype. Both the image and the myth have been rapidly transformed in a roller-coaster ride of style and nerve-pounding action. Leading this revolution is Luc Besson, a talented French screenwriter and director, who produced the two landmark movies, *Nikita* (US title *La Femme Nikita*, 1991) and *Leon* (US title *The Professional*, 1994). Besson introduces us to professional contract assassins who are human beings, who not only bleed, but weep. From the 'hard-as-nails' killers of *The Day of the Jackal* and *The Mechanic* we have reached the time of assassin as a victim, as a humane and compassionate person tormented by a dark career that mars an otherwise decent soul.

Nikita's eponymous heroine is a Parisian drug addict, who, with the rest of her drugged-out gang, is caught by police robbing a store. During the ensuing gunfight, Nikita shoots dead a police officer. She turns out to be the only survivor of the gang and faces execution by lethal injection. However, not all is as it first seems. She later awakens to find herself in a secret government installation. Technically dead, she is reborn as Nikita, a woman who does not officially exist. She is given only one option: to become a government assassin. Bullied, cajoled and enticed, Nikita begins the programme that will turn her into a professional killer. Her training takes many years, and many lessons are learned. Not simply the technical skills of marksmanship, but also the equally important skills of etiquette and deportment. *Nikita* is *Pygmalion* with a savage twist.

Her missions are conducted almost completely without forewarning or briefing. Nikita is given the tools for the job and told to murder X. She is not told why, just how. She obeys without question, although fear and trepidation grip her. In the scene that stands as the defining moment of the movie, Nikita has retired to a hotel bathroom and there puts together a silenced sniper rifle. Waiting to identify a target from the window, she listens to her boyfriend who (knowing nothing of her secret life) chats to her through the door, talking of the future. As she sees the target she must kill and prepares to fire, tears course down her cheeks. The young Nikita is caught up in a web of deceit and death from which she can see no visible means of escape. Finally, however, following a botched assassination, she manages to leave behind the murderous lifestyle that has dominated her life.

With *Leon* Luc Besson goes to much greater lengths to create an assassin who comes across almost wholly as a victim. *Nikita*'s hard edge is replaced with a saccharine coating of warm sentimentality that jars with the movie's hard-edged rationale. A gentle giant, a simple man, outwardly a shy buffoon, Leon the assassin is used and abused by the people for whom he works. Leon is an uneducated and illiterate first-generation Italian. His contracts are handled by Tony, a local restaurant owner with underworld connections, whom we suspect keeps much of Leon's money from him. Leon carries out his obligations to perfection: the 'client' (the victim) will never see him and has no chance of survival unless specified as such within the contract. Utterly professional, Leon is a super-assassin – silent, deadly, untraceable. Unlike Nikita, he has great flexibility in his approach and uses guile and cunning to get into a killing position and then escape.

Scenes from Leon's personal life provide the most memorable moments in the movie. Although he earns thousands of dollars for each hit, Leon lives in a sparse and tiny apartment, alone except for his beloved house plant. He says little, never curses and drinks copious amounts of milk. Leon has the blood of many people on his hands, but it is impossible not to feel a great sympathy with his character. 'No women, no kids ...' is a self-imposed limitation that Leon places on each and every contract.

When Leon takes in a twelve-year-old girl called Mathilda whose parents were murdered in a drugs war, the story retains its credibility. We are in no doubt that Leon is a 'good guy' and that he really would protect this little girl, despite the problems this will cause him. Her vendetta against Stansfield, a corrupt cop who killed her family, leads Leon to give her first advice and then training. She wants to be a 'cleaner' (a hit man) just like him.

Hollywood typically portrays the contract killer as a hard-edged unemotional machine. Most often he is an anti-hero, a character who leads a questionable life but who is forced to perform good deeds by circumstance. Leon is a real hero, with a simple charm, honesty and integrity that belies his deadly profession. The movie is less about his job than about his relationship with Mathilda. Their love and their willingness to die for each other transforms *Leon* from all-action movie to romantic drama. In the penultimate scene Leon saves Mathilda's life, but is then tragically killed by the evil and sadistic Stansfield. Luc Besson has flipped the common conception of the hit man, who here appears as the blameless protagonist, and installed a police officer (Stansfield) as the movie's evil antagonist.

With all the visual style and elegance of *Leon*, the 1995 movie *Crying Freeman* (director Christophe Gans) presents us with the story of a professional killer who is a true hero. *Crying Freeman* is unusual, being a live-action remake of a Japanese animated story. By no means simply 'cartoons', these animated movies (known in Japan as *anime*) pursue adult stories with adult themes. The 'Freeman' is a Chinese assassin, a unique and mystical killer who pursues his victims across the globe. He is a member of an élite Chinese warrior cult called the Sons of the Dragon, a super-secret sect that has vowed to protect the Chinese people throughout the ages. Today that threat comes from the powerful Japanese Yakuza crime syndicate, and the Freeman is dispatched to eliminate a number of key individuals.

The Freeman weeps each time he murders his victim. The profession and his elevated status within the cult have been forced upon him. When his face is seen by a young woman during an assassination, he is ordered to eliminate her in turn. But she has watched him weep over the body of his victim and has fallen in love with him. He discovers this, and the two lovers have then to face the wrath of the Yakuza, who desire revenge, and the Sons of the Dragon, who desire anonymity. Hero, lover, victim – the Freeman is all of these, despite also being a professional killer. He is sensitive and emotional – driven by duty, but riven by guilt and anguish.

A modern audience is sophisticated enough to appreciate that a deadly assassin might actually have a personal life worth exploring. Today's world has been almost purged of good versus evil symbolism, 'black and white' characterization and the notion that 'bad guys always lose'. With these barriers shattered, directors are able to peer into those darker recesses of the human psyche. We know that even the bad guys have their motivations, and modern movie-making now has the freedom to gives us a glimpse of life 'on the other side'. In Hong Kong cinema this is nothing new. The director John Woo has revolutionized the action movie genre, and his heroes are often tough cops going after Triad killers. Alternatively, he depicts Triad killers fighting for honour among themselves on the streets of Hong Kong. Visually breathtaking and packed full of pathos, the movies of Luc Besson, Christophe Gans and John Woo offer a powerful assassination mythology, transforming the professional killer from antagonist to icon.

2. Imperial Rome

olitical life in the Roman Empire was a game played for high stakes. The empire was the known world, and whoever controlled its vast collection of conquered provinces effectively controlled that world. If a contender for the throne actually managed to fight off his rivals to claim the throne, he soon discovered that getting there had been only half the battle. Jealousies, rivalries, petty bickering, wars, disease and the changing loyalties of the Roman legions all conspired against an emperor to bring him down. Relatively few died peacefully in their beds with a nominated heir waiting to step into their shoes.

Politics was a game that the Romans always played well, and assassination proved to be a useful method of ensuring success. Initially used in a piecemeal fashion (as was the norm in ancient societies), political murder later gained a strange acceptance. Under the Roman republic, where all powerful men had a chance to share in the riches of government, assassinations were rare. When the system began to break down, political killings were legitimized as 'proscriptions'. These were lists of political enemies targeted for exile by the ruler of the day. They served a two-fold purpose. First, they eliminated a rival (or potential rival) and second, they provided a free and easy source of income from the victim's villas and estates.

Wielding the proscription in Republican times with horrific effect was an aristocrat called Sulla (138–78 BC). Sulla was an ambitious senator, who had fought a savage civil war in 82 BC and then taken his legions into Rome. As dictator and undisputed master of Rome, he initiated a campaign of selective assassination. Initially, he began with indiscriminate murders, but soon systematized the killings by posting up lists of his political opponents with a fixed bounty. One ancient writer, Orosius, estimated that as many as 9000 senators and other wealthy Romans were murdered on the orders of Sulla. Guarding against revenge, the dictator also debarred the sons and grandsons of his victims from taking up political office. From the households of the dead men, the dictator freed 10,000 slaves and formed them into a private and unofficial bodyguard called the Cornelii. Sulla feared everyone and trusted no one. He retired from political life in 79 BC, and the rising stars of Roman politics, Julius Caesar and Pompey the Great, began to forge their own destiny. Both would die ignominiously at the hands of assassins.

THE MURDER OF POMPEY

In Sulla's wake, three men rose to power who would dominate politics for two decades. They were Julius Caesar (100–44 BC), Crassus (c.115–53 BC) and Pompey the Great (106–48 BC). Pompey had commanded armies in the service of Rome and was both an influential politician and an able general. His commander-in-chief during the civil war had been Sulla. He had helped to crush the slave revolt of Spartacus and had sailed around the eastern Mediterranean in his campaign to defeat the pirates of Asia Minor. One of his greatest military triumphs was the defeat of Mithridates VI, king of Pontus.

In 53 BC the rivalry between Caesar and Pompey increased when the third member of the Triumvirate, the wealthy Crassus, died in battle. Fearful of unchecked power and afraid of Caesar, the Senate backed Pompey in his rivalry with the illustrious general. The antagonism developed into open conflict, and when Caesar brought his troops, fresh from the Gallic Wars, into Italy and across the River Rubicon, the open struggle for power began. Pompey and Caesar were locking horns and only one would survive unscathed. Pompey had command of greater numbers, yet Caesar was undoubtedly the superior tactician and always kept one step ahead of his rival.

At Pharsalus on 9 August 48 BC the two armies clashed and the civil war came to a head. The struggle tore at the heart of Roman society as families fought on opposing sides. Pompey enjoyed numerical superiority with almost 50,000 infantry against Caesar's 22,000, but Caesar's military skill proved to be Pompey's undoing as his troops were slaughtered and then fled. Over 20,000 of his soldiers surrendered, while 15,000 were wounded or killed. The rest fled the battlefield, and Pompey, disgraced by the defeat, was one of them. In victory Caesar was magnanimous. Those who surrendered were spared, and the noble Marcus Brutus, who had fought with Pompey, was to be captured alive or allowed to flee if this was not possible. This decision was to have terrible consequences for the future. Pompey fled across the Mediterranean to Egypt, where armies still loyal to him were waiting. It is also possible that he considered drawing the Egyptians into the conflict.

At Mytilene, *en route* to Egypt, Pompey met up with his wife Cornelia; who urged him to stay. But Pompey insisted on continuing. His advice to Cornelia and her entourage was to surrender to Caesar without fear, and he allayed her concerns with the words: 'Caesar is a man of great goodness and clemency.' When he arrived at Alexandria, capital of Egypt, Pompey anchored the vessels of his tiny squadron. The young pharaoh, Ptolemy XII, brother of Cleopatra, dispatched a boat to bring the defeated Roman general ashore. Caught in a bind, Ptolemy's advisers had been forced to choose a side. While Pompey rode at anchor waiting for Ptolemy's boat, they chose Caesar. Pompey's fate was sealed. As he stepped into the small craft that would ferry him to the royal palace in Alexandria, Pothinus, the eunuch vizier of pharaoh, gave the signal for the assassins to strike. Several servants lunged forward and stabbed the general to death.

When Caesar landed at Alexandria some time later, the Egyptian leaders presented him with the severed head of Pompey. Caesar turned away in tears. He could not know that he would soon face an equally ignominious end at the hand of his own friends and colleagues.

THE MURDER OF CAESAR

> Brutus was elected Consul
> When he sent the kings away;
> Caesar sent the Consuls packing,
> Caesar is our King today.
> > *Graffiti written on Caesar's statue*

The Roman people despised and feared kingship. So terrible had been the legacy of the ancient kings of Rome that the Romans greatly valued their republican system of government. It little resembled the democratic form of government that most Western powers enjoy today. Political power was jealously held by a small number of ancient and highly revered noble families dwelling in and around Rome. The men of these patrician families were granted the right to sit on Rome's Senate, and they spent much of their time fighting bitterly for public office. Practically all Rome's important civil offices, from the chief of aqueducts to the head of the state religion, were held by members of the senatorial families. In military circles, too, the privileged few competed for votes so that they might command a Roman legion. All these offices were temporary, and all were steps on the ladder to ultimate power, the consulship. Few ever made it to the top of this ladder. Two consuls were elected each year, and the posts were undoubtedly the most prestigious that a senator could hold during his career. The consuls acted as Rome's leaders, with the power of one counterbalancing the power of the other. Thus the despotic tendencies of kingship were held in check – or so the Romans believed.

Although a number of ambitious senators had, over the years, sought to monopolize power and attempt effectively to rule Rome alone, it was actually Julius Caesar who destroyed the republican system. The legal loophole that Caesar employed was the emergency office of 'dictator'. To Romans, a dictator was not a tyrannical despot, but a consul who, in times of war, temporarily became the sole head of government. The crucial word here is 'temporarily'. The senators recognized the need for clear and decisive leadership in times of emergency, but they would relinquish their power to a single man only in the knowledge that it would soon be handed back. Julius Caesar used pretext to hang on to the dictatorship, until in February 44 BC, he became dictator for life. The power-hungry, prestige-orientated senators suddenly found the ladder of opportunity (technically called the *cursus honororum*, the circuit of honours) curtailed. Caesar now had a great number of wealthy and powerful enemies who nursed bitter jealousies.

As dictator and sole ruler of Rome, Caesar had honours heaped upon him. Now that he was in total command of Rome's entire legionary army, he could be challenged neither politically nor militarily. He had recently defeated the two most powerful men Crassus and Pompey – with whom the Senate might have sought to oppose him Any open show of defiance to Caesar would be crushed by force. The Senate pandered to Caesar and although he refused title after title, he did accept honour after honour. A statue of Caesar was placed alongside those of Rome's ancient kings, and another statue depicted the dictator standing astride the world. The month known to Romans as *Quinctilis* was even renamed in his honour and became known as *Julius* (July). A golden throne was set up in the Senate house. Caesar was awarded a triumphal robe, and his head appeared on Roman coins, a practice that until then had been current only in the East, where kings were regarded as gods.

That Caesar was beginning to associate himself with the gods is clear. His great hero, Alexander the Great (356–323 BC), had considered himself to be the son of Zeus-Ammon, king of the gods. Julius Caesar had a temple erected to the personification of his own 'Clemency', and a powerful college of priests, the Julian Luperci, was established in his name. A priest was even appointed to him in connection with his new title, Jupiter Julius. The dictator did nothing to appease an increasingly fearful Senate. When senators appeared before him to award him some honour or other, he would refuse to stand and greet them. In this way he would sit and accept the deputation as a Roman gentleman would receive his clients come to beg favours from a powerful patron. Such lack of courtesy rankled with the nobles, who greatly appreciated outward displays of respect.

One final act remained, the completion of which would eradicate the ancient traditions of the Roman republic. That act was for Caesar to proclaim himself king, a momentous step that would undoubtedly be an all-or-nothing gamble. Would he take that final step and overturn five centuries of Roman history? Rumours abounded that he planned to move the capital from Rome to Egypt and marry Queen Cleopatra, leaving his friends to rule Rome. As if to further fuel such rumours, Caesar is said to have acted improperly during an incident in Rome. Returning from a festival on the Alban Hill, Caesar passed by his statue while in the company of two tribunes. A member of the public had placed a royal white fillet, symbol of kingship, upon the statue's head and the tribunes immediately removed the scandalous item and made arrangements for the offender to be imprisoned. It was reported that Julius Caesar severely reprimanded the two men for their hasty actions, and thus the rumours continued that the dictator desired, more than anything else, to become king of Rome. In his defence Caesar declared that the two tribunes had not given him an opportunity to remove the fillet himself and thus prove to the people his genuine disgust of kingship. But the mood of a small group of desperate senators could not easily be swayed by such flimsy arguments.

Today historians cannot agree on the motivations and objectives of Julius Caesar. He knew the perils of kingship all too well and was aware of the Roman mistrust, even hatred, of that particular institution. And yet he openly scorned the previous political high-flier, Sulla, who had, like Caesar, been able to monopolize power with a continuing series of dictatorships. Sulla had relinquished the dictatorship of his own free will, an act that Caesar always considered to be foolhardy and short-sighted. Most likely, Julius Caesar himself did not yet know what form his autocratic power might take in the future. He was engaged in planning a large-scale military campaign that would drive back the immense Parthian Empire in the East. As a general without equal in the ancient world, Caesar's plans for the future governance of Rome were probably secondary to those of his forthcoming military venture. The Parthian campaign again prompted rumours of Caesar's imminent coronation. Even the Roman writer Suetonius, writing only a century or so later, could not be certain about Caesar's bid for kingship. Whatever the facts, there were wild rumours that a friend of Caesar's, Lucius Cotta, was to announce the decision of the keepers of the Sibylline Books (Rome's prophetic texts) that Julius Caesar should be proclaimed king. For the Sibylline Books stated clearly that 'only a king can conquer the Parthians'.

To an alarmed clique of powerful patricians, Julius Caesar was a dangerous tyrant, a would-be king and a man who would grind the traditions of the republic and the senatorial system into the dust. It was the custom for Roman leaders to pardon their opponents once they had achieved power, in order that they might be recruited to the cause and further nullify opposition. Caesar's political opponents refused to accept such proposals, however, and their hostility continued to grow. Plans were undertaken to have him assassinated. Initially there were several tiny factions who burned with hatred, but as their presence became known to one another (so writes Suetonius), they united and planned the murder of Julius Caesar together. In total there were more than sixty conspirators involved in the plot, and they were led by Gaius Cassius, Marcus Brutus and Decimus Brutus. Marcus Brutus came from a well-established Roman family, and it was one of the family ancestors who had actually exiled the last king of Rome, Tarquinius Superbus, in 510 BC. He was brought into the plot by Gaius Cassius, who also recruited a number of other influential senators. Some had lost money from tax-collection schemes in the Roman provinces after Caesar had implemented certain restrictions. They were not happy. Also lending their weight to the plot were a number of his own generals, who were dissatisfied with the distribution of booty from the recently fought wars.

Although there were so many willing hands involved in the plot, the conspiracy held together and Caesar's information network failed to detect it. Several plans were formulated by the conspirators, all involving the shock of surprise as well as the drawn dagger. Speed was required, for Caesar's imminent military campaign against the Parthian Empire, although vast in scale, would undoubtedly bring the general glorious victory and vast wealth. If Julius Caesar had plans for kingship, they would have to wait until his triumphant return to Rome and by that time no one could realistically oppose him. Caesar had to be killed before he left for the East. Eventually the conspirators settled on a plan to kill Caesar at a meeting of the Senate on 15 March, the date known to Romans as the Ides.

With such a groundswell of opposition to his autocracy, Caesar seems to have been forewarned of his impending doom, if only from a series of bad omens. The warning of the soothsayer to 'beware the Ides of March' is legendary, and mentioned by several Roman writers – Suetonius, Plutarch and Appian. He was a man well aware of his own mortality, and wondered not how soon his death would come but what sort of death he should expect. At a dinner party held on the eve of his assassination, when the conversation turned to the subject of death, Caesar cried, 'Let it come swiftly and unexpectedly!' It was the remark of a soldier, who faced the danger ahead of him rather than shying away. Caesar prepared to attend the Senate meeting, but at the last minute he wavered, poor health and the continual warnings causing him to hesitate. Only on the urgings of Decimus Brutus did the leader decide to attend the meeting. Even as he made his way to this rendezvous with death, a friend pushed a note into his hands that gave details of the assassination plot, but he had no time to read personal messages and bundled this note up with the rest of his paperwork.

Julius Caesar took his seat, and the senators began to crowd around him in order to pay their respects. Mark Antony, a loyal friend and staunch ally of Caesar, arrived outside at that moment but was delayed in conversation by one of the conspirators. The first conspirator to attack was Tillius Cimber, who leaned forward as if to ask a question. The dictator held up his hand to cut Cimber short, but the senator suddenly grabbed his shoulders and held him fast. 'This is violence!' shouted Caesar, and another of the assassins, Casca, a tribune, stepped behind Caesar and after pulling out a hidden dagger, cut him just below his throat. Instinctively, Caesar grasped the man's hand and stabbed his sharp writing stylus deep into it. A veteran of countless fights, Caesar kept his head and lunged forward to escape from the mêlée, but as he did so another dagger was thrust into his chest. By now all those senators who were involved in the plot had stepped up to Caesar with daggers drawn. Seeing the hopelessness of the situation and no doubt suffering greatly from the two wounds already inflicted, Caesar readied himself for the *coup de grâce*. Cassius stabbed his face. Marcus Brutus stepped in to stab his friend in the groin. In all, the dictator suffered another twenty-one stab wounds and he fell to the floor, dead, ironically at the foot of Pompey's statue. Some reported that his last words, uttered in Greek to Marcus Brutus as he prepared to strike his blow, were *'kai su teknon'* ('You too, my child').

The aftermath of the most renowned assassination in ancient history did not have the effect the conspirators had hoped. Although they had decided to have Caesar's body flung into the River Tiber and to confiscate all his property, the fear of Caesar's deputies, Mark Antony and Lepidus, resulted in a period of inaction, during which the dictator's body was removed to his house by his own slaves. Within days funeral arrangements were announced and his will was read. The greater part of Julius Caesar's estate was to go to a great-nephew, Octavian, who was to be formally adopted as Caesar's son. News of the assassination had been met by a hostile public reception and the murderers were forced to withdraw to safety. It soon became obvious that they had made a fatal error and that Mark Antony (who held the second of Rome's two consulships) should have been murdered along with Caesar. Cassius had, in fact, tried unsuccessfully to convince Marcus Brutus that Mark Antony also had to die, but it was too late to rectify the situation. During the funeral Mark Antony gave a stirring speech that provoked hatred and anger at Caesar's death and called for revenge on his assassins. Amid the riots that followed, Marcus Brutus and Cassius were forced to flee Rome, leaving Caesar's two lieutenants, Mark Antony and Lepidus, in control. A comet seen at the funeral marked the deification of Julius Caesar – his spirit had travelled to the heavens and he had become a god. Octavian, as adoptive son, was now the son of a god.

The assassination had achieved nothing positive. It had eliminated an unwanted certainty and replaced it with chaos. It would not bring the Roman republican system back to life, but instead it provoked a civil war that would be fought across the empire by Mark Antony, Lepidus and the young Octavian as they struggled not to restore the old system but to take Caesar's place as sole ruler of Rome. The man might be dead, but the position was still vacant.

The Senate quickly sided with the 'boy' Octavian, giving him an official title and command of several legions, and ordered him to engage

Mark Antony and his legions in battle at Mutina (Modena) in northern Italy. Marching with him were Rome's consuls for the year of 43 BC, Hirtius and Pansa. These two men were the 'official' leaders of Roman government now that Caesar was dead and the Senate's only lever of power in the struggles that were about to take place. Unexpectedly, both Pansa and Hirtius died during the conflict, the former of wounds received, the latter while engaged in fighting. Rumours soon circulated that Octavian had been behind the two sudden deaths, his motive being to secure total control over Rome's legions once Mark Antony had been defeated. For a commander to be captured in battle is rare, for a commander to be killed on the battlefield is even rarer. So mysterious was Pansa's death from a wound, that his personal physician, Glyco, was immediately arrested and charged with poisoning the consul. The writer Aquilius Niger even reported that in the confusion of battle, Octavian himself struck the fatal blow that killed the consul Hirtius. That Octavian could engineer such a spectacular pair of assassinations at this early (and precarious) stage in his career is doubtful. Octavian did demand the consulship for himself and duly took over the entire army. Antony slipped away and the Senate declared him a public enemy, but they refused Octavian's outrageous demand. Still supremely powerful, Octavian marched on Rome and was awarded the consulship through intimidation.

Later in 43 BC, Mark Antony and Octavian reconciled their differences and presented a unified front against the Senate. They teamed up with Lepidus to create the Second Triumvirate (Caesar having being the pivotal member of the First Triumvirate fifteen years earlier). In the wake of Caesar's assassination, the three leading men of Rome decided that the murder of their predecessor must be avenged. Both Crassus and Brutus still controlled armies that would fight to protect their leaders, ensuring that a period of violence and bloodshed was destined to follow. These assassins could not evade the wrath of Rome, and both were defeated in battle and killed in state executions that finally avenged the assassination of Julius Caesar.

Some assassinations change the course of history. If Philip II, king of Macedonia and father of Alexander the Great, had not been assassinated in 336 BC, the entire history of the ancient world may have been very different. The shocking murder of Julius Caesar, on the other hand, did not change the course of Roman history. His death proved to be a trial by error for the imperial system. Caesar had failed to smooth the ride from republican to imperial rule and paid the ultimate price for it. His nephew and successor, Octavian, would not make that same mistake and cleverly built on what Caesar had achieved. And he moved slowly and carefully every step of the way. His ambition was tempered by caution – he had no intention of following Caesar to the grave.

The murder of Julius Caesar must rank as one of the best known assassinations in human history, second only to the murder of President Kennedy in 1963. Immortalized by Shakespeare, the killing of Caesar proved to be the ultimate betrayal. The murder is committed by friends and colleagues, face to face with their victim, plunging their daggers deep into the body of a man they have respected and followed, but hated. It is through his untimely and shocking death that Julius Caesar lives on today. Few can say they have never heard of him, and even those who are ignorant of his life are well acquainted with the gory details of his death. Assassination has frozen Caesar at the moment of death. He will be forever remembered in popular imagination as the Roman 'emperor' who ignored warnings of the Ides of March and who was savagely stabbed to death by members of the Senate led by his close friend Brutus. The impact of Caesar on the empire that followed him is far outweighed by the actions and policies of Octavian, the first emperor of Rome. Yet his name lives on. Every emperor in the centuries to follow legitimized his rule by the adoption of the official title of 'Caesar' as a badge of status. The title has even lived on into the twentieth century – the words Kaiser and Tsar are both derived from the word Caesar. That one Roman politician should be so honoured 2000 years after his assassination is quite incredible.

THE FORTUNES OF A DYNASTY

If anyone thought that political murder would come to an end with the rule of a single man they were mistaken. Individual members of Octavian's dynasty, termed the Julio-Claudians, would use assassination as a tool of both intimidation and self-defence. Several members of the family would succumb to the knife of a murderer or to the deadly poison that coated a fruit. Some of the most notorious emperors of the empire followed in Octavian's wake, men like Caligula and Nero. These emperors tested men's loyalty as much as their patience, and the imagined injustices of Caesar's ambition must have paled into insignificance compared with the absurd horrors that these tyrants inflicted on those around them.

Octavian's rule was a long one – 27 BC–AD 14 – and this gave him adequate time to establish all the elements of one-man-rule at Rome in a form that both the Senate and the people could accept. He accepted the title of Augustus and retained that name in historical annals. Like Caesar, Augustus had one of the months of the year named after him, the month in which he was born. Despite his incredibly long and revolutionary rule, no recorded attempts were made on his life, and he could not produce a legitimate heir to the throne of Rome. As old age gripped Augustus, he realized that all the work he had done in reforming the Senate, the constitution and the legions would be in vain if Rome were to be left leaderless at his death. Yet another civil war would tear apart both the nation and the empire. To prevent this catastrophe, Augustus put in train a programme to groom a suitable heir. Little did he know that his attempts would be blocked at every step by a sinister series of assassinations.

Octavian (now Augustus) married three times, first to Claudia, Mark Antony's step-daughter, and then to Scribonia, a relative of Sextus Pompeius. The love of his life, however, and the woman who stayed with him till death was Livia Drusilla. When Augustus first met her she was already married to another man. Her husband could deny Augustus the emperor of Rome nothing and promptly divorced her, allowing Augustus and Livia to marry. He loved her but did not remain faithful to her. Livia, however, tactfully turned a blind eye to her husband's philanderings despite some intense pressure. Livia had two sons, Drusus and Tiberius, from her previous marriage, but Augustus considered neither of them as a suitable heir to the throne. He desperately wanted a blood-relative to succeed him, thus establishing the tradition that would continue after his death. Apart from a premature baby, which quickly died, Livia had not given birth to any children, either male or female, while she was married to Augustus. From his previous marriage he did have a daughter, Julia, and as a blood-relative he pinned on her all his hopes of finding a suitable successor.

His dynastic plans first began to bear fruit in 25 BC when he married Julia to Marcellus, his own sister's son. Marcellus was young, still in his late teens, and could not easily share the throne with Augustus at that time. Within two years, the emperor fell gravely ill and fearing imminent death handed his signet ring to the only person he could trust – his able general and close friend, Agrippa. Had this situation been allowed to continue a serious struggle for power might have ensued, but that same year Marcellus fell ill and died. Without a husband Julia was now available to be matched up with another of Augustus' candidates for the succession. Agrippa became the next obvious candidate, and at the behest of Augustus he divorced his wife and married Julia. Despite the great difference between the two (Agrippa was twenty-five years Julia's senior and had already been married several times) the couple were able to produce five children, three of them boys. Of his new grandsons, the emperor took a great liking to Gaius and Lucius. He quickly selected Gaius to succeed him when he became old enough. Until that time his friend Agrippa would be heir-apparent.

The depth of feeling that Augustus held for the two boys is evident in a surviving letter, reproduced by Aulus Gellius in *Noctes Atticae* ('Attic Nights', XV, 7):

> Greetings my dear Gaius, my dearest little donkey, whom, so help me, I
> constantly miss whenever you are away from me. But especially on such
> days as today my eyes are eager for my Gaius, and wherever you have
> been today, I hope you have celebrated my sixty-fourth birthday in
> health and happiness. For, as you see, I have passed the climacteric
> common to all old men, the sixty-third year. And I pray the gods that
> whatever time is left to me I may pass with you safe and well, with our
> country in a flourishing condition, while you are playing the man and
> preparing to succeed my position.

Gaius was born in 20 BC and was only eight years old when his father, Agrippa, died. Always ill and fearing that death might strike him down at any time, Augustus knew that his young heir would not stand a chance without a powerful guardian of some kind. Still desperately trying to keep the succession within the family at all costs, he turned reluctantly to Livia's son Tiberius. In 11 BC, like Agrippa before him, Tiberius was forced by Augustus to divorce his own wife and marry Julia. He did so under duress since he loved his wife, Vipsania, and resented the forced marriage. Things did not go well for him. He could not quell the precocious and aspiring demands of Gaius and Lucius, despite being awarded all the powers of a tribune in 6 BC. Struggling against the impossible position in which Augustus had put him, Tiberius left Rome for the seclusion of Rhodes. His relationship with Julia was almost non-existent and her two sons were ambitious and unmanageable. Tiberius dropped out of public life.

Gaius and Lucius continued to carve a place for themselves within the

Roman hierarchy. However, a sudden illness struck down the younger brother, Lucius, in AD 2 while he was in the south of France. He did not survive. The previous year, at the age of twenty-one, his brother Gaius had become consul of Rome and had been sent to the East to flex Roman muscle in Armenia. Within a short space of time he, too, was dead; initially wounded during a siege, he slowly lost all his strength and willpower on the return trip to Rome. After all those careful political calculations, Augustus now found himself back at square one, only older, of less certain health and still with no viable heir.

However unpalatable the decision, Augustus adopted Tiberius (now in his forties) as well as the surviving younger brother of Gaius and Lucius, the fifteen-year-old Agrippa Postumus. Because Tiberius had also adopted Augustus' great-nephew, Germanicus, at the same time, the sixty-six-year-old emperor might still be succeeded by a member of his own blood-line. This would take place upon maturity, while Tiberius reigned in the boy's place. Within three years, Tiberius was duly confirmed as the only legitimate successor to the emperor after the young Agrippa Postumus proved to be unstable, violent and dangerous. Augustus had the boy permanently exiled from Rome, and Tiberius' future as the emperor of Rome was secured. When both he and Augustus were travelling to the island of Capua in AD 14, the emperor became sick and both returned to the mainland. Augustus, the first emperor of the Rome, died on 19 August at Nola. Tiberius was emperor now.

Historians have long debated the sinister role of Augustus' wife Livia within the tangled web of politics that was the succession. Could the long list of casualties really have been due to bad luck and disease? Or had Livia been the ultimate 'pushy mother'? Had she engineered an elaborate series of assassinations in order to see her son take up the succession? Rumours abounded that Livia had a hand in the death of Augustus' nephew Marcellus, of his friend and son-in-law Agrippa, and the death of both his beloved grandsons, Gaius and Lucius. The suddenness of these deaths and the fact that they all followed in relatively rapid succession was compounded by the way in which they, one by one, succeeded in eliminating every attempt by the emperor to produce a viable heir.

Later writers no doubt picked up on contemporary gossip that pointed the finger of suspicion at Livia. Just as many modern conspiracy theorists of our own day search for answers and for connections, there were those who asked 'who had most to gain from these deaths?'

Livia was powerful and intelligent, and her ambition far outstripped that of her hesitant son, Tiberius. If she had a hand in this catalogue of murder, she need not have acted alone, for, as the wife of Augustus, she commanded great respect and a degree of loyalty. Livia had asked her son to allow her to be his co-ruler, much to Tiberius' horror. When he received the title of 'Son of Livia' from the Senate, Tiberius refused to accept it, fearing her shadow might one day eclipse his own. Proof of her control came in the hours following Augustus' death at Nola. Livia's bodyguards cordoned off the villa in which he lay and refused to allow people or news in or out until Tiberius could arrive.

One remarkable charge made of her is that she actually murdered her husband, Augustus, for the sake of her son. Near the end of his life he made a secret visit to Planasia, where Agrippa Postumus was living in exile. Livia is thought to have suspected a last-minute attempt to groom the young man for the succession. Obviously Augustus was desperate to avoid placing Tiberius on the throne – it is well known that he disliked him. This move may have sealed Augustus' fate. It was said of Livia in the years that followed that she 'smeared with poison some figs that were still on trees from which Augustus was wont to gather the fruit with his own hands; then she ate those that had not been smeared, offering the poisoned ones to him'.

Livia truly loved her son and, like most Roman women, lived her life through him. She wanted the best for him, and when an opportunity appeared for him to succeed Augustus as emperor, she may have snatched it. Repeatedly blocked by younger, more active and vital candidates, Livia may well have turned to murder as a means to clear the way for her son. Tiberius had been reluctant to follow in Augustus' footsteps, and had once retired from public life to escape his failed marriage. In AD 26, while in power, he retired again, this time to the island of Capri. One of the reasons he fled Rome was to avoid the constant round of disagreements he had with his mother. There is no doubt that she had great influence over Tiberius and was able to exercise some degree of power. Livia may have continued to push and prod her son even after he had become emperor, and that Tiberius could no longer stand. On his accession Tiberius went out of his way to limit the honours paid to her and to curtail her influence. When she died at the age of eighty-six, Tiberius refused to honour her will and did not attend the funeral. This must surely have been a mark of the bitterness and long-running acrimony between them.

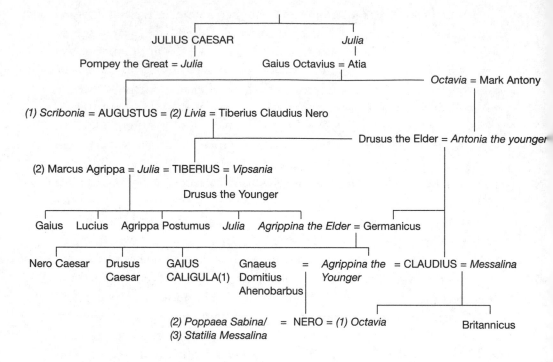

Tiberius was no stranger to assassination, despite his reserved and dour demeanour. Once, when campaigning in Germany during the reign of Augustus, an assassin of the Bructeri tribe was able to sneak into his headquarters disguised as an attendant. The killer was so nervous, however, that he gave himself away and confessed to his intention under torture. At the moment of Augustus' death, Tiberius himself resorted to assassination to secure his own future. He hesitated to announce the death of the emperor, waiting until written orders had reached the officer guarding the young Agrippa Postumus. The orders were to murder the boy. Suetonius records that Livia herself may have written the order and had it sent in her name. When the Senate convened to hear Tiberius' news, he disowned such an order and threatened to have the officer executed. He may have been covering his tracks or he may genuinely not known anything of the plot.

Many people had lost their lives – naturally or unnaturally, we can never be sure – during the scramble for the imperial succession, but as Tiberius began his reign, political murder became a tool of state, a hidden dagger with which rivals or would-be rivals could now be successfully eliminated without the horrors of civil war. The first to suffer was Germanicus, the great-nephew of Augustus who had been grudgingly adopted by Tiberius. Germanicus had a certain star quality that reflected badly on Tiberius. Not only was he related by blood to Augustus, but he had married Agrippina, Augustus' granddaughter. He fought several military campaigns in Germany, quelling a mutiny in the legions and recovering some of the legionary standards that had been lost in a military disaster some years earlier. In AD 16 he was recalled to Rome and entered the city in triumph. In AD 18 he became a consul of Rome and the colleague of the emperor. It was clear that Germanicus was the most likely candidate for the imperial succession, but no sooner had he become consul than he was bound for the East to solve a number of problems in the provinces there. At some point he ran foul of the Syrian governor, Gnaeus Piso, and also made waves when he visited the imperial province of Egypt without Tiberius' approval. Egypt proved so vital to the empire, providing much of Rome's corn supply, that Augustus had forbidden any member of the Senate (which included Germanicus) from visiting the province.

Germanicus fell ill while he was in Syria and died in Antioch on 10 October AD 19. Gnaeus Piso was immediately suspected of poisoning him, and he was arrested and tried for murder. Although he took his own life, as was the way of the Roman nobility, some doubt remained as to his motives. Some thought he had acted on orders from Tiberius who, out of fear, had wanted Germanicus killed. Drusus the Younger, Tiberius' only son, now became the heir apparent. Like Germanicus, he had spent time in the provinces, and he held the governorship of Pannonia in AD 17. On his return to Rome he, too, was awarded one of the consulships (Tiberius held the other) and, like Germanicus was suddenly struck down by illness, dying in September AD 23. Several years later it was discovered that his wife, Livilla, with help from Sejanus, the head of the Praetorian Guard, had conspired to poison him. Sejanus was later killed after other plots were revealed, to be replaced by Macro, a man of equal ambition.

It was at the seaside retreat of Misenum, in one of the emperor's many villas, that the succession for the imperial throne was again played out. Incapacitated by illness while on a tour of Campania, Tiberius finally gave up the ghost on 16 March AD 37. Caligula, the only son of Germanicus, was with his step-father at the end, and he stepped out to be surrounded by a congratulatory crowd. His reign as the third emperor of Rome had begun. Suddenly panic broke out when someone reported that Tiberius was alive and asking for food that he might recover from his faint. Caligula stood in shock and terror, but Macro, realizing that the point had already been crossed, stepped back inside the emperor's bed chamber and smothered the old man with a pillow.

An assassin's hand may have ended Augustus' life; it certainly ended that of Tiberius. Caligula in turn would become so hated in such short a period of time that he too would become bound up within a web of conspiracy that would see him hacked to death by his enemies. Caligula is known as one of the cruellest and most sadistic of the Roman emperors. Born Gaius Caesar Germanicus in AD 12 – his name was actually a nickname, *caligula* meaning 'little boot' – Caligula was the son of Germanicus and nephew of Tiberius. Tiberius had been hated in his later years, and his death provoked rejoicing and celebration. The reign of young Caligula was greeted with optimism, and the people and Senate hoped that the youth might show some of the heroic promise of his father.

Following a strange and acute illness, Caligula's character changed. The young emperor was afterwards stricken by nightmares and he began to be consumed by paranoia and suspicion. Most historians agree that Caligula was, to some indeterminate degree, insane. His sadism is legendary. Men of noble birth who slighted him in some minor fashion, whether by accident or design, suffered horribly. He had them branded, or held in tiny cages in which they were unable to stretch out; he even had men sawn in half. He took a genuine pleasure from the pain and humiliation of others, and his favourite quotation was: 'Let them hate me, so long as they fear me.' One of his interests was in murder and poison. He had a large collection of different poisons and cruelly fed one of these concoctions to a Thracian gladiator called Columbus instead of medicine. Columbus had been lightly wounded in a duel but had won nevertheless. The gladiator died quickly, and Caligula named the poison that had killed him Columbinum in his honour. 'At any rate, that was how he described it in his catalogue of poisons,' remarks the writer Suetonius.

Caligula had incestuous affairs with all his sisters, treated his favourite racehorse, Incitatus, with incredible luxury and considered himself a living god. He had succeeded Tiberius in AD 37 and within three years had provoked anger and resentment among the Roman establishment. He could not disguise his sincere belief in his own divinity, and this repelled the nobility. As a sign of this obsession, Caligula had statues of Roman gods and goddesses decapitated and his own head mounted on their shoulders. He spoke out loud to the gods and engaged them in conversation. He even claimed that he could sometimes see and hear them. At every opportunity he would dress up as one of the gods, or dress in any manner which suited his warped temperament – in military garb, in boots, in women's dress, in outlawed silks or in flowing robes. In many ways Caligula began to resemble the Eastern kings, men who routinely considered themselves sons of gods, living on earth.

Even more offensive to the Roman aristocracy than claims of divine kingship was financial ruin. Expenditure on such a lavish scale had never been witnessed in Rome before, and in only three years Caligula succeeded in squandering the riches of the world's greatest empire. Tiberius had left his successor over 3 million sesterces, but this was quickly spent in a constant round of chariot races and banquets. He had immense pleasure barges constructed that featured banquet halls, mosaics, colonnades, trees and even heated baths. On board these floating palaces he would cruise along the coast of Campania. One vast enterprise of the emperor was inspired by the pronouncement of a soothsayer that Caligula had as much chance of becoming emperor as riding dry shod over the Bay of Naples. He paid for a fleet of merchant ships to be anchored across the bay, lashed together in a double line stretching from Bauli to Puteoli, a distance of over 3 kilometres (about 2 miles). He had this floating bridge paved with a roadway of earth and timber purely for his own amusement, and for two days the emperor held a lavish festival, riding across the bay dressed as Alexander the Great and returning by chariot. One of his most peculiar and expensive habits was the drinking of vinegar in which pearls had been dissolved.

The expense of his exotic and ruinous lifestyle was maintained through crippling taxes (which Caligula even extended to the city's prostitutes). He reinstituted the practice of proscriptions so that he could have the wealth of condemned men gobbled up by his treasury, and also under took to seize the large legacies left by wealthy Romans. The pocket of Rome, as well as its pride, suffered from the emperor's uncontrolled excesses. A conspiracy to assassinate him was hatched in late AD 40, but before the plotters could strike, they were discovered, and several members of the Senate were executed as a result. A second plot proved more successful. Both the Senate and the influential Praetorian Guard were involved in the murder, which was to take place on 24 January AD 41, as the emperor left a theatre during the midday interlude. He was to be cornered and set upon in a narrow passageway that led out of the auditorium. At the appointed time the assassins were in place, armed with knives and swords, but Caligula failed to appear. They waited in tense expectation while the emperor's friends tried to persuade him to ignore the stomach pains that were troubling him and to take his midday meal as usual. He soon gave in to their requests and left by the passageway. Gaius Sabinus and Cassius Chaerea, both Praetorian officers, stepped towards Caligula as he watched a group of dancers rehearsing in the passageway. Sabinus ordered several centurions involved in the plot to move the crowds away and then he approached the emperor to ask for the day's password. 'Jupiter' was his reply, at which point Chaerea brought his sword down on Caligula's head, splitting the jawbone. As he struck, he shouted 'So be it!' (since Jupiter dealt sudden death from the heavens). The emperor fell, but shouted out that he was still alive, which resulted in shouts of 'Strike again!' The assassins hacked and stabbed at Caligula until he was dead. The emperor's German bodyguard appeared on the scene too late to save their master but succeeded in killing a number of the assassins as well as several innocent, and unlucky, senators.

The evil and malicious sadism of Caligula was so potent and the terror that he had inspired was so strong that the people of Rome dared not show any emotion when the news of his death swept the city. Many feared that this was yet another cruel trick of the emperor designed to identify as traitors those who celebrated his murder, who would then be tortured and executed.

The only Julio-Claudian successor able to take the throne was Caligula's uncle Claudius, a man who had been mocked by the imperial court for his ridiculous clumsiness and stammering. Discovered hiding in terror within the imperial palace following Caligula's assassination, Claudius was proclaimed emperor by the Praetorian Guard. This they did on no more pretext than they needed to make a living. Apparently the Senate was hastily drawing up a republican constitution, which planned to do away with the role of emperor. But without an emperor, reasoned the soldiers, who would the Praetorians guard?

Claudius was to be the penultimate emperor of the Julio-Claudian dynasty and, like his predecessors, would not be allowed to die a natural death. Well aware of the risks to his person, he took great care to have everyone who approached him searched for hidden weapons. Although he took such precautions, several ill-executed attempts were made on his life by individuals. Claudius was never regarded as a suitable imperial candidate. His limp, his stammer, the way in which he sometimes frothed at the mouth when he spoke and his partial paralysis marked him out as a fool, an idiot, a joke. His reign, however, although rudely thrust upon him, proved to both Senate and people that Claudius was no fool. Like many emperors – and many Romans – he displayed a taste for cruelty, but he was in many ways a competent ruler. As commander of Rome's armies he was able to take the credit for the conquest of Britain in AD 43, he was a passionate historian, and he sought to cut taxes and correct many of the unjust laws imposed by his tyrannical nephew.

The enemies of Claudius were not the legions or their commanders, nor the senators jealous of his power, nor the people of Rome unhappy with his rule. Rather, his enemies were to be his own wives. Claudius had a disastrous personal life and was married or betrothed to a string of women. His third wife, Messalina, bore Claudius a son, Brittanicus, but she proved to be more than a handful. She began to make false accusations against members of the senate and others whom she regarded as potential enemies. Messalina's killings were matched only by her adulteries, of which there were many, from high-born senators to the lowliest Romans. It is not known if Claudius knew of these infidelities and kept quiet or if he really knew nothing about his wife's activities, which even included a 'duel' with a Roman prostitute to discover who could satisfy the most men in a single night. Messalina is reported to have won.

In the year 48 her adulteries culminated with a 'marriage' to Gaius Silius. Claudius heard of this outrage while he made sacrifices at the port of Ostia, and he hurried back to Rome. There, fearing a coup, he retreated to the comparative safety of the Praetorian camp and had Silius dragged before him. Silius was summarily executed. The emperor then had Messalina, her admirers, supporters and lovers executed for their disloyalty. Although he vowed never to remarry, it is a testament to the wiles of a young woman called Agrippina that she persuaded him to forgo that vow and marry her.

Agrippina was, in fact, Claudius' niece, the daughter of his brother Germanicus, and the emperor had to seek special permission from the Senate before he could marry her. With her came Lucius Domitius Ahenobarbus, her young son from a previous marriage, and Agrippina began to show all the maternal concerns that Livia had shown for Tiberius. She was determined to see that her son should succeed Claudius, rather than Britannicus, his own son by Messalina. Only three years older than Britannicus, Ahenobarbus (who took the name Nero), was officially adopted by Claudius and rapidly earned many honours. While his mother schemed behind the emperor's back to install 'friendly' officers and advisers, Nero was making his mark, and successfully keeping Britannicus out of the spotlight.

Although Claudius was ill and in all probability would not live much longer, Agrippina could not afford to wait for fear that her husband might replace Nero with another candidate for the succession. When he was heard to mutter that it was his destiny to suffer and finally punish the infamy of his wives, she dared not wait any longer and in AD 54 hired the services of Locusta, a notorious poisoner. Agrippina acquired the poison she needed and had the chief taster, Halotus (who was, like many others in the imperial palace, loyal to Agrippina), sprinkle the deadly concoction over mushrooms that she knew Claudius, a slave to his stomach, could never resist. The poison took hold and Claudius retired to his chamber suffering from diarrhoea, but he seems to have vomited up the poisoned mushrooms. There, as he lay incapacitated, he was poisoned again by the doctor Xenophon, this time fatally.

Nero was the last of the Julio-Claudians to rule Rome. His reign is notable for its cruelty and barbarity, which seemed so much more savage when contrasted with Nero's obsession with the arts. Agrippina continued to manipulate her son as he took his place at the head of the Roman Empire, just as Livia had refused to give Tiberius the freedom he had desired. At first Nero ruled well and honoured the Senate, but the sixteen-year-old was soon corrupted by the immense power that his position gave him. His crimes were many. They included the persecution of the Christians following the Great Fire of Rome, a catastrophe that swept through the city in AD 64. Rumours abounded that Nero had actually started the fire himself to make way for a new building scheme he had planned for the centre of Rome. Many died in the fire, and hundreds of others died during the merciless round of executions that was instigated by the paranoid ruler. His enemies were both real and imagined. Like Caligula, he spent inordinate sums on wasteful extravagances and was forced to turn to the confiscation of property to pay for his pleasures.

He soon alienated the Senate and the Roman aristocracy, first, by these confiscations, and second, by his devotion to the Greek arts of music and theatre. Nero considered himself an artist of some skill and composed many verses. He began to perform in front of members of the imperial court, and forced his talents first on the people of Naples and then on those of Rome. Towards the end of his reign Nero embarked on a grand tour of Greece, and he participated in many of the province's artistic competitions. Of course, he won them all. He even had the Greeks bring the Olympic Games forward from the year in which they should have been staged so that he might compete – and win. This open display of love for Greek culture and his open disinterest in government sickened the establishment. Several conspiracies against Nero were uncovered before the plotters could vent their anger on him, and all involved were either executed or exiled. Again, members of the Praetorian Guard were an integral part of one assassination plot (in AD 65), which was a clear indicator that the emperor's life would never be entirely secure. The Praetorian Guard always stood between the emperor and all those who wished him dead. With their loyalty in question, Nero was a marked man.

Two notorious assassinations carried out in his name damned Nero's reputation irredeemably. There were some things that the Senate, the army generals and the people of Rome could forgive, but the murders, on Nero's orders, of his own mother and his step-brother, Britannicus, could not be ignored.

Britannicus, as Claudius' own son, stood little chance of survival once Nero had been formally adopted and nominated as the emperor's heir. Because he posed no immediate threat did not mean he would not challenge Nero's power at some point in the future. And if the Senate or the legions needed someone around whom they might rally, Britannicus would be a logical choice. It remains a mystery why Claudius would have favoured his newly acquired step-son Nero and left the young prince Britannicus with nothing but a dangerously weak position and a powerful enemy who wished him dead. Nero took steps to have him removed, and for this sordid business he turned to Locusta, the poisoner who had done such a good job in dispatching Claudius. Agrippina had previously made use of her talents – she had even been sentenced to death for her activities – but now Nero approached her with the problem of killing Britannicus. The brew she created was duly administered, although with unexpected results, for the fourteen-year-old boy fell ill with severe diarrhoea but survived.

Enraged, Nero had Locusta brought to him and he beat her with his own hands, complaining that she had given Britannicus a laxative instead of a poison. He dragged her into one of his chambers and stood over her while she prepared a more potent and more rapidly acting poison. Nero fed this to a goat, and the two watched it die over a five-hour period. Still not satisfied, the emperor forced her to boil down the poison, increasing its potency until he was sure it would kill in an instant. This second batch was tested on a pig, and to Nero's delight the animal dropped dead instantly. This was the poison for Britannicus. All that remained was to somehow get past the servant who always tasted the boy's food and drink. The plan was ingenious. Later that evening as dinner was served, Nero had a hot drink handed to his rival which the servant duly tasted. Britannicus complained that it was too hot to drink and so cold water, containing the lethal poison, was added to the drink and passed back to him. Within seconds of the first sip, Britannicus began to convulse, then slumped down dead. Some of the guests panicked, others, understanding the reality of the scene they were witnessing, froze and stared numbly at Nero. Agrippina looked on in horror but controlled herself; she knew that she had just witnessed a murder. Octavia, the sister of Britannicus, was also present, but she, like Agrippina, showed no emotion, lest she make herself the next target of Nero's insane wrath. The emperor calmly addressed his guests, informing them that the youth had long suffered from epileptic seizures. Without pomp or ceremony, Britannicus was removed. The next day, in pouring rain, Claudius' son was buried quickly without fuss or lamentation.

Nero was pleased with the result of Locusta's work and granted her a free pardon. From then on he even began to send students to her who might learn the secrets of her dark and deadly craft.

Nero's mother, Agrippina, had openly clashed with Nero and had even threatened to join forces with Britannicus, but in order to murder her the emperor was forced to turn to an alternative method. Agrippina's suspicious nature and familiarity with poisons meant that three attempts to poison her failed because she had taken an antidote each time. He had an ingenious booby-trap rigged up into her bedchamber so that the ceiling panels would fall on her as she slept. Agrippina's informants tipped her off, however, and she was able to avoid the attempt on her life. Finally Nero turned to an even more audacious contraption. In AD 59 he conspired with Anicetus, commander of the Roman fleet, to have a small sailing boat designed and built that would collapse, killing its passengers. Nero's plan was to have his mother drowned in an accident at sea. He invited her to join him during the festival of Minerva at Baiae, and on her arrival cleverly had her galley involved in a collision that rendered it unseaworthy. For the return voyage he presented her with his booby-trapped boat. Although Agrippina may have suspected something, she said her farewells to Nero at the quayside and boarded the ship for Rome. After it had sailed a short distance through the darkness, the mechanism was activated and a weighted canopy crashed down on top of her. Although her attendant was crushed to death, Agrippina survived, thanks to the raised sides of her couch, which miraculously protected her. The ship capsized and sank, but Agrippina seems to have been a good swimmer and although she was suffering from a shoulder wound, she managed to make it to shore.

Nero had gambled everything on this floating death-trap, a mechanical stunt that must surely have been inspired by the clever stage effects he had witnessed in the theatre. He had to be careful not to be seen to sanction the murder of family members, because there was a line over which not even emperors of Rome could cross. Agrippina, resting at one of her villas, sent word to Nero that she had by divine mercy survived a catastrophe. She recognized the plot for what it was and had decided that the only option open to her was to feign ignorance. When the message reached Nero, he was devastated. His hand had already been played, and it was now too late to pretend that the assassination attempt had never occurred. The plan had failed disastrously, but he did not hesitate to finish it one way or another.

The freedman Anicetus arrived at the villa with a column of soldiers. They arrested all the house slaves who stood in their way and found Agrippina resting in her bedchamber. Anicetus stood before her, with two naval officers behind him in the company of a group of soldiers. 'If you have come to visit me,' she said, 'you can report that I am better. But if you are assassins, I know my son is not responsible. He did not order his mother's death.' At that one of the officers lunged forward to club her in the head, and the other drew his sword ready to deal the fatal blow. As he approached her, Agrippina pointed to her womb and shouted, 'Strike here!' The soldiers chopped at her body until they were sure she was dead.

The emperor was now free of his mother's torments, but, too late, he realized the enormity of the crime. Although his friends rejoiced on his behalf, the emperor, like Macbeth, imagined himself to be haunted by her presence. Nero's excesses later intensified to such an extent that in AD 68 the legions rebelled and marched on Rome. Abandoned by the Praetorian Guard and by his staff, Nero fled from the palace and was led to a private villa by one of his servants. There the soldiers found him —

Nero had been betrayed. He committed suicide with the help of his private secretary.

With Nero died the Julio-Claudian dynasty and the hope that a legitimate succession of Roman rulers could be continued. A year of violent civil war was to follow, a clear indication that the fortunes of the imperial house now rested with the candidate who could boast the greatest number of legions, and not the strongest blood-ties to the previous incumbent. This would become painfully apparent during the turbulent years of the third century, when the right to rule would rest in the assassins' hands.

MAXIMINUS AND THE GORDIANS

If the Julio-Claudian dynasty had been an ignominious beginning to the imperial system of government, then the so-called Time of Chaos in the third century was the heart of the imperial disaster. Over a period of fifty years from 235, anarchy, civil war, destruction, plague, persecution and terror ravaged almost every part of the Roman Empire. All the while the enemies of Rome, mainly the Gothic hordes and the Persian Empire, fought bloody battles along Rome's weakening frontiers. In the period between 247 and 270 (equivalent in length to the entire reign of the emperor Tiberius), the legions proclaimed thirty different generals as emperor of Rome – the equivalent of one every nine months.

A climate of distrust slowly spread over the empire. After AD 200 military police officers (secret police) became a formal part of the establishment. Spies, informers and secret agents proliferated with every twist of the government screw. As policies became more rigid and taxes more rapacious, a network of hated secret agents grew up to enforce them. Writing of the third century, one Roman author noted that: 'Many spies had gone round all the cities listening to what people were saying. All temperate and just speech was destroyed and everyone trembled at his own shadow.'

There were many political killings, and a number of emperors or usurpers were murdered by their own troops as fickle loyalties swept first one way and then another. At the centre of the chaos, the Senate remained relatively powerless as armies volunteered their own generals for the post following some military victory. It seemed that anyone with a large enough army might toss his hat into the ring. Yet the ultimate force was still the Praetorian Guard, the élite body of politically orientated soldiers who were still able to make or break a candidate for the imperial throne. Any pretence of a succession quickly slipped away in the late third century. There are two episodes, in particular, from the Time of Chaos that illustrate the terrible problems of this period and show us how the empire had become dominated by the act of assassination. The start of this turbulent period is dominated by the imposing figure of Maximinus Thrax, a powerful general whose legacy proved to be pain and torment for a generation.

Severus Alexander, whose thirteen-year-long reign began in 222 when he was only fourteen years old, was considered to be a 'good' emperor by the ancient historians. Not only was he a prolific builder who greatly helped to restore Rome, but he moved swiftly against the growing power of the Persian Empire in the East. His campaign against the Persians began in 231, and although not entirely successful, it discouraged that state from making further pushes into Roman territory. His campaign against the Germans in 234 did not go quite as well and, in fact, resulted in his own death. After crossing the Rhine with his armies, Severus opted to gain time by buying off the enemy tribes with Roman coinage. His intentions were no doubt honourable, but some elements of the army turned against him for this apparently unheroic act. Inflamed by other grievances, part of the army that was camped near Mainz switched its allegiance to the officer Maximinus Thrax (the Thracian), a massively built soldier who had worked his way up the ranks. As this imposing figure strode onto one of the training grounds, recruits approached him with a cloak of purple and threw it around his shoulders, proclaiming him emperor. It is doubtful that this act was spontaneous; more likely, it was a carefully prearranged affair that was intended to have the appearance of a popular revolution. Maximinus at first feigned surprise, but then organized an attack on the emperor, who was encamped at nearby Bretzenheim.

Severus received news of Maximinus' uprising before the disloyal officer and his troops arrived. Immediately he panicked, an act that destroyed any chance he had of rallying his troops around him. We are told that he ran from his tent 'weeping and trembling and raving against Maximinus for being unfaithful to him'. Any loyalty the troops had felt for their terrified emperor quickly evaporated once the rebellious army was sighted, and they stood back to watch the events unfold. Severus had nowhere to run except back into the imperial tent, and there he clung to his mother, whom he cursed for his predicament through tears of despair. Outside, Maximinus had entered the emperor's camp with his troops. The army there willingly hailed Maximinus as their emperor. His first act was to send a tribune into the imperial tent with a guard of centurions. Drawing their swords, they turned on Severus Alexander, his mother and those attendants who had remained with him and stabbed them all to death. Rome was now in the hands of a common man, a rough barbarian from the backward region of Thrace, who had entered the auxiliary army as a common soldier. This was an unprecedented development, and one that could not bode well for the future of the empire.

The Senate had no realistic option but to ratify Maximinus Thrax as emperor, although it hated to see the governance of the empire in such lowly hands, and a number of bold senators conspired with friendly elements in the Rhine army to assassinate the usurper. The new emperor planned to continue the German war and had constructed a pontoon bridge across the Rhine, which gave his army access to enemy territory. When the time came for Maximinus to cross this bridge in the company of his bodyguard, the conspirators were going to sever the ropes that held it fast on the west (Roman) bank, thus stranding him in hostile territory. However, the audacious plan was exposed and all those involved were executed without trial. This did not discourage another group that was opposed to Maximinus' rule from concocting a second assassination plot. But this, too, was discovered and crushed. With those elements of the army brave enough to stand up to him now purged, the emperor could turn his attention more fully to the German campaign, which he fought with vigour. Maximinus was an able general, who mercilessly taxed the Roman propertied classes in order to pay for his military expeditions. The rich and influential, who had opposed the accession of Maximinus in the first place, now had even less liking for him. When he turned to the poor for revenue, the resistance in Rome that had begun to develop had, by 238, blossomed into an organized revolt.

The tragic events of 238 would seal the fate of Rome for half a century and prove to the world how impotent the Senate had finally become. In North Africa a group of young nobles had taken as much as they could stand from the imperial tax collector, and in January they staged a demonstration with their followers and tenant farmers. The official in question had been efficiently stripping the province of its wealth to pay for the war in Germany and when the demonstration took place, he was out assessing the olive harvest. The young noblemen chose their moment carefully and approached the official. When they were up close they murdered him. Unless they could get their crime sanctioned by someone in a position of power the men were doomed, and they turned to the governor of the province, Gordian, urging him to support their revolution and to claim for himself the imperial throne. Although Gordian was an old man of eighty, he agreed and rode into the provincial capital, Carthage, as if he were emperor already. When it heard of the coup, the Senate immediately recognized Gordian as the legitimate holder of the imperial throne.

Gordian came from a distinguished family that could trace its ancestors back to the days of the republic, before Caesar. He was a man of noble birth who had held a number of important offices. The Senate threw their weight behind both Gordian and his forty-six-year-old son, also called Gordian. Following tradition the senators awarded both Gordian I and II the honorary title of Augustus, adding an air of legitimacy to their claim. Vitalianus, the Praetorian commander in Rome, had been a loyal follower of Maximinus and had to be quickly disposed of. Several officials sent by the Senate met with Vitalianus and, after stabbing him to death, ran with bloodied hands through the streets.

Maximinus reacted angrily and swiftly when he heard of the developments both in North Africa and in Rome. He immediately marched on Rome in an effort to 'persuade' the Senate to reconsider its loyalties. Before he could reach the borders of Italy, however, events overtook him. In North Africa, not all were pleased to accept Gordian I as the new emperor. Capellianus, governor of neighbouring province Numidia, had never liked the Gordians, and he assembled the troops garrisoned within his province. In addition, he had what the Gordians lacked, a fully equipped legion, which marched on Carthage with units of the Numidian frontier force. The poorly equipped and inexperienced citizen militia that sought to oppose them failed. Gordian II died from wounds sustained in the fighting, and when his father heard the news he retired to his room. There, he slipped off the belt from his tunic, tied it to the ceiling and hanged himself. The pretenders had reigned for a mere twenty days, but the revolution had still not run its course.

Rome was still threatened by the army of Maximinus, which was rapidly marching on the city. The Senate decided to stand against the Thracian general and elected two of its number, Pupienus and Balbinus, to oppose him. According to some estimates these men were both in their sixties or seventies. Between them they had several lifetimes' worth of military and civil experience, and the Senate put their trust in them. The

51

people of Rome had other ideas, however, and stormed the Capitol demanding that an emperor be chosen to lead Rome – a member of the Gordian family. The Senate backed down and had the thirteen-year-old Gordian III inaugurated as the emperor of Rome, honoured with the ancient title of 'Caesar'.

In early February, with the boy in place to keep the mob happy, Pupienus and Balbinus got their defence of Rome underway. Pupienus led an army north to the city of Aquileia, which Maximinus had besieged. The defenders of the town were fighting bravely and would not easily give in. The spirited defence made a number of Maximinus' troops (especially the Italian units) reconsider their loyalties. They had fought barbarians on the frontier for an emperor who was now ordering them to murder their own countrymen. Members of the Praetorian Guard and of the Second Legion conspired to assassinate Maximinus. Bursting into his tent, they pulled down his portrait hanging there and killed Maximinus and his son.

The assassins rode out to meet Pupienus and his army at Ravenna and presented the heads of their victims to the senator: it seemed that a civil war had been averted. The murder of Maximinus at that crucial moment had prevented the two armies from coming to blows. Pupienus was able to disband both armies, and he returned to Rome with the Praetorian Guard. Rome welcomed him with open arms, but that in itself would not guarantee the survival of the two old men. The Praetorian Guard defended not just the physical body of the current emperor (until such time as it grew tired of that emperor) but also the imperial office itself. Its soldiers were an integral part of the imperial system, which traditionally tugged against the power of the Senate. They disliked emperors being made without their participation, and they had no real respect for either Pupienus or Balbinus. A group of guards stormed the emperor's palace and kidnapped both men. They were stripped of their togas and dragged naked through the streets of Rome. Terrified and publicly humiliated, the two elderly senators were taken back to the Praetorian camp. After having their eyebrows and hair torn out, they were savagely beaten and then killed.

The young Gordian III was more to the Praetorians' liking, and they hailed him as the rightful emperor of Rome. Only thirteen years old when he came to power, the boy had others rule for him in his stead. Who they were is not clear – they may have included his mother and a military officer named Timesitheus, to whom Gordian gave command of the Praetorian Guard, a sign that he was a trusted friend and adviser. The Persian Empire, which had caused trouble during the reign of Severus Alexander, now began to renew its attacks on Rome's eastern boundaries. When Timesitheus died from illness during a campaign against the Persian forces in 243, he was replaced as Praetorian commander by Philip the Arab. Philip may, in fact, have been responsible for the death of Timesitheus, as some ancient writers suspected. Young Gordian's protection from the fickle Praetorian Guard (the deadliest imperial assassination organization in the empire) had vanished.

Philip desired the throne for himself and attempted to engineer a mutiny against Gordian among the armies in the East. All the while, Philip sought to enhance his own position and soon gained the trust of Gordian, becoming his regent. According to one version of events, the nineteen-year-old emperor, who was camped with his troops in Syria, discovered just how deep the division and disharmony ran. It was 244, and the young emperor decided to gamble everything on a direct appeal to his soldiers. He stood up before them in the camp and demanded that they choose between Philip and himself. This brave and desperate move failed. The troops chose Philip and Gordian was murdered. Philip the Arab returned to Rome as emperor and his first act was to place his son by his side as co-emperor. Within five years, both had been murdered by the army. And so the endless round of assassinations continued, with emperors, co-emperors and challengers dying at the swords of their own dissatisfied troops.

Why so many men stepped forward to fight so desperately for such a dangerous political position has long been a historical mystery. To be declared 'Augustus' or 'Caesar' seemed to be tantamount to committing suicide. Perhaps the much vaunted glories of past emperors, men like Augustus, Hadrian and Trajan, continually inspired these ambitious and foolhardy men. Perhaps some day one claimant to the imperial throne would gain the respect of his armies and the backing of the Senate. This man would surely survive for more than a couple of months or years. When that man eventually emerged onto the deadly stage of Roman politics, he surprised everyone with the way in which he reformed the system to eliminate the government-by-assassination that had preceded him. After fighting so hard to gain the empire, he went on to give it all up in order to tend his garden vegetables in the provinces. This man was Diocletian (d.316).

Diocletian dominates Roman history as much as Caesar or Augustus, yet he was of humble origins, the son, some said, of an ex-slave. He entered the army and rose through the ranks to become one of a group of influential officers. In 283 Diocletian accompanied the emperor Carus on his Persian campaign. By this time, he had been promoted to the trusted position of cavalry commander of the imperial bodyguard, and this powerful post gave him as much access as he needed to manipulate events in his favour. The two sons of Carus were Numerian and Carinus. The elder son, Carinus, was granted co-rule with his father and was given the western half of the empire to administer. Both were titled 'Augustus'. Meanwhile, Carus and Numerian would attend to the government of the East and keep the ambitions of the Persian Empire in check. In 283 Carus launched an attack on Persia, marching to the shores of the River Tigris and capturing the Persian city of Ctesiphon. It was here that a calamity befell Carus, although we cannot be sure what exactly it was. According to one writer, Carus was in camp within his tent when he was struck dead by a bolt of lightning. His own secretary bore witness to the event:

> Carus, our dearest emperor, was confined by sickness to his bed, when a furious tempest arose in the camp. The darkness which overspread the sky was so thick that we could no longer distinguish each other; and the incessant flashes of lightning took from us the knowledge of all that passed in the general confusion. Immediately after the most violent clap of thunder we heard a sudden cry that the emperor was dead; and it soon appeared that his chamberlains, in a rage of grief, had set fire to the royal pavilion, a circumstance which gave rise to the report that Carus had been killed by lightning.

Historians have suspected that the story of the 'lightning' may have hidden a more sinister plot to do away with Carus. The emperor had two politically minded sons, and paternal loyalty had always been a rare thing in third-century politics. Today, suspicion falls on either Aper, commander of the Praetorian Guard, or Diocletian, commander of Carus' cavalry bodyguard.

Numerian, ruling the East jointly with his father, now inherited his father's place at the head of the expedition. Technically he was still the junior partner (a 'Caesar') of the imperial throne, with Carinus ruling as the senior partner, the 'Augustus'. The first order Numerian gave was the Roman withdrawal back into Syria – the Persian campaign had been successful and the troops would be happy to return. The thirty-year-old could not travel in triumph on horseback, however, because of a debilitating eye infection, which forced him to return to Rome carried in a closed litter. At some point on the road to Nicomedia in Asia Minor, the co-emperor was assassinated and his death kept secret. Each day the litter was carried further along the road, and each day the crime remained undetected, until at Nicomedia in November 284, the awful smell coming from the decaying body of Numerian could no longer be disguised. Immediately Aper, the praetorian commander, was arrested and charged with the murder. On a platform in full view of the army, Aper, bound in chains, was condemned by a military council of generals and tribunes, and the army, gathered around, proclaimed Diocletian emperor and successor to Numerian. According to one version, Diocletian addressed the army. 'This man,' he said, 'is the murderer of Numerian,' and without hesitation he drew his sword and plunged the blade deep into Aper's chest, with one blow eliminating a dangerous rival and, if Diocletian was responsible for the murder of Numerian as is suspected, disposing of the only man who could incriminate him. Diocletian had now to overcome Numerian's older brother, Carinus, the emperor of the West.

Carinus celebrated several military victories during his first years as emperor, but as time passed he allowed his base instincts to rule his head. Later writers paint a picture of Carinus as a seducer of young boys and of other men's wives. He is alleged to have married nine times and to have had prostitutes, actors and pimps in attendance at the imperial residence in Rome. He replaced friends and advisers of rank and noble birth with a gang of commoners and gave huge banquets for all these hangers-on. In the summer of 285 Carinus' sexual vices caught up with him at a most unexpected hour. The emperor was leading his army eastwards to meet the army of Diocletian coming the other way, and the two forces met on the River Margus (the modern Morava). Carinus enjoyed numerical superiority, and it seems that his army was successfully gaining the upper hand over Diocletian's troops, when Carinus was assassinated. At that moment news of the emperor's sudden death spread and his army gave up the fight immediately to join forces with Diocletian.

Who had murdered Carinus? It seems likely that a number of Carinus' own officers nursed bitter grudges against the emperor. Their wives had been victims of the emperor's voracious sexual appetite, and one or more had been looking for just the right moment to strike. Either revenge, or fear of what Carinus might do when he returned to Rome, drove the killer, a tribune, to act. For Diocletian, who would reign as emperor for another twenty years, the murder was a blessing, and for a change it was not a murder that had been instigated by him.

Diocletian completely reformed the government and administration of the Roman Empire, introducing many of the innovations that would survive into the medieval period. It was his far-sighted reforms and his careful choice of supporters and lieutenants that enabled the empire to enjoy a respite from the chaos and anarchy of the previous half century. By many standards his rule was warlike, bloody and despotic, but by the standards set by the century in which he lived, Diocletian achieved what no one had even considered a reality in a long while – stability.

In May 305 Diocletian abdicated with his co-emperor in an attempt to create a peaceful succession for the empire. Both men had juniors who would step forward to take up the throne in their stead. Diocletian did not want to hang on to power until the bitter end, ending his life with a dagger in his chest and his military commanders squabbling over the spoils of empire. To some degree he succeeded, but the ambitions of Roman leaders could not be cooled so easily so quickly. He had, however, introduced a workable system for succession that did not depend on either blood-ties or military might. Diocletian introduced the Tetrarchy, the system of having two emperors, co-emperors, who ruled the two halves of the Roman world, East and West, and who were both known as 'Augustus'. Each Augustus would nominate an heir, a joint ruler known as a 'Caesar'. Thus there were, in effect, four emperors, not one or two. These juniors would inherit the title of Augustus when the present incumbent died or retired and these rising stars could be assured of a place in the leadership at some point in the future. Long gone were the days where one man jealously hoarded power and influence, staving off rivals with legions, spies and assassins.

3. Religion, Power and Murder

The fall of Rome did not see an end to the terrible power of assassination. Where the use of this bloody instrument of succession and elimination proved to be most startling, however, was the Christian Church. Under the murderous Borgias, Renaissance Rome and the Vatican trembled in fear, and centuries earlier Thomas à Becket became perhaps the best known Christian cleric to have died at the hands of assassins. The Crusades had been plagued by a unique cult of deadly Muslim assassins. In the far east, while the Church dominated life in Europe and assassination dominated the Church, the ninja waged a secret war on behalf of Japanese warlords. Cut off from society (and religion), the ninja became a prominent lever of power, working for first one feudal lord and then another.

THE KILLING OF THOMAS À BECKET

Canterbury Cathedral is a mighty and impressive edifice, a monument in stone that testifies to human belief in something far greater than mere existence. The cathedral towers over the small English town, imbuing the narrow streets with a rich sense of history. This building has cast its shadow over Canterbury for almost a thousand years and may continue to dominate the town for hundreds of years to come. The fascination of this religious monument for modern pilgrims and for tourists, British and foreign alike, lies partly in the magnificent medieval architecture, partly in the city's prominent position as the centre of English Christian worship and partly in its reputation as the site of Britain's most notorious assassination.

Thomas à Becket was the fortieth Archbishop of Canterbury, and shortly after the accession of Henry II in 1154 he became the monarch's royal chancellor, a position of great power and prestige. He acted as one of the king's foremost advisers and statesmen and often sided with him in disputes with the clergy. Becket had studied canon law and was also deeply and sincerely religious, but he nevertheless became a good friend and political ally of the king. Physically, Thomas à Becket was tall and imposing; his occasional fits of temper were moderated by a civil and generous nature. As part of his training, Becket had served under Theobald, the Archbishop of Canterbury, and on Theobald's death in 1161, the king decided to install Becket as his successor. As the trusted friend and confidante of Henry, it was thought that Becket would be able to give the king almost total control over the Church and its lands, and the wranglings with the clergy would at last come to an end. Henry II received an unpleasant surprise, however, when his old friend began to act counter to his expectations. Educated in Church law, Becket had great respect for the position that he now held, and refused to demean the title by pandering to the political requests of the king. He changed overnight, even resigning from his post as chancellor. Thus the powerful friends became powerful enemies. The two men were constantly at odds, and Henry realized that Becket would prove to be more of a problem than a solution. Following a long period of prevarication, Becket refused to consent to the Constitutions of Clarendon, important acts that defined the king's power over the realm's ecclesiastical courts. He demanded that the king hand over Church territories seized by William the Conqueror and insisted that clerics were subject only to the law of the Church and not to the courts of the king.

For this and other confrontations, Thomas à Becket fled from England in 1164 for the safety of northern France. A conference at Fretteville attended by Becket, Henry and the French king, Louis VII, seemed to restore the friendship that had once existed between the two men, but this was not to last. King Henry had decided that his son should be crowned as king of England during his own lifetime, and with Becket's continued absence in France, the coronation was performed by his ecclesiastical rival, the Archbishop of York, assisted by the bishops of both London and Salisbury. Thomas à Becket was furious at being cut out of such an important ceremony, and he had the pope excommunicate both bishops and suspend the Archbishop of York from his duties. By December 1170 the king had managed to come to terms with Becket, and the exiled archbishop landed at the Kentish port of Sandwich. A short journey saw him within the city walls of Canterbury, and Becket was welcomed with rapture by the citizens. By this time, however, the letters of

suspension and excommunication had reached the clerics who had offi-
ciated at the coronation of Henry's son, all of whom were with the king
in Normandy. Henry was beside himself with rage and publicly criti-
cized his courtiers for lacking the bravery to rid him of 'this turbulent
priest'. Henry's flippant and open challenge to the mixed party of courtiers and knights unexpectedly hit its mark. Taking the heartfelt wish of
their king as a direct order, four of his most loyal knights decided to
assassinate Becket.

The knights – Richard le Breton, Reginald Fitzurse, Hugh de Morville
and William de Tracy – crossed the English Channel by separate routes
and assembled at Saltwood Castle in Hythe, Kent. From there, after a
period of intense debate, they set out on the road north to Canterbury,
accompanied by a small staff of servants and retainers. On arriving in
Canterbury, the knights had to find a way of surprising the archbishop.
They were able to gain access to Becket's quarters and confront him, but
after an angry argument the four knights left to recover the swords they
had hidden under a tree in the courtyard. Now armed, the assassins
returned to the archbishop's chamber, but finding the way barred had to
force an entrance through a window that was being repaired. Finding
the archbishop's quarters unoccupied, the knights turned towards the
cathedral and pursued Becket and his entourage through the beautiful
cloisters. Becket fled from the knights. He fully understood their purpose, and with his companions made his way to the cathedral itself,
refusing to allow the doors through which he passed to be barred behind
him. Thomas à Becket suspected the fate that awaited him and bravely
decided to face that fate unflinchingly.

The archbishop entered the cathedral from the cloisters through the
chapel of St Benedict at the northwest transept. It was now growing
dark and a lamp on the altar illuminated the grisly scene that followed.
The knights rushed into the chapel from the cloisters in pursuit of the
prelate, and one shouted out: 'Where is the Archbishop?' According to
one account, Becket turned around as he was about to mount the steps
that led out of the chapel and declared: 'Here I am, no traitor but a priest
of God, and I marvel that you have entered the church of God in such
attire. What do you want with me?' One of the knights answered: 'That
you should die; you cannot live any longer!'

Becket is supposed to have said: 'I accept death in the name of the
Lord, and I commend my soul and the cause of the Church to God.' A
tussle ensued, with some of the knights trying to drag the archbishop

away, but a crowd of townspeople gathering outside for worship prevented an easy escape. It was the knights' intention to get him away
from the church and off holy ground. None of the knights wanted to
commit sacrilege. When Becket refused to leave, William de Tracy drew
his sword and brought it down on the archbishop's head. At the last
minute, in an effort to protect his master, a clerk of the church sprang in
front of Becket and took a terrible blow on his upraised arm. The force
of the blow was slowed but not stopped, and Becket was cut on the
head. A second sword blow knocked him to his knees, a third left him
sprawling on the floor of the chapel, bleeding heavily. Richard le Breton
brought his sword down with all his might on Thomas à Becket's head,
completely severing the crown. So powerful was the killing blow that
Richard's sword snapped as it hit the stone floor.

Finally, one of the group put his foot on the dead man's neck and
stuck the point of his sword into the top of his head. With a twist of his
hand he removed his sword and blood and brains splashed over the
chapel floor. 'Let us go, knights,' he said, 'This fellow will not rise again.'
Sheathing their bloody swords, the knights, accompanied by their attendants, left the cathedral.

When they believed the coast to be clear, a crowd of monks and clerks
gathered around Becket's bloody body. The large crowd of worshippers
outside had by now entered the cathedral and also gathered around,
shouting and weeping. After some time the archbishop's head was
bound and his body placed at the high altar. Some members of the staff
returned to the chapel of St Benedict to scoop up what they could of the
blood and brain matter into a basin. Later the body was buried within
the crypt, where it became a focus of worship for the pilgrims who
flocked to Canterbury. On 21 February 1173 Thomas à Becket was can-
onized as St Thomas, and miracles of healing were alleged to take place
around his tomb.

Henry II at first denied any knowledge of the plot to assassinate the
archbishop. The whole of the Christian world had been shocked by the
killing; many considered it an outrageous act, compounded by the fact
that it had taken place within the cathedral itself. The king insisted that
his call for the removal of the archbishop had been nothing more than a
rhetorical question. At the orders of the pope, however, Henry was
forced to atone for his crime – the king of England had to walk barefoot
through the streets of Canterbury dressed only in a simple pilgrim's
gown. At the site of the murder, the king knelt to kiss the sacred stone

on which Becket died. He then moved on to the tomb, where he confessed and asked for forgiveness, then he bared his back while every monk in the cathedral lashed the king three times.

The assassination of Thomas à Becket had little effect other than to turn Canterbury into one of the foremost pilgrimage sites in Christendom. The king failed to prosper from his murder, although he was free of Becket's interminable opposition.

THE BORGIAS

The name of Borgia carries with it a special mystique, a mystique that embraces courtly conspiracies, double-dealing, treachery, incest – and murder. The family name seems to embrace everything abhorrent to the human condition. At the highest levels of state in the fifteenth century the Borgias played the most deadly game of all with cunning and a cold heart. Standing at the head of this most infamous of families was the Spaniard Rodrigo de Borja (1431–1503). In order more easily to pursue a career in the church, Rodrigo changed the spelling of his name to the Italian Borgia. In Rome he entered the bitterly fought contests for power and influence within the corridors of the Vatican. Both his skills and his personality marked him out for great things, and in 1457 he attained a position of immense power as vice-chancellor of the Holy See, the right-hand man of the pope of the day. He hoarded power, traded in favours and could see his long-term plans maturing over the years through the careful application of bribery, force and opportunism. As a power-monger of the first order, Rodrigo earned the praise of no less a contemporary than Niccolò Machiavelli (1469–1527), the Florentine politician, who made the study of power his life's work.

Rodrigo had already murdered. At the age of twelve it was said that he had turned on a boy his own age in Valencia and stabbed him to death on the pretext of having been mortally insulted. He grew up proud, defiant, clever and bold. In 1492, after a fiercely fought political battle, Rodrigo Borgia became pope. As is customary, he took a new name, which was Alexander VI. Carried with him into the halls of papal power were two of his children, Cesare and Lucrezia Borgia, the son and daughter on whom Alexander pinned the Borgia future. With Alexander reigning as pope at a time when the papacy was more akin to a kingship than a religious office, Rome was set to become a Borgia city. The family citadel, employed as place of refuge, was the ancient Castel Sant'Angelo.

Cesare (c.1475–1507) in particular benefited from his father's far-reaching influence. He first became absentee bishop of the Spanish city of Pamplona and then a cardinal, much to the disgust of the Sacred College, the Vatican's staff of incumbent cardinals. Cesare Borgia had obviously no interest and no spiritual desire to enter the priesthood – he was an attractive, high spirited and worldly young man who possessed the same keen ambition that had served his father so well.

Cesare might have inherited his father's desire for power, but it seemed to him that it was always the younger sons, Jofré and especially Juan, who received much of Alexander's attention. This burned within the proud and arrogant Cesare. He could not stomach a rival, especially if it were his own brother. With Alexander's sons Cesare, Juan (1476–97) and Jofré (1481–1517), and his son-in-law Giovanni Sforza, lord of Pesaro, in positions of some importance, the papacy amounted to a Borgia Mafia, with the Spanish pope heading the clan as the puppet-master and godfather. But like any Mafia organization, the threats and dangers come not just from without but also from within.

In 1497 Alexander's beloved son Juan was murdered by professional assassins, a perfect, deniable murder that ended the young man's seemingly inexorable climb to power. Someone wanted Juan Borgia out of the way. But who? Of all the murders carried out during the Borgias' reign, the death of Juan Borgia has remained one of the most mysterious and enigmatic. The finger of suspicion pointed to Cesare, but was he responsible?

Of the pope's sons, Juan was undoubtedly the favourite, but initially Alexander had rested his hopes on Pedro Luis, another son from a previous affair. Pedro received the dukedom of Gandía and seemed destined to reach the pinnacles of power. His death in 1488 left the way open for Cesare. Older than Juan, he expected to take over the reigns of power while his younger brother would be shepherded into the Church, which was the normal practice. It was Juan, however, who became Alexander's next choice, leaving Cesare to face a lifetime of service to the Church. Power corrupts, and the power-soaked cardinals of the Vatican, close to the pope and the source of ultimate power within the Papal States, were far from chaste, honest and virtuous. Cesare's lifestyle was such, however, that even he would scandalize Rome with his immoral excesses.

The degree of trust that Alexander VI placed in Juan can be gauged by his appointment as the commander-in-chief of the papal armies in 1496. The pope made plans to use this army to extend the Vatican's earthly influence, but Juan's soldiers suffered a defeat near Bassano in 1497. Cesare could not hide his joy at the news of the defeat. Later that year the two brothers arranged to eat dinner together with their mother, Vannozza dei Cattanei. As well as two footmen, the brothers were accompanied by a mysterious masked man, a friend of Juan's. This man, who had been seen several times in Juan's company on social occasions, always wore a distinctive mask. When the meal had finished, Cesare and Juan rode away, with the masked man sharing Juan's horse. It was growing dark, the narrow lanes were dangerous at night, and despite the protestations of his older brother, Juan insisted that he and his friend were going in search of further pleasures. The two men vanished (into the arms of certain young women, it was thought) and Juan was never seen alive again.

That night a boatman on the River Tiber named Giorgio Schiavi, who had been awake guarding his property, remembered seeing several people on the bank that night. Then out of the woods came a horse and rider, a body slumped over the saddle. Harry Edington's book *The Borgias* includes Schiavi's description of what he had seen:

> Having reached the point where refuse is thrown into the river, the horseman turned his horse so that its tail faced the river, then the two men who were standing on either side, taking the body, one by the hands and arms, the other by the feet and legs, flung it with all their strength into the river.

The cloak was then sunk with rocks. The boatman heard the words 'yes, my lord' uttered by one of the men, when he was asked if the cloak had sunk. Based on this evidence, Alexander had the River Tiber dragged, and Juan's body was soon recovered. He had been stabbed eight times, his throat had been cut, his hands were tied behind his back and a rock had been tied around his neck to take him to the bottom of the river. There was no evidence of robbery – Juan had been assassinated. When asked why he had not come forward immediately after he had witnessed the unusual activities on the riverbank, Schiavi gave a chilling answer to the investigators: 'In the course of my life, on various nights, I have seen more than a hundred bodies thrown into the river right at this spot, and never heard anyone troubling himself about them.' So ran the course of Rome's turbulent political life in the late fifteenth century.

The chief suspect for the killing of Juan Borgia was the Borgia family rival, the Orsini. There was a long-running feud in progress, and since

Viginio Orsini had recently met his death from Borgia justice, they lacked no shortage of motive. Within three weeks of the murder that shook Alexander and Rome, the investigation was brought to a close. Many believed that the Orsini (or more likely contract killers in their pay) had murdered the pope's favourite son, and that Alexander knew it. By winding up his investigation, it was thought he was trying to prevent a state of open civil war on the streets of Rome. Still others regarded the sudden end to the proceedings as strange, considering the fact that Juan's murder broke Alexander's heart. Had his agents uncovered other, darker secrets he could not bear to consider?

His mourning over, Pope Alexander began a period of vigorous reforms, almost as a method of atonement for the sins of his earlier regime. His good deeds did not last long, however, and still in desperate need of a trusted lieutenant, Cesare was, at long last, pulled out of the college of cardinals to serve his father. Some historians cast doubt over the contemporary allegations of gossipmongers that Cesare had his brother assassinated in order that he might take his rightful place by the side of the pope. The real truth will never be known.

The Borgia name continued to carve a disreputable name for itself. Cesare's sister, Lucrezia (1480–1519), enjoyed an unsavoury reputation and was known as 'the greatest whore there ever was in Rome'. She was rumoured to have had a succession of lovers that included not only members of the Vatican establishment but also her own brothers. As she was being divorced from one husband to be remarried to another in one of Alexander's political marriages, Lucrezia became pregnant by a gentleman named Perotto. Like Juan, he suddenly vanished – and re-emerged in a fisherman's dragnet, the victim of another contract killing. The envoy from Venice put down his thoughts on the terrible event: 'With his own hand, and under the mantle of the pope, Cesare murdered Master Perotto so that his blood spattered in the face of the pope, of whom Master Perotto was a favourite.'

Gutter gossip carried the rumours through Rome and across Italy. One man, a monk named Girolama Savonarola, dared to oppose the Vatican's resident godfather. His invective pulled no punches as he called for change, accusing Alexander of immorality, of uncounted crimes and of monstrous and abominable behaviour. The pope thought it prudent to ignore this madman, but the torrent of abuse reached such levels that he could take no more. In 1498 he had Savonarola arrested, charged with heresy and executed. Opposition to Alexander's corrupt rule could not be tolerated. Cesare was soon dispatched on papal business. He married into the French aristocracy and formed an alliance with the French king, Louis XII, which made it possible for Cesare to lead a French army into Italy. Its aim was to seize those Italian states that remained hostile to the Vatican, especially Milan and Imola.

The countess of Imola, Caterina Sforza, stridently opposed Cesare Borgia and his army. Bold and beautiful, Caterina was a Renaissance Boudicca, riding into war at the head of her army. Even the redoubtable Catarina could not resist the forces ranged against her, although she tried one tactic that could slow, if not halt, the invasion. She wrote to Pope Alexander and had the deadly message wrapped in bandages taken from the corpse of a plague victim. Although ranking as perhaps one of the most unusual assassination attempts in history, it failed. Cesare Borgia heard of the plot and dashed to Rome to warn his father. He found Alexander in good health. When he heard Cesare's terrible news he ordered that messengers be arrested and burned at the stake, even though Caterina's letter had been transported within a sealed container. Perhaps this was one instance in which the bearers of bad news had to die for safety's sake or perhaps the pope was simply venting his anger and frustration on those unfortunates who had so nearly been the agents of his own death.

Meanwhile Lucrezia had remarried the Duke Alfonso of Bisceglie, whose family had suffered at the hands of the Franco-Borgia alliance. Alfonso fled from Rome and was persuaded to return only after considerable effort on Alexander's part. When Cesare returned triumphant to Rome he knew that he would not be able to trust his new brother-in-law, Alfonso. The young man might be able to convince the pope to ease the military pressure on Naples and Milan. Cesare's ambitions were founded on these recent military manoeuvres, and the Borgia master-assassin coldly decided that his sister's husband must die.

Following a family meal on 15 July 1500, the nineteen-year-old Alfonso made his way across St Peter's Square towards his home at the palace of Santa Maria. As he approached the halfway point across the square, a shout echoed out and five men, whom Alfonso had initially mistaken as innocent pilgrims asleep on the steps of St Peter's, jumped up and ran towards him. He failed to draw his sword in defence as the men attacked him with their swords. He quickly fell under a storm of cuts, slashes and stabs that seriously wounded him in the head, shoulder, arms and legs. As he lay there, the assassins tried to drag him towards a group of accomplices who were waiting to carry him off on horseback, but friends of Alfonso who had been following at a distance were able to scare off the attackers. Alfonso miraculously survived the attack, but was terribly scarred. He was carried back to the Vatican where he received the best medical attention in Rome. So fearful were Lucrezia and Alfonso that their apartments became a virtual fortress, guarded night and day. Accompanied by Alfonso's sister, Sancia, Lucrezia helped her husband recover his health, yet she knew that as he grew stronger, the likelihood would increase that the assassins would try to finish the job. She even insisted on preparing all his meals, for fear that he would be poisoned.

Cesare Borgia was rumoured to be behind the attack and was reported to have sneered, 'What is not done at lunch can be done at dinner,' a veiled threat of a repeat attempt on Alfonso's life. That attack came on 18 August when Michelotto, a professional killer and one of Cesare's close associates, burst into Alfonso's chamber and seized both the young man's uncle and the envoy of Naples who were at his bedside. Incensed by this outrageous act, Lucrezia left to petition her father. While she was gone, Michelotto strangled the bed-ridden Alfonso. Guards were posted and Alfonso's sudden but 'natural' death was quickly announced. This fooled no one, however, and Cesare was immediately implicated, along with the pope. While the Vatican reeled at such cold-hearted evil, father and son worked hard to cover their tracks. They concocted lies and had suspects arrested. Alfonso's doctors were questioned intently, and his servants were tortured in an attempt to force a confession from them. A story was circulated that the young duke had fallen from bed and aggravated his head wound. Then a different story was put about: the teenage duke had risen from his sick bed and attempted to shoot Cesare with a crossbow as he walked in the gardens below. If Cesare was implicated, therefore, surely it was self-defence. These pathetic attempts failed to convince anyone, so the pope was now implicated in a political murder not of his own making. Cesare may well have convinced his father that Alfonso had been plotting against the Borgias, and with the duke's death there was no one alive who could contradict him.

From that moment on, Cesare Borgia's name became a byword for assassination. Unsolved murders were ascribed to him (irrespective of where Cesare was at the time), and he soon became the most feared and reviled man in Italy. One unfortunate rumour-monger was arrested by

Cesare and had his right hand amputated and his tongue cut out. Both tongue and hand were gruesomely hung on the bars of the man's cell as an example to others. The pope tried to play down his son's murderous activities. 'The duke is a good-hearted man,' he commented apologetically, 'but he cannot tolerate insults.'

Rome was swept by a plague of malaria-carrying mosquitoes in the hot summer of 1503 and both Alexander VI and Cesare came down with the disease. Both seemed close to death, and Alexander eventually succumbed on 18 August. After recovering his health, Cesare found his position precarious. The Borgia empire had been masterminded by Alexander, and with his death it all began to come apart at the seams. Cesare lost his position as captain-general of the papal army, and the new pope, Julius II, could not allow the Borgias to regain their former stranglehold on power. Imprisoned in one castle after another, Cesare eventually made a dramatic escape attempt from a Spanish fortress in 1505 by trying to kill the prison governor. He attempted to throw him from a parapet, and then climbed down a rope of knotted sheets. Unfortunately for the cunning prince, he fell and fractured his shoulder. A second attempt from an even more secure castle by exactly the same means succeeded a year later. Cesare died in Navarre, December 1507, while fighting in a civil war on the side of the Basque king, John d'Albret. The king laid Cesare Borgia's body to rest beneath the following inscription: 'Here, in a scant piece of earth, lies he whom all the world feared.'

Machiavelli, who had known Cesare Borgia personally, held the thirty-one year old to be 'an example to be imitated by all who by fortune and with the arms of others have risen to power'. Lucrezia died in childbirth twelve years later, and history remembers her as an incestuous harlot, and a poisoner who murdered her husbands one after the other. Pope Julius was greatly to blame for some of the bad press that the Borgias (and especially Lucrezia) received and are remembered for. He had the Borgia apartments sealed, and they were re-opened to a curious public only some 300 years later. In the popular imagination, Lucrezia remains the most notorious of the Borgias, a myth perpetuated by Donizetti's opera *Lucrezia Borgia* and Victor Hugo's play of the same name. The Borgia name was feared by beggars and kings alike during the family's heyday in Rome, and the terror it inspired long outlived those bearing that name. Cesare is one of history's greatest assassins. He became a deadly knife in Pope Alexander's hands, and the arch-intriguer Machiavelli even considered their father-son partnership to be one of Italy's lost opportunities. The supreme power and authority of the Borgia pope, coupled with his son's deadly cunning, might have been the key to a united Italy.

CRUSADERS AND ASSASSINS

Not every political murder of medieval times was carried out by an ambitious nobleman. Two groups of professional assassins were active in the centuries that separate the Roman world from our own. They were the Muslim Assassins and the Japanese ninja. Both earned for themselves reputations that long outlived the organizations themselves. The killer cult known as the Assassins created such an aura of fear and terror about it that even today the word for an act of political murder is taken from its name.

Their profession was murder, and they took it seriously. For the Assassins of medieval Syria it was, in fact, part of their religion. The group, properly known as the Nizari Ismaili, formed a dissident religious sect, a splinter cult of Shia Islam. The Shias believe that every age has its own divine prophet (or Imam) who has been authorized by God to lead the faithful. Who these Imams were and who should inherit their title became the subject of conflict between competing Shia sects, and the Nizari Ismaili was just one of several sub-cults. A small group, it was forced to resort to secrecy to survive, and this secrecy would eventually become the group's greatest asset. Hasan-i-Sabbah (Hasane Sabbah; d.1124), who commanded the cult, was a friend and mentor of Prince Nizar, the son of the powerful caliph of Egypt, and a devoted follower of the Ismaili religion. The group believed Ismail to be the rightful eighth Imam, and the members were distrusted and persecuted for their heretical beliefs. Hasan studied the tenets of the cult in Egypt and travelled to the mountains of Persia (modern-day Iran), where he established himself as an Ismaili missionary (known as a *dai*).

Hasan's power base spread successfully from town to town as he preached the group's heretical message in the 1080s. He was clever, subtle, devious and frighteningly persuasive. With his followers, he travelled across the inhospitable district of Daylam in northwest Persia. They needed a secure base from which to operate and so put into operation a plan that would catapult them from the status of wandering preachers to that of an established power within Persia. They decided to seize a fortress. Hasan had more on his mind than finding a place of security, however; he had dreams of conquest far beyond Persia. Dominating politics in the Middle East at the time was the Seljuk dynasty of the Turkish Empire. At its height, this empire stretched from the Turkish heartland to the mountains of Persia. The cult's leader resolved to free Persia from the domination of this hated power, and in so doing his passionate religious mission became a political one.

The castle at Alamut (from *aluh-amut*, meaning the Eagle's Nest) became their chosen target. It occupied a prominent position in the Alamut valley, amid the Elburz range of mountains that was itself an important defensive feature. Alamut had virtually impregnable natural rock defences, which made it an ideal location for the secret cult Hasan was planning to establish. Built originally in the 860s, it included an array of outlying watchtowers and frontier forts that considerably enhanced its usefulness. Rather than take Alamut by force, Hasan sent trusted Ismaili missionaries to infiltrate the fort. This approach would characterize both the man himself and the cult of mysterious killers he was later to establish. In the year 1090 these dusty pilgrims settled in the villages around Alamut one by one and set about slowly converting the unsuspecting inhabitants. Soon these missionaries were able to teach the Ismaili doctrine inside the castle, and they made numerous converts to the faith. All the time these missionaries posed as the purveyors of some other, legitimate, trade or craft. When enough of the fort's inhabitants had been converted, Hasan himself was smuggled into the castle, and he lived there secretly for a while under the name Dihkuda.

It was only a matter of time before the fort's ruler discovered the subterfuge occurring all about him, but by then it was too late. The proud Persian chieftain was allowed to leave Alamut with the few followers that remained loyal to him. Hasan had achieved his first victory, and from this first bloodless conquest, he would continue to expand, sending *dais* into the surrounding mountains to repeat the success. Towns, villages and castles fell to the Ismaili campaign of infiltration and persuasion, a campaign that would be repeated centuries later by other, similarly charismatic leaders – men like Mao Zedong, Ho Chi Minh and Che Guevara. Where guile and cunning failed, the cult employed force. The Ismaili could train warriors as well as wandering preachers, and these led villagers in rebellious uprisings. Three areas came under Hasan's immediate control: Alamut and its surrounding district of Daylam, the southeast portion of Quhistan and the Girdkuh region. Where defiance to Seljuk authority existed to only a limited degree, Hasan's Assassins could exploit, manipulate and control it. His missionaries were ranked according to seniority, with the lowest office known as *dai*; the *dai'l-kabir* (superior missionary) ranked above this; and the *dai'd-duat* (chief missionary) at the head of the organization. Hasan and his successors occupied the post of chief missionary, although it was known to Western contemporaries as the office of Grand Master.

The Seljuk authorities could not ignore these fanatical bands of religious zealots for long. In 1092 the Seljuk vizier, Nizam al-Mulk, sent armies against the two Assassin strongholds at Alamut and Quhistan. Neither force could dislodge the cultists from their positions, and the guerrilla tactics that the group was pioneering came into play. Local forces were raised in the neighbourhood, and these troops ambushed the vizier's army around Alamut. This gained the Assassins a breathing space, which Hasan wanted to use to his advantage. He would initiate a reign of terror that would propel the Assassins from being just a tiny mountain cult to one of history's most feared group of assassins. From guerrilla warfare, Hasan decided to switch his campaign to one of selective political murder. He planned to overthrow the Seljuk domination not by a campaign of territorial gains but by eliminating key Seljuk officials. This strategy would eventually prove to be the downfall of the Assassins. History has since shown that in order successfully to overthrow a regime it is necessary to have popular support in towns and villages. As the Baader-Meinhof terrorist gang discovered to its cost in the early 1970s, assassination on its own will not bring about revolution. Assassination produces a vacancy that can be filled. The identity and agenda of the man who fills that vacant post is the crucial factor; yet the Grand Master's brutal political killings were the precursors of modern urban terrorist attacks. Hasan was a 'Carlos the Jackal' of his day, the world's first international terrorist.

The first Seljuk victim to die by the hand of an Assassin was Nizam al-Mulk (c.1018–92), the vizier to the Turkish sultan who had been dispatched to find and kill Hasan. Legend says that the two were great childhood friends (along with Arab hero Omar Khayyám). Each agreed to share any adult fame and fortune with the others, but this was not to be. Nizam al-Mulk was the first to achieve a position of some importance, when, in 1073, he won high office in the sultan's court. As agreed, he duly awarded Hasan with a degree of power, but the young man incurred the sultan's displeasure and Nizam and Hasan became deadly enemies. Hasan fled from the sultan's court, his long flight eventually ending at the fortress of Alamut in 1092. Perhaps inspired by (or perhaps even despite) the former friendship they had shared, Hasan sent a trusted Assassin, named Bu-Tahrir Arrani, to kill Nizam al-Mulk. The assassination had all the hallmarks of later murders – the Assassin dressed in the guise of a Sufi holy man and carried out the shocking murder during the holy festival of Ramadan. Within seconds of impaling the vizier on the point of his concealed dagger, the Assassin was dead, struck down by the iron scimitars of the panicked bodyguard. These elements – the hidden dagger, the innocuous disguise, the use of religious festivals or buildings and the suicidal attack by only one (or sometimes two) faithful members of the cult – would become the standard operating procedure that could not be stopped. There was absolutely no protection against this kind of suicidal murderer, a fact quickly understood by Seljuk officialdom – much to its dismay.

Two years later, in 1094, Prince Nizar was arrested and later killed. Hasan had regarded Nizar as the legal claimant to the (Ismaili) caliphate of Egypt, and with his death the Ismaili sect divided. Hasan refused to recognize the caliph's successor, and his band of fugitive Ismailis high in the Persian mountains became known as the Nizari Ismaili. History remembers them as the Assassins. From this moment, Hasan's doctrines, teachings and policies were his own. He represented no one. He was his own spiritual master and free to pursue his aims, without regard for religious ideologics abroad. The Persian Assassins devoted themselves to an endless struggle, not just against an oppressive dynasty but against the rest of the Islamic religion.

The sophisticated cult of religious killers became known as Assassins through the practices of its later Syrian branch. Ismailis had lived in Syria during the early years of Hasan's Persian campaign, but the branch achieved notoriety under the leadership of Rashid al Din Sinan (d. 1192) during the Crusades. From 1162 onwards, this medieval Moriarty spun a web of intrigues, alliances and plots that enabled the Syrian Assassins to survive amid the turbulent and chaotic politics of the Crusades. His reputation earned this Grand Master the title 'Old Man of the Mountain'. Hasan and most of his successors far away at Alamut were harsh, dogmatic and almost monastic, but Sinan used every conceivable lever to enhance his power. Politics, money and influence were Sinan's motivations, and his gang of Assassins shifted their alliances from one employer to another as fortunes waxed and waned. Hasan was a religious leader, an Ismaili prophet, leading the faithful in a terror war against the Seljuk forces of tyranny. Sinan was chief of a mercenary brotherhood.

According to legend, the Syrian Assassins were regular users of the locally grown drug hashish, thus giving them the name 'hashishin', the origin of the modern word 'assassin'. Sinan is reputed to have used the drug to instil loyalty, doping up a new recruit and allowing him to spend a few hours inside a secret 'Garden of Paradise' within the castle walls. With sumptuous foods, drinks and women, the unforgettable experience was afterwards explained as a trip to heaven. At the moment of death in the service of the Assassins, Sinan was able to convince his followers that they would return to that paradise.

So effective was this conditioning that the Old Man of the Mountain was able to command absolute and unquestioning loyalty. A Crusader, Count Henry of Champagne, once visited the Assassin fortress of Kahf to accept the Grand Master's apology for the murder in 1192 of a crusader called Conrad of Montferrat. While walking with Sinan around the castle, the Grand Master declared that no Christian knight was as loyal as his Assassin warriors. To prove his point he signalled to two Assassins high on a battlement. Without an instant of hesitation the two men threw themselves off the wall and to their deaths. With good reason was the regular Assassin warrior named a *fidai* (devoted one). Those cult members with a greater knowledge of doctrine were known as *lasiq* (adherent). Above the *lasiq* stood the more senior rank of *rafiq* (comrade). Each of these titles reflects the importance of group loyalty. The powerful and persuasive missionaries ranked above these fanatical warriors.

It was the assassination in 1152 of Raymond I, count of the Crusader state of Tripoli, that brought the Assassins to the attention of the Europeans. From the moment of his murder, Crusaders and Assassins became enemies. Until then, the Christians had ignored the hermit-like cult, huddled away in mountain fortresses dotted throughout the mountains of Syria. Although his actions sometimes failed to help the Assassin cause, the Grand Master Sinan continued to target the Christian aristocrats. In 1192 Conrad of Montferrat, the prince of Tyre, was walking through the crowded streets of that city to visit the Pishop of Beauvais. Turning a corner, the count was met by two Arab youths brandishing daggers – both were known to him. A fight ensued, in which Conrad suffered a mortal wound. Conrad's bodyguard was able to kill one of the Assassins in retaliation, but the other made his escape through the streets. One source says that Conrad, close to death, was hastily carried to a nearby church. It was there, by a stroke of misfortune, that the second Assassin had taken refuge in his flight. Seeing Conrad there, he moved in for the kill and finished the job that his Grand Master had sent him to perform.

Conrad of Montferrat had been an important and influential man. The great Arab leader, Saladin, sultan of Egypt and Syria, had conquered Jerusalem in 1187, and Conrad was seen as the ideal Crusader to lead the Christian forces in an attempt to retake the city. Like many assassinations throughout history, the identity of the instigator of the murder was the subject of speculation. Sinan's gang were well known as mercenaries, killing as much for profit as for self-interest. Rumours abounded that Saladin himself had approached the Grand Master with an offer of 10,000 gold pieces if he sent 'devoted ones' to assassinate both Conrad of Montferrat and Richard the Lionheart, king of England. It was said that Sinan agreed only to have Conrad murdered. Nevertheless, Richard himself became inextricably associated with the deadly order of killers when he was rumoured to have hired the Assassins for his own personal vendetta against Conrad! This rumour may have been started, or at least spread, by Philippe Augustus, king of France, who was a bitter rival of Richard's and who could only profit from such a defamatory story, which stuck – true or not. One French poet immortalized the connection in a poem that features the king teaching English boys how to commit murder, Assassin-style!

A later French king did not treat the cult so lightly. News of plans for a new crusade, to be launched in France by Louis IX (1226–70), reached Syria in 1237, greatly unnerving the Assassins. The Old Man of the Mountain of the day sent two 'devoted ones' to the coast to secure passage on a ship. Travelling in disguise, the two killers took a ship to Marseilles in southern France, where they prepared to travel north to Paris. There they would ambush the king of France and assassinate him, probably dying in the process. The Assassins soon learned, however, that a band of warrior-monks, the Knights Templars, with whom they were often on good terms, were to be involved in the coming campaign. This may explain why the Grand Master dispatched two, more senior, Assassins to pursue the first pair and stop them. They met each other in Marseilles, and legend has it that a grateful king sent the Assassins back to the Holy Land with gifts and peace offerings.

When campaigning near Acre in the Holy Land in 1250, Louis IX came face to face once more with members of the dangerous cult. This time, however, the Assassins warned him of the terrible fate that awaited him if he refused to pay off the cult. They told him that several other European nobles, including the emperor of Germany and the king of Hungary, were already paying protection money – money that provided immunity from the razor-sharp knives of the Assassins. At the following meeting, the king ensured that he was accompanied by a guard of Knights Hospitallers, formidable holy-warriors, similar in many ways to the Knights Templars.

Saladin may well have sought the services of the Syrian Assassins, but this did not mean that he was immune from their sinister attentions. While the sultan laid siege to the city of Aleppo in 1175, the city's ruler, Gumushtakin, hired the Assassins to murder Saladin, thus bringing to an end the siege. Several 'devoted ones' were able to enter Saladin's camp in disguise and prepare to move in for the kill. Before they could enter the sultan's tent, an emir, one of Saladin's officers, recognized the men as Assassins he had dealt with previously. Foolishly, he approached them to ask their business in the camp. They drew their daggers and killed him. This attempt to conceal their intentions failed, and during the struggle to capture them, the Assassins killed several guards. Every one of the cult members died during the fight. Saladin himself was unharmed. A similar assassination plot a year later was more successful, and only Saladin's armour saved his life as the killers tried to stab him. As happened at the siege of Aleppo, all the Assassins died rather than surrender to the sultan's bodyguard.

Neither the Persian nor Syrian Assassins had much of a long-term future. Isolated and feared, both groups succumbed to larger and more organized forces. In Persia the Mongol hordes led by Hulegu, brother of the Great Khan, laid siege to the castles of the cult and in 1256 sacked Alamut. The last Persian Grand Master, a young man named Khwurshah, was taken into captivity, dying a short time later. The Nizari Ismaili were not beaten yet – the Syrian members of the cult were still holed up in their mountain retreats, but they were faced with a foe just as terrible as Hulegu. Within twenty years even these tenacious and fanatical warriors would be crushed under the tremendous pressure of the Mameluke Empire. This new and powerful force in the Muslim world began conquests in Syria and the Holy Land under the leadership of the ambitious sultan Baibars I (Baybars; 1223–77). Baibars ruled from Egypt, and his growing conquests formed the basis for a new Islamic empire. There was no place within for a fanatical band of professional mercenary assassins who could infiltrate an enemy camp or palace with ease and murder counts, viziers or kings. Baibars laid siege to several Assassin fortresses in the early 1270s and by the end of 1273 had conquered all their strongholds. The most feared and reviled organization of the day had been crushed, never to rise again.

THE ART OF NINJUTSU

The Japanese warlord Fugasiti was ever mindful of the threat from an assassin. Accordingly he protected himself with a tough bodyguard of samurai warriors and had his castle constructed to provide every possible defence. The moat was wide, the walls high, and every corridor was wide and easily defensible. Every possible entrance and exit was guarded by alert and competent samurai warriors, and in Fugasiti's bedchamber his most trusted samurai watched over the lord while he slept. All to no avail. One morning the lord was found murdered in his bed and the lone warrior set to guard him had been similarly dealt with. No one in the castle had seen or heard any intruder during the night, yet one man, a ninja assassin, had somehow penetrated the multi-layered defences of the fortress in order to carry out the crime.

No study of assassination would be complete without reference to the Japanese ninja. The ninja need practically no introduction. They have survived the centuries in story, legend and image – to be recreated in low-budget martial arts movies, in comics and cartoons, at fancy-dress parties and on the shelves of toy shops. The ninja myth has eclipsed the fact of the ninja phenomenon: from the seventeenth century onwards (if not earlier), truth began to become distorted. The black-garbed men of mystery, these deceptive and silent martial artists were ascribed strange powers of invisibility, of magic and of illusion. They began to be portrayed as Japanese folk heroes, righters of wrongs, honourable (if secret) warriors, fighters for the *status quo*. Several modern *ryu* (schools) of ninjutsu exist today in Japan, and all profess to teach ninjutsu as a wholesome martial art. The truth is very different.

The ninja were members of a number of Japanese families who made a living by hiring out their services as professional murderers and saboteurs. They were assassins of the highest order. No group of humans in the history of mankind can have matched the same level of professionalism and dedication by which the ninja earned their grisly reputation. The emergence of the ninja myth really took hold after the Japanese feudal warlords (the *daimyo*) were united under the leadership of Tokugawa Ieyasu (1543–1616). His dominance of Japanese politics put an end to internecine squabbles and thus ended forever the role of the ninja as mercenaries for hire. In fact, Tokugawa Ieyasu was so afraid of the ninja clans that he took 300 of their number into his castle guard. What better way of stopping an assassin than to employ an assassin to stop him!

For perhaps five centuries the ninja had occupied a niche that existed in Japanese feudal society. Dominating both Japanese politics and war were the samurai, the loyal warrior-retainers of the feudal warlords. The samurai, who lived by a strict code of honour (*bushido*), fought their opponents fairly, without trickery or deception. As we know today, there are many ways to fight a war, but the samurai were limited to only one – an honest and fair fight. All the advantages of secret warfare – spying, sabotage, arson and assassination – were denied to them. But the independent families living high in the remote and mountainous provinces of Iga and Koga were not so concerned with honour and honesty. These clans hired themselves out as mercenary killers, men who were capable and willing to carry out all the unsavoury jobs that a samurai would never even admit to supporting. The clans of these two provinces virtually formed the ninja cult that was to so terrorize the Japanese aristocracy. Among the most powerful of the ninja clans were the Wada, the Hattori and the Oe, and they reached their peak during the Age of the Country at War (the *sengoku-jidai*), which lasted from 1450 until 1615.

In 1560, during this violent period, the rebellious leader Dodo, vassal of the *daimyo* Rokkaku Yoshitaka, was besieged by his lord. Yoshitaka realized that he could not take Dodo's castle by conventional means and turned to the services of ninja from Iga province. The leader of this mercenary band stealthily penetrated the castle and was able to steal a paper lantern from the fortress. These lanterns were typically decorated with the *mon* or heraldic badge of Dodo's forces. With this as a model, the ninja created more of them. Then, dressing as the defenders and carrying their freshly painted lanterns, the ninja brazenly approached the castle gates and were allowed in. Once inside, they used an established tactic – they set fire to buildings, causing chaos and confusion. During the panic, several members of the ninja unit were able to carry out their intended mission, and then make their escape.

The victorious Yoshitaka was also a target of ninja from Iga, as well as an employer. This time the ninja were hired by the rival Asai family, an event that illustrates the real mercenary nature of the ninja killers. At the siege of his castle at Futo, however, the ninja acted only as a covert raiding force much as they had done at Dodo's fortress, and once they had set the castle on fire, signalled for the Asai army to attack. In most cases the names of individual ninja are not known to us – fame attracted arrest and execution, and a famous ninja was a dead one, cooked alive in a vat of boiling oil – but a century before the time of Rokkaku Yoshitaka, the identity of a ninja named Yamoto was preserved. In 1478 the trained assassin was given the task of killing the high-ranking samurai Herrito. Yamoto was able to scale the walls of his well-guarded house and stealthily avoid the patrols who kept a look out for intruders. Eventually, he entered Herrito's empty bedchamber and climbed up into the rafters of the low ceiling, to await the samurai's entrance. As soon as his target came to bed and fell asleep, Yamoto planned to drop down, silently murder him and then make his escape. Things did not go as planned, however. Herrito arrived with two friends, and the men proceeded to relax just beneath the ninja and begin a game of *go*. The game continued for five hours, with Yamoto only 3 metres (10 feet) away all the time, hanging from the rafters above their heads! At last the three men finished the game and Herrito was left alone to retire to bed. Within the hour, after carefully listening to the samurai's breathing to make sure the target was not feigning sleep, Yamoto quietly dropped, drew his *ninjato* sword and killed him with one well-aimed sword thrust.

The ninja clans were modelled on the tightly structured samurai clans, but they were cloaked in secrecy. Not only was the identity of the clan leader, the *jonin*, kept secret from the ninja, but the techniques and fighting skills of the group were shrouded in mystery. Techniques were grouped into distinct schools, or *ryu*, so there was the Iga *ryu*, the Koga *ryu*, the Nakagawa *ryu*, and so on. The schools guarded their secrets jealously. It was said that when members of the Nakagawa clan practised in one corner of a lord's castle, no one outside of the ninja clan was allowed near them for fear he might see the secret techniques of the cult. Anyone who disseminated these techniques was often the target of immediate assassination by the ninja themselves. This deadly threat did not stop some later writers committing ninja skills and types of equipment to paper. The *Bansen Shukai*, the most authoritative original work on ninja to have survived, was written by Fujibayashi Yasutake in 1676.

The training regime that prospective ninja underwent was tough.

77

Beginning at an early age (sometimes as young as five years old) the boys would be trained in ninja skills by their fathers or trainers. Flexibility, co-ordination, strength and stamina were developed to incredible lengths, and the boys found that their entire lives revolved around the perfection of their physical abilities. They learned to hang from trees for hours, to dislocate their own joints to enable them to squeeze into small spaces, to stay under water for minutes on end and to travel cross-country up to 160 kilometres (100 miles) in one day. Ninja agents had a reputation for superhuman feats because they had been moulded into supermen. One story relates how a ninja stumbled into a trap laid for him in a castle corridor. Fearing imminent detection and unable to free his foot, the brave man cut off his own foot and made his escape. Strength, stamina and suppleness do not a ninja make, however. The real art of ninjutsu centred on the assassin's ability to avoid detection going into and getting out of the target location. If such a thing as a ninja philosophy existed, it certainly focused on the myriad techniques of deception.

One method of getting close to a potential victim was through the adoption of a disguise, and the ninja clans used seven major identities to this end. These Seven Ways of Going (*shichi ho do*) were:

Akindo – merchant
Hokashi – musician
Komuso – wandering priest
Ronin – masterless samurai, wandering warrior
Sarugaku – actor or entertainer
Shukke – Buddhist monk
Yamabushi – mountain warrior-monk

Some of these innocent disguises allowed the agent to carry a weapon of some description. A musician's flute could be weighted and used as a club, the warrior-monk could easily carry a staff that held some sort of blade, and both the *yamabushi* and the *ronin* could carry a blade openly. The ninja were adept at concealing weapons within innocuous items – a metal fighting chain was sometimes hidden within a staff – and such a weapon would have the advantage of great surprise, coming as it did from a musician, priest or other 'harmless' traveller.

For the assassination attempt, the ninja would need a more effective costume, most likely a stolen uniform from the army guarding the castle. This would enable the agent to continue the deception up until the moment of the murder and then assist in his escape. More famously, the ninja adopted night-black head-to-toe costumes, complete with mysterious face-masks, which rendered the ninja almost invisible beneath moon- or starlight. There were supposed to be brown, green and even snow white versions of this costume for work in different terrain. Some evidence has come to light of chainmail sleeves being worn by some ninja under their costumes, affording them limited protection in a sword fight, but contrary to popular myth, the ninja were not great warriors and carried little offensive equipment and rarely any armour. The ninja philosophy of deception scorned open combat. That was left for the samurai, who were trained almost from birth to take down an opponent in a fair sword fight. Ninja avoided fights whenever possible; it was always better never to have to deal with an enemy than to face him in combat. And when this was unavoidable, they never fought fairly.

Nobles devised several techniques to counter the stealth of the ninja, who was trained to walk without sound. One was the use of a simple but effective string of bells hung across a darkened corridor; another was a specially constructed wooden floor that was designed to squeak when trodden on. A working example of this 'nightingale flooring' still exists at Nijo castle in Kyoto. For crossing moats ninja were able to hold their breaths for considerable periods, and they could improvise snorkels from reeds or the scabbard of their *ninjato* sword if necessary. Other equipment also came in useful. Collapsible ladders, ropes and grappling hooks were used to scale the monumental walls of the Japanese fortresses. Within the castle walls guards had to be dealt with immediately, especially during the ninja's escape. For this purpose the clans were reputed to have mastered various chemical formulae. Smoke bombs and flash bombs were said to have been used by some agents as a means of blinding their pursuers. Others threw down *tetsu-bishi*, tiny, multi-pronged spikes that passed easily through the straw sandals of the average samurai, impaling his foot and taking him out of the chase. If immediate escape from the castle seemed impossible following the assassination attempt, one more tactic was open to the ninja with nerves of steel. He could remain in the castle, within the victim's chamber, close to the body! This audacity more than once saved a desperate ninja from detection as he squeezed into a closet or chest while the *daimyo*'s samurai searched the grounds for the murderer.

Although both the Muslim Assassins and the Japanese ninja were professional killers, greatly feared for their political murders over some considerable time, they differed greatly in method. The Assassins found that their interests were best served by infiltrating the staff, especially the bodyguard, of an intended victim. They could get close to their target and then strike with ease, shock multiplying violence to achieve a long list of kills. Most Assassins were cut down by the victim's bodyguard within seconds of carrying out the assassination. Little if any thought was given to ways in which the successful killers could escape the scene of the crime. Detection after the fact was irrelevant, and through the conditioning of faith (or drugs) the Assassins considered every assassination a suicide mission, a one-way trip to paradise. The ninja could not think like this. They were not driven by blind faith or a belief in the afterlife, their prime motivation was professionalism. It is doubtful that any but the *jonin* actually made any money from the assassination trade. Escape was as important a part of an assassination as the infiltration and murder itself. No ninja wished to be caught, to be tortured and beaten, and finally to be boiled in oil. This survival instinct made life much harder for the Japanese shadow warriors than for their Middle Eastern counterpart. This accounts for the wild profusion of techniques, tools and weapons employed by the ninja clans.

As well as the *ninjato* sword, the ninja were reputed to have employed a wide variety of lethal weaponry in the course of their trade. Their arsenal included blowpipes, *bo* staffs, medieval hand cannon, daggers and *jo* clubs. The staff, made of hollowed bamboo, could conceal a weighted fighting chain (*shinobi-zue*), and this chain might itself be attached to a dagger (*kyoketsu-shogei*) or a sickle (*kusarigama*). The combination of chain and weapon was unique to the ninja fighting style. Either the weapon or the chain could be used in attack, or both might be employed to attack and entangle or disarm an opponent. Combining the concept of both weighted chain and club was the *nunchaku*, two heavy rods connected by a piece of chain. The chain gave power and speed to the blows of the *nunchaku*. Exemplifying the versatility of ninja weaponry were the *nekode*, iron claws mounted on bands worn around the hands that assisted in climbing yet could double up as a nasty improvised weapon. Of all Japanese weapons, however, one stands out above all others as having a ninja origin – the *shuriken,* or throwing stars, were wholly a creation of the ninja clans. Each metal disc had an edge of razor-sharp blades, and when thrown at an opponent might wound him badly if it struck him in the face. The small stars were thrown either overhand or Frisbee-fashion and could be coated with an improvised contact poison, greatly increasing their lethal qualities.

So valued was their deadly expertise that, as the final contest for ultimate power played itself out in the late sixteenth century, the ninja were used at every stage. The most remarkable assassination of any political leader anywhere took place during this period. A ninja who had been sent to assassinate the *daimyo* Uesugi Kenshin (1530–78) discovered that the leader took extensive security precautions, making the murder attempt a difficult one. But the resourceful ninja found a way. The justly paranoid *daimyo* was only ever alone during his visits to the toilet, and so the hardy ninja secretly found a way into the cesspit beneath his lavatory. At the appropriate time the killer stabbed Uesugi Kenshin through the anus with a spear. He did not die immediately, but staggered to his bed and died, in silent agony, several days later.

One of Japan's greatest historical figures, Oda Nobunaga (1534–82), was the target of several ninja assassinations (twice by primitive guns), but he survived to make war on the ninja clans of Iga province for harbouring rebels who had defied him. The war that followed in 1579 is known as the Iga Revolt, and it ended with the destruction of the Iga ninja clans. Their members dispersed across Japan to form new *ryu* and find new masters. Iga would never again be the centre of ninja strength and the role of the ninja as freelance mercenary assassins was itself weakened by the episode. The last recorded use of ninja (by the all-conquering shogun Tokugawa Iemitsu; 1604–51) was during the Shimabara Rebellion in 1638, when they were employed to infiltrate the rebel fortress, start fires, steal maps and one of the enemy's banners and learn passwords. From 1640 until the end of the feudal system of government in 1868, the role of the samurai declined with the decline in conflict and warfare. Intimately connected with the fortunes of the samurai and their love of violent conflict, the ninja discovered that their time, too, had come and gone.

Although some martial arts schools of today claim to teach the techniques and skills of the ninja (often claiming a direct link to the scattered ninja of Iga province), they little resemble the murderous clans of history. Without the mercenary attitude, the exotic weaponry and the use of terror, assassination and arson to advance the client's political goal, what is left? Ninjutsu was always about deceit, lies, deception and death. It is doubtful that any ninja considered that his profession could help develop his inner spirit and bring order to his life. The true inheritors of ninjutsu are not the tiny numbers of martial artists claiming such a link, but the special forces soldiers, SWAT teams, commandos and counter-terrorist teams of the modern world. Armed to the teeth with deadly high-tech weapons, such as laser sights, silenced sub-machine-guns, night-vision goggles, rappelling ropes, ballistic jackets, breaching charges and long-range sniper rifles, these black-clad killers display all the resourcefulness, strength of mind and professionalism that characterized their distant cousins, the ninja. Today's feared shadow warriors are the soldiers of the SAS, Spetsnatz, Green Berets and GSG-9.

4. The Role of Assassins in Warfare

Assassination is often considered a phenomenon of peacetime, but there have been many incidents of wartime assassination. The Second World War saw a remarkable proliferation of para-military groups and special operations, and for the first time in Western warfare 'honour' and 'fair play' were discarded as outmoded concepts. It was now deemed strategically sound to 'cut the head off' of a particular military unit in order to render it useless. The delay involved in replacing a military commander with a suitable successor was thought to gain time and create disorder among the enemy. Some military leaders were so talented that no one could have stepped into their shoes, and these commanders were particularly sought out as targets for assassination by both the Allied and Axis powers. General Reinhard Heydrich, Admiral Isoroku Yamamoto, General Erwin Rommel, Winston Churchill and Adolf Hitler were all intended victims in various wartime assassination plots.

Prime Minister Winston Churchill had only a single bodyguard, a former police detective called W.H. Thompson. Churchill also trusted his life to a Colt revolver from his personal collection – and practised with it often at Chequers, the prime minister's official country residence in Buckinghamshire. He realized that his position would almost certainly invite the unwanted attentions of a Nazi assassin and once commented grimly: 'The Germans believe I am one of their most formidable enemies. They will not stop short of assassination.' Although Hitler never did send out a hit team to kill Churchill, one incident illustrates how vulnerable the British Prime Minister was. Within a few weeks of the Allied Casablanca conference attended by Churchill in 1943, the Luftwaffe shot down a plane (BOAC 777a) flying from Lisbon to England. The Germans had been convinced that the plane was carrying Winston Churchill. Although he was not on board, it had contained another passenger of international note – Leslie Howard, the British actor.

In that same month, a remarkable historical coincidence occurred. The United States military decided to make an attempt on the life of the celebrated Japanese commander, Admiral Isoroku Yamamoto (1884–1943). Yamamoto had masterminded the extraordinary attack on Pearl Harbor in 1941, which forced the United States to join the war. Yamamoto had been the first naval strategist fully to integrate the power of the long-range bomber with the mobility of the aircraft carrier. His surprise attack on the US naval base at Pearl Harbor had depended entirely on the carrier for its shock value. He understood that the armoured battleships of old were dinosaurs and that naval battles were now air battles. He had complete confidence in his own tactical abilities but knew that the Japanese government and its ponderous military machine would not be able to wage war with the United States on equal terms. None of the Japanese naval encounters with the US Navy was ever as successful as Pearl Harbor, and, despite his brilliance, the admiral was forced to face one defeat after another.

Yamamoto's infamy and his skill made him a valuable target for the Americans, and as luck would have it, they had been able to crack Japan's secret and 'uncrackable' military code. In this way they were able to monitor radio traffic in the Pacific and to plot the admiral's movements, enabling the US Pacific High Command to become aware of his itinerary during a forthcoming inspection tour of the Japanese forces in the Solomon Islands. At Tassafaronga Field on Guadalcanal eighteen, hand-picked fighter pilots were ordered to prepare their aircraft for an interception. They were going to assassinate Admiral Yamamoto over the Pacific Ocean. Long-range fuel tanks were rushed in from Port Moresby in time for the start of the mission. On 18 April 1943 Major Mitchell of 199th Squadron led the planes out on a two-hour flight that successfully intercepted the admiral's plane (a Sally transport aircraft). Its six Zero fighter-escorts were dealt with by the squadron's powerful, two-engined Lightnings, while one pilot, Lieutenant Lanphier, closed in on the fleeing Sally. Yamamoto's plane had been chased out of formation and was flying low, trying to force the Lightning to overshoot. The ungainly transport made an easy target, however, and after receiving a number of direct hits, it crashed into the ocean. There were no survivors. The coded message, immediately radioed back to headquarters by the American commander to signal a successful mission, was 'Pop goes the weasel'. The Imperial Japanese Navy had lost its finest commander;

the United States had lost its most formidable opponent of the war.

A number of attempts were made, in North Africa and France, to assassinate Germany's outstanding commander, Field Marshal Erwin Rommel. His known headquarters were targeted by Allied air-strikes, and commando raids attempted to catch him at suspected locations, but, as it had with the assassination on Yamamoto, luck would play a part in the most successful attempt. In 1944 Rommel was given a command in France. When a unit of British commandos was captured during a beach reconnaissance (several months prior to the D-Day invasion) the field marshal insisted on interviewing the prisoners himself to try to find out at which section of the coastline the Allies planned to launch their impending invasion. Outside his headquarters, at a chateau near La Petite Roche Guyon, one of the British prisoners happened to get a glimpse of a road sign. Although he was transferred to a POW camp, he was able to smuggle out the location of Rommel's headquarters, and it eventually reached Britain. Remarkably, the British high command acted on the tip-off and a flight of Allied fighter-bombers is reputed to have made strafing runs on Rommel's staff car outside the chateau. Rommel survived the incident, however, and lived to die by his own hand after D-Day and the failure of the officers' plot against Hitler.

NIGHT OF THE LONG KNIVES

Adolf Hitler instituted a bloody purge of his own National Socialist (Nazi) Party long before the war itself began. Hitler's fascination and obsession with power and control drove him to take every precaution. Even by 1934 he had travelled a great distance along his journey to ultimate power. The year before that, the Nazis had gained complete control of the German government. Hitler would soon set in motion his plans to restructure the social life and psychology of the German people, but first he had to eliminate any potential rivals within the party.

The Sturmabteilung (SA) had been the iron fist with which Hitler had seized power. The rough tactics and violent reputation of its 400,000 members gave it a discernible, intimidating aura. From their distinctive uniforms the paramilitary thugs were known as 'Brownshirts', but their official title said it all – they were the Nazi Party's 'stormtroopers'. In command of this powerful organization was Ernst Röhm (1887–1934), a professional soldier who had been invited by Hitler to step in and reorganize the SA, which the Führer believed to be getting out of hand.

With such tremendous power at his command, Röhm played a pivotal role in the Nazi bid for domination. Gregor Strasser (1892–1934) was another figure who seemed destined for great things. His easy, affable manner made him popular with the local Nazi groups he supervised, and some members of the party suspected he might well make a better leader than the crude Austrian corporal. The Führer never fully trusted Strasser and was quite content to let him bicker with Joseph Goebbels, since this lessened the chances of any conspiracy against himself. Hitler's paranoia was such that he would match enemies against each other within his own cabinet.

The SA had grown to vast proportions (2.5 million members) by June 1934, and its influence and power now rivalled that of the army. High-ranking military officers were alarmed by what the ideologically driven SA had become. What was more, the leaders of the SA had even greater ambitions, many wanting a second 'revolution'. Röhm presented to the new Nazi cabinet a proposal to create a new People's Army. Hitler dismissed this idea, which enflamed Röhm and his supporters. To appease those people who feared and hated the SA (including a wide variety of business interests and, of course, the army), Hitler plotted to cripple the organization. This was to be part of a 'moderating' campaign, which the Führer found necessary to forge wider and deeper links into the lucrative German business world.

To prevent the SA from rising up against him before he could fully implement his planned reforms, Hitler (ruthless as always) first set out a one-night assassination operation designed to purge the SA of its most formidable leaders and the Nazi Party of Hitler's most feared rivals. This bloody massacre, which was carried out on 30 June 1934, became known as the Night of the Long Knives. The killings were carried out by members of Heinrich Himmler's Schutzstaffel (Defence Squads) or SS, the Nazi agency tipped to take over the SA's role. During that night as many as 1000 key SA Brownshirts were cornered and shot to death. The real target of the purge, Ernst Röhm, was captured and imprisoned in a Munich gaol. Attempts to persuade him to shoot himself failed, and so Röhm bravely faced the two SS killers as they entered his cell, guns drawn, and shot him to death. With Röhm now silenced and the SA in complete disarray, Hitler could effectively make the alliances he wanted without further interference. His hold over the party was now complete. One of his aims had been to curry favour with the German army, but in a move to prevent his own party thinking that he was dancing to the army's tune, Hitler also had two generals, General von Scleicher and General von Bredow, assassinated during the purge.

Just as he had key figures in the Nazi far-right assassinated, Hitler also ordered that Gregor Strasser, representing the Nazi Party's left-wing, also be murdered. It was said that Strasser always considered the 'social-ism' in National Socialism to be far more than just a meaningless label for propaganda's sake. His calls for the nationalization of certain businesses forced the influential financial backers of the party to demand that Hitler kept his house in order. Strasser had to go. The Führer's devotion to the cause and his utter ruthlessness resulted in Strasser being arrested by the Gestapo at his home in Berlin and shot a few hours later. Violence reigned in those few fear-crazed hours, to be followed almost immedi-ately by the veneration of Hitler by the army. President Hindenburg even congratulated him for his 'energetic and successful action' in sup-pressing 'high treason'. Hindenburg went on to thank the Nazi leader for rescuing 'the German people from great danger'. No one wanted civil war, and now that this seemed to have been deftly averted the guard of the German people dropped. Where the SA had vainly sought to tread, however, the burgeoning SS would step without fear of objection. And the SS would become a far greater rival to the German army than either the SA or Ernst Röhm could ever have dreamed.

HANGMAN HEYDRICH

With much of western and eastern Europe in Nazi hands after 1940, many of the continent's legitimate governments fled to Britain. Some, in particular the French, were able to maintain secret links with resistance movements that had sprung up under the Nazi occupation. Churchill helped to establish a secret organization that enabled Britain to liaise with these desperate resistance groups, to supply them with weapons and equipment. This organization was the Special Operations Executive (SOE). In many cases the SOE was able to recruit agents in Britain who were well acquainted with a particular occupied nation. An agent – Pol-ish, French or Dutch – would be infiltrated back into his or her country of origin to link up with resistance fighters and to help co-ordinate some sort of armed struggle against the Nazi war effort. There was no more spectacular show of resistance during the Second World War than the assassination of Reinhard Heydrich (1904–42).

As chief of the Sicherheitsdienst (the SD, or secret service of the SS)

Heydrich was deputy chief of the Gestapo and the Acting Protector of Bohemia and Moravia (part of pre-war Czechoslovakia). In 1941 the Protector (the *Reichsprotektor*) was given indefinite sick leave, and Heydrich naturally stepped into his shoes. The SS commander certainly made an immediate impression, authorizing the execution of 300 Czechs. His expertise in the art of terror resulted in a number of flying visits around Europe. He was continually in need to crush incidents of sabotage – and he did this quite ruthlessly, executing hundreds of suspects and quickly earning himself the nickname of 'Hangman Heydrich'. No man was more hated in Czechoslovakia. Yet the unadventurous resistance movement seemed reluctant to conduct sabotage and terrorism against Heydrich's brutal regime. Being so far from Britain it was poorly supplied by the SOE and felt that it was better placed to provide intelligence rather than resistance. And with the Soviets close by, it must also have had an eye to the future and that distant day when Czechoslovakia would be liberated.

President Benĕ of Czechoslovakia, it now appears, may have been embarrassed by criticism from the SOE, which noted that the Czech resistance movement seemed particularly inactive. It seems that an audacious operation to assassinate Heydrich was planned by the SOE without consultation with the Czech resistance fighters. Jan Kubis and Josef Gabeik, two members of the free (exiled) Czech army, were parachuted into the country by the SOE. The assassination team was able to ambush the Nazi commander on 27 May 1942 in a Prague street as he was being driven back to Hradschin Castle – his sumptuous billet. One of the team stepped out of cover with a Sten sub-machinegun and prepared to spray Heydrich's car with bullets – but it jammed. As befits his violent and reckless nature, Heydrich ordered the car to stop and pulled out his own pistol. As he stepped from the car one of the assassins threw a grenade, which wounded the Nazi chief. Heydrich died a week later from a gangrene infection of his wounds.

The assassins had managed to escape the murder scene under cover of a smoke screen. They fled with a large number of other resistance fighters to the Karel Boromejsky (Karl Borromaeus) Church. Unfortunately, the killers were betrayed by one of their number and a battle followed, which resulted in the death of several members of the resistance. Trapped in the church crypt, some of the group committed suicide. Eventually, the Nazis ordered that the Prague fire brigade flood the crypt, thus drowning any resistance fighters who were still alive.

Altogether, 120 people were killed in the assault on the church.

The Czech resistance movement had been dealt a terrible blow, and the killing had barely even started. In retaliation for the assassination, the Nazis began a terrible cull of the Czech population. A former prime minister joined over a thousand other innocent civilians in death — victims of summary execution. Worst of all, the village of Lidice was utterly destroyed, its men were executed and the women and children were shipped to Nazi concentration camps. In Berlin on the day of the attack, Goebbels rounded up 500 of those Jews who were still free and when Heydrich died a few days later, he had 152 of them executed. The blood spilled by the two SOE assassins seemed still to be spreading.

It was clear that any advantage gained from Heydrich's murder had been immediately and brutally obliterated by the retaliatory bloodbath that it provoked. Security measures were greatly increased, and a later attempt to assassinate the Minister for Education and Propaganda failed. The Germans made an even greater effort to crush the Czech resistance and terrorize the nation, reducing still further the spirit of the people. So what were the benefits? Beně had wanted to make a show of Czech resistance, not just to the British but also for the benefit of the Soviets, who had been urging Beně to try to stimulate more vigorous opposition to the Nazi occupation. In the end it was ordinary people who just wanted to avoid the war and all its effects who were to become the unintended victims of a fruitless propaganda exercise.

OPERATION FOXLEY

On 23 July 1998 a dossier of remarkable wartime secrets was declassified by the British government and released to the Public Record Office. It provided full details of an audacious (and untried) plan to assassinate Adolf Hitler. The SOE was again involved, and their proposal was to prove far more controversial than the murder of Heydrich. The idea was first suggested in a secret cable from the SOE station at Algiers on 19 June 1944. The organization had learned that Hitler was due to stay at a chateau in the south of France, and it proposed an attempt to assassinate him. Both Prime Minister Winston Churchill and Foreign Secretary Anthony Eden were briefed on the proposal, but no such attempt was made.

From that first spark the SOE, under the guidance of its commander-in-chief Major-General Colin Gubbins, worked feverishly on a plan to murder the Führer. He briefed his officers about the proposal in a War

Office meeting room on 28 June. An enormous amount of intelligence needed to be gathered, and as the SOE began to learn more about Adolf Hitler, his habits, his routines and his location, a number of different plans were tentatively suggested. But there were those in the War Office who spoke out against the idea. Hitler had been an undeniable failure as a military strategist and had been responsible for some of Germany's most serious errors of the war, including his failure to move against the British Expeditionary Force trapped on the beaches at Dunkirk, his decision to switch from attacks on RAF airfields to cities during the Battle of Britain and his crucial decision to open up a second front against Russia while he continued to wage a war against the British. There were many more. Major Field-Robertson, head of the SOE's German section, argued convincingly that Hitler probably served the interests of the Allies better alive than dead. Further strategic blunders might actually help to shorten the war by a large margin. And what about the ethical considerations? Were not the Nazis notorious assassins? Hitler had himself masterminded the murder of his friends and colleagues during the Night of the Long Knives. The conclusion that the SOE came to, suggested by Air Vice-Marshal A.P. Ritchie, was that the war in Europe was driven solely by Hitler's personal ambitions and that Nazi Germany would effectively fall apart without him. This view won the day, and the SOE was given the go-ahead to create a mixed bag of plans to assassinate the dictator. The historic decision to attempt to murder the Führer was code-named Operation Foxley.

Within three months, the Special Operations Executive had prepared a 120-page document that detailed every aspect of Hitler's personal life, his tastes, and little-known aspects of his daily routine. Maps and diagrams were included, as well as a collection of valuable reconnaissance photographs. All this information was intended to support one of three assassination options.

The first option was based on the fact that for much of the war Hitler was known to reside at Berchtesgaden, high in the Bavarian mountains. This remote and beautiful retreat was to have been penetrated by a lone assassin, a sniper named as Captain E.H. Bennet, who was a British army officer serving as military attaché in Washington. The plan called for Bennet to kill Hitler with a long-range sniper rifle while the Nazi leader took his regular morning walk. Warned of the immense dangers involved in the plan, Bennet is reputed to have 'showed even greater keenness'. Alternatively, a small team would be infiltrated into Berchtesgaden with an anti-tank rocket launcher (a 'bazooka') with which they would blow up Hitler's limousine (an armoured Mercedes touring car), killing him instantly.

The second option focused on the vulnerabilities of the Führer's personal railway train, the Führerzug. Hitler's carriage could be identified by a white stripe running beneath the windows. By one means or another it could be targeted, either by derailment as it passed through a tunnel or by throwing a suitcase of explosives onto the track from the platform as it sped through a station on its route. When the SOE scientists considered the use of chemical or biological weapons, the Führerzug again featured in their plans. The location of the tank supplying drinking water to Hitler's coach was discovered, and one idea proposed poisoning this supply with a fatal toxin. Since he was thought to drink copious amounts of tea, it was hoped that Hitler would quickly succumb to the poison. Other outlandish ideas included the use of a poison-filled syringe disguised as a fountain pen or the contamination of Hitler's clothing with a deadly germ, ideas that would later find favour with the CIA in their attempts to assassinate Fidel Castro. One of the major arguments against using poisons or deadly viruses was the difficulty in administering them. A potential assassin had to be able to carry the syringe or pen or other container carrying the agent with him and negotiate countless body searches.

The third option favoured a more traditional military approach – a heavy bombardment of Hitler's residence, the Eagle's Nest, immediately followed by a parachute assault by a battalion-sized unit of commandos. The purpose was to eliminate any remaining resistance and ensure the success of the mission – that is, to locate Adolf Hitler and kill him if he had survived the bombing. By luck, full details of the area, of the Führer's house and his security arrangements were handed over to the British by a German POW who had served as part of Hitler's bodyguard at Berchtesgaden.

The option to assassinate Hitler with a well-placed agent using a sniper rifle received the greatest attention from War Office chiefs. Captain Bennet was approached for the mission in March 1945, but before plans could progress, the war reached its climax. Berlin was surrounded by the Allies, and Hitler, cornered in his command bunker, committed suicide rather than be captured alive. Had Hitler died earlier, before the Allies reached German soil, the course of the Second World War may have been dramatically altered. Is it right to assume that the death of

Adolf Hitler would necessarily have ended the war? There were many able and fanatical men ready to step into the Führer's boots, including Joseph Goebbels, Herman Göring, Martin Bormann, Albert Speer and others. The war might have been continued under better leadership and with greater German persistence thanks to the 'martyrdom' of Hitler by an assassin's bullet. Nothing would have changed for the better.

Even worse, the war might have been ended in a fashion that would have been far from satisfactory for the Allies. With Hitler out of the way, one of the Nazi leaders who were hoping for a peaceful resolution to the war might have taken control. If this had happened shortly after D-Day there is a distinct possibility that Nazi Germany might have survived in some form or other after it had relinquished its hold on all the territories it had seized since 1939. Field Marshal Rommel approached Hitler in 1944, a month after the massive D-Day offensive to liberate Europe, with a proposal: 'The unequal struggle is nearing its end. I must ask you immediately to draw the necessary conclusions.' Hitler would not listen. During the final few days of the war it became clear that there were others, too, who were willing to negotiate rather than fight Hitler's bitter and futile war to the end. On 23 April Göring sent a telegram to Hitler's bunker that announced his intention to negotiate with the Allies (on Hitler's behalf). Hitler, beside himself with rage, paranoia and frustration, denounced Göring as a traitor. The SS chief, Himmler, also had serious doubts and on the evening of 23 April met with Count Bernadotte of Sweden at the Swedish consulate in Lübeck. There he told the count that Hitler was dead (or would be in a matter of days) and that he would be willing to capitulate on the Western Front to Allied forces. He was negotiating the surrender of Germany in the hope of keeping the nation intact. He had even sketched out plans for a Party of National Union, which would replace National Socialism in the post-war era. Of course, these meetings came to nothing, and Himmler was informed that the Allies would accept nothing less than the unconditional surrender of the German people. Who can say what might have happened if such overtures had been made in the early years of the war?

In this way the assassination of Hitler, had it taken place, could have backfired on the SOE and the British government. The SOE, of course, had already gravely miscalculated the repercussions of the Heydrich assassination in 1942. Thousands had died as a result of that error. Successful assassinations are successful only if the outcome of that murder is the one desired, whether the target survives or not. In February 1944, for example, a four-man SOE team was infiltrated into Nazi-held Crete and successfully kidnapped the commander of the island's German garrison, General Heinrich Kreipe. Kidnap was a more troublesome, but potentially more rewarding, alternative to assassination. The agents, two British army officers and two Cretan freedom fighters, set up a bogus police road-block on a narrow road and brought the general's limousine to a halt. Dressed in German military police uniforms the SOE agents held a gun to Kreipe's chest and marched him up into the mountains. After several days of running from German search parties, the kidnap team rendezvoused with a Royal Navy launch and made their escape. Kreipe was so hated by the Cretan population, however, that his disappearance was a blessing in disguise to the German forces on Crete. Although the mission had been a total success, the repercussions were unforeseen and undesirable.

STRIKING AT THE DICTATORS

Despite the fanatical loyalty commanded by Adolf Hitler during his years in power, several attempts to assassinate him were made – all by native Germans. The most bizarre took place before the outbreak of war in 1939. Hitler always attended the annual commemorative celebrations of the Beer Hall Putsch, which had taken place on 8 November 1923 and which had propelled Hitler and his new-born party into the political arena. That evening in 1939 Hitler made his usual speech to the faithful few who had participated in the event, but he cut short his address and left the stage. Twelve minutes later a bomb planted within the pillar directly behind the speaker's podium exploded, killing seven people and wounding more than sixty others. None of Hitler's close advisers was among the dead or wounded.

Hitler's own fascist newspaper (and no other) ran the full story of the attempted assassination, and blamed British secret service agents for the attack. William L. Shirer, an American correspondent in Berlin during those tense pre-war days, wrote in his diary about the event: 'The attempted "assassination" ... undoubtedly will buck up public opinion behind Hitler and stir up hatred of England ... Most of us [foreign correspondents] think it smells of another Reichstag fire.' The fire to which Shirer referred had burned down the parliament building on 27 February 1933, and many later suspected that the new Nazi government had begun the fire deliberately to show the communists in a bad light and to gain some public support. Hitler and Nero both were distinguished arsonists as well as notorious tyrants.

In support of these claims in the *Voelkischer Beobachter*, Heinrich Himmler ordered one of his top men, Walter Schellenberg, to arrest two British secret service agents and to blame the bombing on them! Schellenberg had made contact with the agents in Holland, posing as an anti-Nazi conspirator in order to lead the spies on. Now Himmler had another use for them. On 9 November, outside a café in the town of Venlo, the two spies, Captain S. Payne Best and Major R.H. Stevens, were held up by German security men, bundled into a waiting car and driven over the border into Germany. Twelve days later it was publicly announced that the organizers of the Beer Hall bomb, Best and Stevens, had been apprehended and that the actual bomb manufacturer had been a thirty-six-year-old mechanical expert called Georg Elser.

Elser was a disturbed and simple man who never denied planting the bomb that could have killed Hitler. Later, as he fought for survival in Sachsenhausen concentration camp, he related a strange story. While he had been an inmate of Dachau camp, on charges of being a communist sympathizer, Elser had been approached by unnamed officials who offered him the job of murdering Hitler's enemies with a bomb, just after Hitler had finished speaking at the Beer Hall. In return, he was promised better treatment in the camp until the murder was carried out, and he was to be given his freedom at the Swiss border. Everything went to plan. Elser was taken to the Beer Hall before the day of the commemorative celebrations to plant his bomb and then driven to the Swiss border. There he was handed incriminating evidence and set up to be immediately arrested by the Gestapo.

Elser spent the next six years in Sachsenhausen and Dachau camps and was probably murdered by the Gestapo in April 1945. They had claimed on 16 April that Elser had actually been killed in an Allied bombing raid, only three weeks before the death of the man he had almost murdered. The truth about Elser's death and his bomb may never be fully known. Some historians consider Elser to have been no more than a psychologically disturbed attention seeker, and feel that his years of imprisonment, torture and interrogation point to the doubts and suspicions of the Führer – a man who saw conspiracy and intrigue everywhere. Others, like Shirer, believe that Hitler felt he could not execute a man who had helped boost his own popularity to even greater heights. But Elser had to die – his bizarre story had to remain a secret.

If Hitler had truly believed that Elser represented a conspiracy to assassinate and replace him, his fears were not misplaced. A number of military leaders, angry at the Führer's frequent demands for success, regardless of the cost or the risks, were preparing to kill Hitler in their own way. A group of disillusioned generals had been disheartened by the Allies' massive show of strength on the beaches of Normandy and were stunned by Hitler's dogged determination to fight until the bitter end. These senior officers were not fanatics or political animals; they were soldiers trying to make the best out of a bad job. Rommel had already cautioned Hitler against continuing the bloody conflict, without effect. These officers, including Fabian von Shlabrendorff, Erwin Lahousen, Friedrich Olbricht, Wilhelm Canaris and Hans von Dohnanyi, were led by General Ludwig Beck and planned to assassinate the Führer, seize control of the German government and kill or imprison all his loyal Nazi advisers. Initially, they had put their hope in the field marshals but, after realizing that they would never turn against Hitler, decided that assassination was the only way forward.

The conspirators tried several unsuccessful attempts in early 1943 to blow up their leader. In one attempt two bombs were carried under Colonel von Gersdorff's coat, and he intended to explode them as he walked with Hitler around an exhibition hall. Unfortunately, his target cut short the visit, denying Gersdorff enough time to carry out the assassination. Another bomb (disguised as a bottle of brandy) was put on board Hitler's plane by Shlabrendorff but failed to go off. Between September 1943 and January 1944 there were another half dozen unsuccessful attempts to try and kill the Führer. Hitler understood the dangers that he faced. He never fully trusted his generals and always made sudden changes to his itineraries. He cancelled appearances or cut them short, arrived on a different date or by a different route. The assassin requires three things to commit political murder, and one of those is opportunity. Hitler did his best to deny the scheming generals this necessary 'leg' of the assassination tripod.

The attempt that came tantalizingly close to success was carried out on 20 July 1944 by Colonel Klaus von Stauffenberg, deputizing for General Olbricht. Stauffenberg had once been badly injured when his staff car had run over a mine, and now the colonel had a patch over one eye and had lost his right hand. The experienced and trusted staff officer nursed a long-running hatred for Hitler. Backing him up were a number of other high-ranking (and aristocratic) military officers, each of whom had his own reasons for joining the conspiracy. Stauffenberg made several abortive attempts to get a bomb close to Hitler for detonation, but each time the plan was foiled. At last, on 20 July, it seemed as though the conspiracy was about to get lucky. The Führer had called a top-level meeting at Rastenburg in East Prussia, which was to be held within a wood and concrete headquarters block. Stauffenberg's briefcase was not checked (which was normal) and he entered the hut for the conference. The case contained a bomb that had been activated by the colonel before he stepped inside. Now he placed it under the desk, and after a short period, apologized for having to make an urgent telephone call, and left the hut. He carried on walking for quite some distance and then heard the terrific roar of the explosion.

Stauffenberg assumed that Hitler could not have survived the blast. Immediately he tricked his way past the large security screen around the headquarters to the airfield and flew directly to Berlin. But Hitler was not dead; in fact he was not even seriously injured. Another officer, wanting more leg room, had discovered Stauffenberg's briefcase under the table and moved it behind a large wooden pillar. This may have lessened the effects of the blast on those in the building. Four people had been killed and several were quite seriously wounded, but Hitler had come away with nothing more than minor burns and shock. As Hitler reeled from the horror of the moment, the plotters failed to make any headway in Berlin. No attempt was made to take over the government, despite Stauffenberg's assurances that Hitler was dead. When reports to the contrary began to arrive in Berlin, one half-hearted conspirator, General Fromm, tried to arrest the other plotters, but was himself taken prisoner. Then the reports were confirmed – Hitler was alive. Fromm escaped and soon took charge, arresting the men who had dared to challenge the awful might of the Nazi war machine.

The aftermath of the attempted assassination was predictably bloody. Several officers (including Stauffenberg) were executed by military firing squad, and as many as 2000 others were arrested and executed in the months that followed. Even General Fromm was executed the following year – the guilt of his complicity had outweighed the loyalty of his quick 'about-face'. Erwin Rommel, who had not disguised his criticism of Hitler's wartime strategy, was also implicated in the Stauffenberg plot and was given the option of a well-publicized show trial or suicide by poison. Rommel knew what the chances (for both his family and himself) would be under Nazi justice and wisely chose poison.

The bomb had exploded at precisely 12:42 on 20 July 1944, only four hours before Hitler was to greet the Italian dictator Benito Mussolini. That afternoon, both men surveyed the destruction of the Rastenburg barracks. The two proud Axis partners had begun their conquest of Europe so energetically, but now had the opportunity to muse over their current situation. Hitler had survived (another) assassination attempt by his own military advisers, and Mussolini was left little of his country to rule, having recently been rescued from captivity by an élite unit of German commandos. Mussolini had been been unexpectedly summoned to the royal palace in Rome on 25 July 1943, where the king summarily dismissed him from office. The fascist dictator was immediately arrested, driven ignominiously to a police station in an ambulance and imprisoned. A new non-fascist government was installed in his place, and the Italian people showed no inclination to try and prevent it. Mussolini was eventually moved to a secret location high in the Abruzzi Apennines. On 13 September an audacious glider landing was made by German commandos led by Otto Skorzeny, and Mussolini was bundled into a Fieseler-Storch observation plane. After a terrifying take-off down a rock-strewn slope, the dictator was flown to Vienna and safety.

Benito Mussolini had been no stranger to assassination attempts. His ruthless and speedy rise to power in the early 1920s had earned the balding political heavyweight many enemies. His 300 bodyguards were not enough to prevent a number of assassination attempts, although none inflicted serious wounds. They included the use of bombs, revolvers, knives and even poison – an Italian favourite that harked back to the days of the Borgias and the Roman emperors. He was fanatical about his own protection – and he had to be. In one incident Mussolini's chauffeur was killed by a bullet meant for him, in another his secretary was wounded by a bullet that had also been aimed at the dictator. And in an attack reminiscent of that on Archduke Franz Ferdinand twelve years earlier, one terrorist threw a bomb at Mussolini's car, killing eight people in the explosion. Mussolini was not one of the eight and was not even wounded. Later that year, however, another shooting incident actually drew blood (on Mussolini's nose), but the injury was a mere flesh wound.

As the Allies moved in on Berlin almost two years later, however, and the Second World War approached its end, Hitler heard the news that Mussolini, who was travelling by convoy towards Switzerland, had been captured by partisans. While Mussolini was held in captivity with his mistress, Clara Petacci, partisan chiefs at the Milan headquarters arranged for a fanatical communist guerrilla to assassinate him. This would-be killer was Walter Audisio (going under the name Colonel Valerio). The local partisans, who wanted Mussolini to face a war crimes trial, opposed Valerio's mission and tried to prevent him from carrying out his orders. But on 28 April 1945 the communist agent tricked the defeated fascist leader into accompanying him by posing as a loyal fascist who had come to rescue Il Duce. Left with no realistic alternative, Mussolini and Petacci followed Valerio out of their locked room. Away from the hide-out, the couple soon found themselves held at gunpoint by their supposed liberator. Valerio tried to shoot Mussolini but, by chance, both his weapons jammed. The leader stood stock-still, awaiting his fate, as Valerio grabbed a sub-machinegun from a companion and fired a burst into the dictator. Petacci was similarly dealt with. On the following day their bodies were mutilated by the crowds in Milan and publicly displayed along with the bodies of a dozen other captured fascists. The awful treatment of the bodies of Mussolini and his mistress made a deep impression on Hitler who was holed up in his Berlin bunker, and he made a point of arranging for his body to be burned once he had committed suicide. At 3:30 on 30 April 1945, Hitler shot himself in the mouth with a revolver, bringing his 'thousand year Reich' to an ignominious end after only twelve war-torn years.

LOW-INTENSITY WARFARE

A state of war brings its own rules of conduct that are followed, to a greater or lesser degree, by the combatants. Both the First and Second World Wars were 'total' wars that were fought not just militarily on some remote battlefield, as wars had been in the days of Rome and Greece. They were 'total' wars in that every single citizen had to become involved. The scale and the cost of war involved a nation's entire economy, and this economy and the people who were involved in it (the citizens of that nation) thus became legitimate targets of war. They were often targeted in indiscriminate air-raids, even though the front line of the war was fought hundreds, if not thousands of kilometres away. Total war required these two complementary struggles: the military war effort and the civilian war effort. With nation fighting nation, the opportunity to single out a particular enemy leader and pick him off in order to advance the war rarely appeared.

In the post-war period, with total war a grim nightmare of the past, a new form of conflict began to spread across the globe. In military-speak, these innumerable struggles were defined as 'low-intensity warfare'. This effectively meant that the fight was waged not between one armed nation and another but that one of the belligerents was in fact a guerrilla army. Such an army is an irregular (that is, unofficial) and highly politically motivated military force, which recognizes no front line and none of the traditional 'conventions' of modern armed conflict. Guerrillas operate within 'friendly' towns and villages and are often able to retire to remote wilderness areas in order to avoid the attentions of the regular army units trying to eradicate them. In such a war, assassination becomes a real option available to the guerrilla commander. His teams can interpenetrate the urban populations and move freely from one place to another without being recognized for what they are. Often they are able to get dangerously close to commanders of the regular forces.

In post-war Malaya a communist-inspired uprising put into practice all the tactics of a classic guerrilla operation. Hundreds of innocent civilians had been murdered by the Malayan Races Liberation Army (MRLA), and in 1951 the movement staged its most audacious act of the conflict. During a carefully laid roadside ambush the fighters assassinated Sir Henry Gurney, the British High Commissioner. He had introduced the efficient emergency measures that were only just beginning to isolate the terrorists from the general population. His successor, however, proved to be an even more formidable opponent of the MRLA and, with his appointment, the tide of the Malayan Emergency turned. A direct effect of Gurney's assassination and the jungle fighting that ensued was the creation of 22 Special Air Service (SAS) Regiment. This highly skilled unit of commandos was put to immediate use in the jungles of Malaya, tracking and ambushing communist terrorists (CTs) on punishing long-duration missions. The success of the SAS in this kind of conflict stemmed from the regiment's approach – adopting the tactics of the enemy. Like the CTs themselves (and unlike the regular army units), the SAS troopers learned to live for long periods within the rainforests of Malaya.

Nowhere has assassination been put to such callous and brutal use as in Northern Ireland. Tit-for-tat murders have dogged the conflict since it escalated in 1969 with the commitment of British troops onto the streets. The struggle has a long and bloody pedigree, with the result that violent events that occurred up to three centuries ago regularly spark off fresh incidents of bloodshed. Here there are no front lines, no enemy territory to speak of and no uniformed enemy. It has often been said that the British government knows the names and identities of many killers, both republican and unionist, but is prevented from arresting them because of a lack of evidence. The SAS were deployed into Northern Ireland at an early stage to gather information for the regular army. Again, they made every effort to 'blend in', wearing plain clothes, carrying concealable handguns and driving unmarked Q cars.

In 1995 a former SAS trooper, Paul Bruce, alleged in his book *The Nemesis File* that his unit had operated in Northern Ireland as a secret assassination squad. This stunning revelation detailed how the SAS had used IRA informants throughout the 1970s to locate and murder members of the terror group. The bodies were disposed of in deep, unmarked graves. Unsurprisingly, the British government of the day dismissed Bruce's claims, but several members of Parliament began to push for a more detailed inquiry. One opposition MP, Ken Livingstone, wrote to the prime minister on the matter, and the Minister of State for Northern Ireland responded to his letter, claiming that an investigation was already under way. If Bruce's allegations are indeed true, they would explain the circumstances surrounding the arrest of two British servicemen on 5 May 1976.

Out of uniform, the two men denied any connection with the SAS. Yet the security forces found a military logbook in their Triumph car, along with an SAS commando knife, a Browning 9mm handgun and a British army 9mm Sterling sub-machinegun. Following an armed confrontation, two more cars were intercepted later that night and six soldiers were arrested. Again they denied any connection with the SAS, yet their vehicles contained a haul of weaponry that included another commando knife, a pump-action shotgun, two Browning handguns and three Sterling sub-machineguns. Both cars also had military logbooks. Following the intervention of the Minister for Northern Ireland, the men were released and the weapons handed over to the British government. A satisfactory explanation of their activities and intent was not given – until the publication of *The Nemesis File*.

Even in the early 1980s there were growing doubts about the official policy of the security services within Northern Ireland. Three incidents occurred in 1982 in which members of the Royal Ulster Constabulary (RUC) shot six suspected IRA terrorists, and killed all but one of them.

There were allegations of a 'shoot to kill' policy among the RUC, and in 1984 a Manchester police officer, John Stalker, was sent to investigate. The 'Stalker affair', as it became known, resulted in Stalker being dropped from the case just before he was ready to reveal his findings. This was viewed as an unsubtle attempt to cover up the facts and it predictably attracted the full glare of media attention. Stalker's conclusions, when finally published, found that the RUC had not operated an 'unofficial' murder policy, but that some officers had shown an inclination to shoot first rather than make an arrest. In January 1988 the British attorney general, Sir Patrick Mayhew, declared that there was reason to believe that some members of the RUC were in fact guilty of 'perverting the course of justice', but that no charges were to be made.

That same year SAS troopers made another shocking appearance in the newspaper headlines and their actions seemed to make a mockery of the whole Stalker affair. On 6 March three IRA terrorists, two men (Daniel McGann and Sean Savage) and one woman (Mairead Farrell), were ambushed in Gibraltar by a team of plain-clothes SAS soldiers, shot at close range and killed. The terrorists were not innocent civilians but an active service unit about to plant a car bomb where it could do most damage – next to a ceremonial parade ground. With the car bomb just over the border in Spain, the terrorists had 'reserved' a parking space next to the parade ground by parking another vehicle there temporarily. This atrocity would have been a repeat of the 1987 Enniskillen cenotaph massacre in which eleven people died and fifty-five people were wounded, many of them children. When reports of the Gibraltar shooting began to circulate, it became clear that the IRA terrorists had not been armed, did not pose any immediate threat to the SAS soldiers and were denied the opportunity to surrender. Further investigation revealed that one soldier finished off one of the bombers with two or three more shots as he lay on the ground. There was an outcry, and in its defence the government claimed that the terrorists had 'made suspicious hand movements', which were interpreted as an attempt either to draw a gun or activate a radio detonator.

The Gibraltar controversy raged for some time, with the government trying desperately to stifle any debate on this most sensitive subject. It had, however, illustrated exactly how members of 22 SAS were being employed in the fight against terrorism. Until that time most people had associated the SAS with hostage rescue, and it was the regiment's spectacular success during the Iranian embassy siege of 1980 that had turned the clandestine SAS into a household name. Gibraltar gave a new slant to the image of the SAS. Clearly its troopers were in some way involved with the monitoring of known IRA agents (a well-known SAS activity in Northern Ireland), but the Gibralter debacle also illustrated how ruthlessly efficient the SAS could be.

Much of what the United States military knows about low-intensity warfare, it learned from its experiences in the Vietnam War. Here, the US Army and Marine Corps were faced with an invisible enemy that seemed to fight on its own terms and at times of its own choosing. When the firefights came to an end members of the local guerrilla movement, the communist-inspired Vietcong (VC), simply disappeared back to their villages. Like most irregular forces, the Vietcong carried little in the way of rank or insignia. Without actually capturing a member of the organization with a weapon in his hand, it was often impossible to determine friend from foe.

Before 1968 the American forces made every effort to force the VC to fight their kind of war. Sometimes entire US divisions would take to the field on 'search and destroy' missions, but only a few hundred Vietcong bodies would be recovered. Why hadn't they come out to fight? In January 1968, during the Vietnamese Tet holiday, they did just that. Every South Vietnamese city erupted into full-scale violence, and the Vietcong offensive looked likely to overwhelm the Allies. But the combined strength of the US, Australian, Thai and South Vietnamese forces was able to repulse and shatter the Vietcong insurgency.

After the Tet offensive the objectives of the war were scaled down and a massive pacification programme was put into operation. The authorities in the capital, Saigon, could never hope to win the war unless the population relinquished its support for the Vietcong. This was often referred to as the battle for 'hearts and minds'. The greatest obstacle to the civic aid project was the large number of communist cadres still at large in the towns and villages. These cadres disseminated communist propaganda, collected 'taxes', organized resistance, recruited for the VC and helped to assassinate or abduct teachers, engineers, doctors and anybody else who could argue against their cause. One estimate put their numbers at 2 per cent of the total population – some 360,000 individuals. With these hidden activists in place, the dream of 'hearts and minds' could never become reality.

What the CIA proposed was a counter-terrorist operation carried to the rural areas. The names of many communist activists and recruiters were handed to the CIA via a network of carefully cultivated informers. Now the Agency proposed a plan to silence these VC agents and cut off their lines of communication with the populace. It would work through the various South Vietnamese intelligence services. This plan was called Phoenix – the best Western translation of *phung hoang,* which was a mythical Vietnamese bird possessing god-like powers. In overall command of the secret programme was William Colby, a former CIA chief who ran it alongside the broader (and more wholesome) activities of America's large-scale pacification effort.

The Phoenix programme revolved around the abduction or assassination of communist suspects. A team of commandos would ambush the terrorist leader (who would often be posing as a member of a teaching or farming association) and then kidnap him. Following the abduction he would undergo lengthy interrogation by CIA intelligence specialists. The jails began to overflow with suspects. Phoenix offices were established at the district level and were run by South Vietnamese intelligence experts. An American official was also present at each office. These offices used informers to identify possible suspects and would pass on this information further up the chain of command. If the CIA had proof of a suspect's collusion with the Vietcong, there was no need for him to be picked up – he could instead be assassinated. If action was thought necessary, a Provincial Reconnaissance Unit (PRU) was dispatched to carry out either an abduction or an assassination. Each PRU was made up of Vietnamese killers, often convicted criminals, VC traitors, mercenaries and other disreputable types who had no political allegiance.

There had always been a strong VC presence in the Rung Sat swamps (known as the Forest of Assassins) to the south of Saigon. Here the irregular assassination squads often worked in tandem with the US Navy's élite commando unit, the SEALs (the title is an acronym derived from their theatres of operation, *sea, air* and *land*). SEAL teams were composed of three to seven well-motivated and highly trained special warfare experts, each of whom had mastered a military trade. Between them, the team members carried a formidable arsenal of weaponry, including pump-action shotguns, Stoner light machineguns and grenade launchers. They also carried Smith and Wesson 'Hush Puppy' silenced pistols, which were specially made for the SEALs (fewer than 200 were manufactured) and which proved invaluable for the teams after they had silently infiltrated their target village and located their target. The

SEALs had their own peculiar customs, as much to inspire terror into their enemy as to foster team spirit. There were reports of SEAL killers painting the faces of their victims with green camouflage paint and even cutting out the livers of their victims (which the Vietnamese believed denied the dead entry into the afterlife).

However precise the intelligence, mistakes were made. Sometimes the wrong victim, the wrong hut or even the wrong village was selected by the strike teams. Many innocent civilians got caught up in the chaotic crossfire of the night-time assassinations. If stealth could not be relied on, the PRUs or SEALs had to hit fast and hard in order to retain the element of surprise. More than one family died in a single night as the victim of a Phoenix attack.

There have been many critics of Phoenix, including some who were actually involved with the programme from the start. One such man was Barton Osborne, who said that the programme 'was not serving any legitimate function that I know of, but rather had gone so wrong that it was the vehicle by which we were getting into a bad genocide programme'. Osborne insisted that suspects were regularly tortured to reveal information. Inefficiency coupled with abuse and corruption conspired to turn a legitimate tool of pacification into a murder weapon. Sometimes it was found that individual Vietnamese, either informers or operatives, had personal axes to grind when it came to the selection of potential suspects. Even more damaging was the fact that district offices were ordered to fulfil a monthly quota of suspects. In this way many innocent people fell victim to the programme.

Another detractor of Phoenix, Frank Snepp, remembers seeing a bodycount for Phoenix in 1970 totalling around 20,000 killed. Colby himself, testifying at a Senate hearing in 1971, announced that indeed 20,000 of the enemy had been assassinated, 28,000 had been abducted and 17,000 had surrendered. By the time the programme came to an end it is estimated that a further 10,000 Vietcong sympathizers had been liquidated by the Phoenix strike teams. It was almost inevitable that the corruption and escalation of standard military practice in Vietnam would also infect the 'supra-legal' Phoenix programme. Jeff Stein, who was working within Phoenix, once provided first-rate intelligence on the name and location of an unconfirmed suspect, as well as a suitable day and time for his the kidnap and interrogation. He later discovered a strategic B-52 bomber had been ordered to unload its bombs over the target's village at the time he had specified. That is an example of how an assassination programme was sadly misused.

So did the authorities use a sledgehammer to crack a walnut? According to the post-war testimony of surviving VC leaders, Phoenix did work. The VC chief Madame Nguyen Thi Binh told the American journalist Stanley Karnow that Phoenix had been 'very dangerous'. Her troops had never been frightened by the thought of facing enemy troops in battle, 'but the infiltration of a couple of guys into our ranks created tremendous difficulties for us'. Another former Vietcong officer estimates that the guerrilla movement lost thousands of its agents to the assassination programme. Although anti-war protesters condemned Phoenix, many of those who supported it pointed to the tens of thousands of assassinations already carried out by the Vietcong since the start of its terror campaign in the early 1960s.

The US Navy SEALs and the British Army SAS are both élite special operations units capable of taking on a wide variety of unconventional missions during wartime. Assassination is just one of these tasks. Many other nations are also able to boast some type of special operations capability, and one of the most renowned (and the most feared) of these élite units is the Russian Spetsnaz commando force. The Spetsnaz are unique in modern warfare in that one of their primary missions during a full-scale conventional or nuclear war is to conduct a campaign of terror and assassination behind enemy lines. After the collapse of communism in the Soviet Union, the Spetsnaz have been more fruitfully employed in anti-terrorist and border defence missions within the former republics. The selection of recruits is still rigorous, however, and the Spetsnaz can boast of more than one Olympic-standard athlete among their ranks.

In the event of war, Spetsnaz teams of between six and eight men were to be parachuted behind enemy lines or infiltrated by submarine along the coast. Once in enemy territory, the soldiers had been trained to wear the uniforms and carry the weaponry of NATO soldiers if required. During the Cold War era, Sweden had always been seen by the Kremlin as a high-priority target, and over the years the Soviet military practised many methods of surveillance and infiltration within that country. Intelligence agents are even believed to have posed as door-to-door salesmen in order to determine the daily routines of key personnel targeted for Spetsnaz assassination if war should ever break out.

The practical use of such training and preparation bore fruit during the period of revolution that swept through the Baltic republics of Estonia, Lithuania and Latvia (1989–91). Spetsnaz troops were seconded to the KGB Border Guards Directorate where they formed élite alpha teams. During the civil unrest these alpha teams infiltrated the three republics as regular paratroopers and carried out a number of abduction, sabotage and assassination missions. Prominent journalists, political agitators, key border guards and police officers were targeted by the ruthlessly efficient Spetsnaz troops.

Some of the skills taught to Spetsnaz recruits are highly unconventional. They are taught how to pick locks and break into buildings, and how to be ruthless with people who get in the way of a mission. This applies even to their own comrades. It is drilled into each man how important it is not to leave behind a wounded comrade – he must be killed rather than allowed to fall into enemy hands. But as a professional assassin, the Spetsnaz should not find his conscience overly troubled. According to Russian intelligence sources, a Spetsnaz unit caught in an ambush sprung by Mujahidin guerrillas in Afghanistan was forced to murder fifteen of its own men – wounded soldiers who could not escape on foot. Other training includes the mastery of one specialist subject (communications, demolition and so on) and one or more foreign languages. To retain the unit's aura of secrecy, the Spetsnaz do not have a distinct uniform of their own; instead, it masquerades as another Russian military unit. The Spetsnaz are truly the ninja of the modern world – specializing in sabotage, murder and infiltration, and all the while in disguise.

Some Spetsnaz rarely wear any uniform at all. These plain-clothes troops are known as Headquarters Companies, and their job is to infiltrate an enemy country by scheduled air transport during the build-up to war. There they are given the task of assassinating key individuals, both military and political, in the war effort. Once war is declared, they are to strike hard, murdering members of government, influential industrialists and high-ranking police and military officers. The aim is to create panic, to shatter law and order and to demoralize a nation's (already anxious) population. In peacetime this Spetsnaz ultra-élite lives and works away from its parent unit. Formed into 'athletics teams' of the Central Army Sporting Club (ZSKA), members of the Headquarters Companies are free to travel to Western countries to compete at international level, to get a feel for Western life and how to operate there. Of course, these 'athlete-assassins' have also won many competitions, and among their number are record holders and Olympic medallists. One such is Valentin Yerikalin, a Spetsnaz operative and world-class rower, who won the silver medal at the 1968 Olympics. Many years later Yerikalin was arrested by Turkish police in Istanbul because he had been attempting to recruit members for a Spetsnaz intelligence network within the country. His Spetsnaz unit worked with the Soviet Black Sea fleet, and the Turkish network would have provided valuable intelligence for the navy.

The Spetsnaz imperative is maximum effect with minimum force. Rather than fight a war of attrition, men against men, machine against machine, the Kremlin has in this unique unit a body of men who can subvert the art of war. Where the SOE and SAS have occasionally turned to assassination during times of conflict (high or low intensity), the Spetsnaz have made it their *raison d'être*.

5. Assassination by Decree

State-sponsored assassination has been a fact of life for centuries. Only with the modern revolution in transport, however, has the extension of a nation's tyranny been quite so easy. The twentieth century has been dominated by the rise and fall of the Soviet Union, an empire in the old tradition that proved to be the first and most far-reaching experiment in communism. The Soviet state sat astride the globe like a malevolent octopus, and its long arms touched virtually every nation on the globe, not just those countries forming the communist bloc, Russia's vassal states, but also the 'free' nations of the West and the supposedly 'neutral' countries of the 'Third World'. Where foreign policy could not reach, the sinister agents of the KGB, the feared secret police, stepped instead. KGB – the initials alone conjure up images of hardened killers moving in the shadows of Western governments, unseen surveillance teams and untraceable murders.

VICTIMS OF THE GREAT TERROR

Although only officially established in March 1954, the Committee of State Security (*Komitet Gosudarstvennoi Bezopasnosti*, KGB) had a much longer history under a variety of names – from 1917 until 1922 it was known as the Cheka (All-Russian Extraordinary Commission for the Suppression of Counter-revolution and Sabotage), for example, and from 1923 until 1934 it was known as OGPU (United State Political Administration).

Joseph Stalin (1879–1953) led the Soviet Union through its bloodiest period, turning Lenin's communist dream into a totalitarian police state, governed through fear and terror. The organization that perpetrated this reign of terror on Stalin's behalf was the much feared People's Commissariat for Internal Affairs (*Narodny Kommissariat Vnutrennikh Del*,

NKVD), which was established in 1934. No more powerful body existed in the Soviet Union, integrating as it did all the powers and responsibilities of border troops, internal troops, the regular police force, criminal investigators, political (or secret) police and the intelligence service. This immensely powerful body answered directly to Stalin, and in his terrible hands it was used to root out, apprehend and suitably reward 'enemies of the state'. Like all tyrants, Stalin suspected enemies everywhere, and his paranoid fears were transmitted via the NKVD to the population in general. His most notorious purges occurred between 1934 and 1937 when all opposition, both real and imagined, was crushed.

One murder at the start of this Great Terror established the ground rules for the bloodletting that was to follow. Sergei Kirov (1886–1934) was the head of the Communist Party, the second most powerful man in the Soviet Union and Stalin's greatest rival. Throughout the early 1930s Kirov had supported the policies of his leader, but the two soon began to differ. Although still a hard-liner, Kirov had suggested a period of reconciliation with the Soviet people and was even named as a replacement for Stalin during a failed attempt to revive an entrenched government. To the paranoid Russian leader, this marked Kirov as a deadly rival and an enemy. His supporters had also to be eliminated in some fashion, since they had masterminded the failed plan.

Sergei Kirov was assassinated on 1 December 1934 as he left his office at the Communist Party headquarters in Leningrad. The killer came up behind the official and shot him in the back of the neck with a revolver. Immediately apprehended, the gunman turned out to be highly deranged. His name was Leonid Nikolayev and he seemed to believe that he was the successor of the populist assassins who had murdered Tsar Alexander II in 1881. There was no doubt that Nikolayev had pulled the trigger, and no doubt that he was indeed an unbalanced individual with a deep-seated grievance against the authorities in Leningrad. What was strange, however, was that he had been able to penetrate the strict NKVD security to murder Kirov. Even stranger, it transpired that he had been planning to kill the party chief for some time and that he had, in fact, been arrested twice while shadowing Kirov and had been carrying a revolver on both occasions. Nikolayev had twice been released without charge by the most feared and brutal secret police force in the world, and each time on the direct orders of Ivan Zaporozhets, the organization's deputy head in Leningrad.

It is widely believed that the order for Kirov's assassination came directly from Stalin, but that he bypassed Yagoda, the chief of the NKVD and directly approached the Leningrad NKVD, which he thought he could trust. Following the death of Kirov, Stalin travelled to the city and made a show of publicly slapping Medved, the city's NKVD chief, in the face. Faced with Kirov's corpse, the leader kissed it and seemed to be overcome with grief. As a reward for their involvement in the crime, both Medved and Zaporozhets were fired for criminal negligence. Although both men found other jobs in the NKVD, neither survived the purges, both meeting their ends at the hands of Soviet executioners in 1937. Their deaths during this era of bloodletting served only one purpose, as Russian leader Nikita Khrushchev later suggested, 'to cover up all traces of the organizers of Kirov's assassination'. Questioned by Stalin in the aftermath of the assassination, Nikolayev would not give his reasons for killing Kirov. Instead, the gunman pointed across the room at the assembled NKVD officers present and told Stalin to ask them instead. Nikolayev was quickly silenced and removed from the room.

'The evil murder of Comrade Kirov,' said Stalin some time later, had revealed 'many suspect elements within the Party.' With the eager assistance of the NKVD, Stalin now planned to use this engineered murder to initiate his Great Terror. The purges began immediately. Within three weeks of the Kirov murder, a fabricated conspiracy was uncovered and crushed. The assassin Nikolayev, it was announced on 22 December 1934, belonged to an underground terrorist cell led by the former opposition leader Grigori Zinoviev (1883–1936). The Latvian Consul-General was also supposed to have been involved, and it was his evidence that 'proved' that there was a link between the Zinoviev terrorists and the exiled communist leader Leon Trotsky. Careful fabrication on Stalin's part tried to enmesh as many of his opponents as possible, thereby justifying later persecution. Arrest, torture, imprisonment and execution were the methods by which those whom Stalin considered his enemies were dealt with. In 1935 the purge gathered a macabre momentum. Party officials began confessing to failings and weaknesses in the hope that this would satisfy the party hierarchy, ever hungry for victims.

Members of the Communist Party from the left, the right and the centre were all suspects, and many were murdered on Stalin's orders. The purges were also used to fill his forced-labour camps with inmates. The officials Zinoviev, Lev Kamenev (1883–1936) and Nikolai Bukharin (1888–1938) were the three main 'conspirators' whom Stalin tied into the Kirov assassination. They were all executed, after being made to confess to their part in the 'Trotskyite-Zinovievite Terrorist Centre'. This confession stated that they had operated on instructions from the exiled Trotsky through a long line of secret agents, and that Kirov's murder was to be the first in a series of assassinations of party leaders, culminating with the killing of Stalin himself.

The fourth major conspirator, Leon Trotsky, was in exile in Mexico and in this way was able to survive the terrible purges. Trotsky and Lenin had been the actual architects of the Russian Revolution in 1918 and following the death of Lenin in 1924, Stalin emerged to challenge Trotsky. The two were opposed to one another's policies. Trotsky favoured a continuous world revolution, while Stalin wanted to consolidate Russian communism. Stalin was a shark who allied himself first with whoever would serve his purpose. Soon Trotsky found his support cut off, and in 1929 he was expelled from the Soviet Union. Stalin reigned supreme. By 1939, when the eighteenth All-Union Party Congress met, there were no survivors of Lenin's original Politburo left alive with the exception of Stalin and the exiled Trotsky. Within a year only Stalin would remain.

The Russian dictator's obsession with Trotsky was profound. A standard question put to political prisoners by NKVD interrogators was: 'Do you agree or do you not that Trotsky is the chief of the vanguard of bourgeois counter-revolution?' Almost everyone who was expelled from the Party and survived was branded a Trotskyite or Zinovievist. For Trotsky this was good news for it meant that a growing opposition was beginning to rally around his name. Both men were deluding themselves. Stalin, for his part, invented for his own purposes a vast conspiracy of Trotskyite followers who formed an entrenched underground of political activists. Trotsky in turn believed these followers to be real, and strove to enflame these 'masses' to revolution. He wrote books with titles such as *Stalin's Crimes* and *The Stalinist School of Falsification*, and this provided Stalin with an even greater excuse to persecute the imaginary conspirators.

Trotsky became a political demon with which the Russian leader galvanized the nation's fears and suspicions. He became the primary enemy of the state, a role parodied by George Orwell in his brilliant novel *Nineteen Eighty-Four*. Orwell's Trotsky is Goldstein, a political terrorist, who continually appears in Big Brother's broadcasts as the enemy of the people. Stalin unmasked a second back-up conspiracy known as the 'Anti-Soviet Trotskyite Centre', in January 1937. This cabal was supposed to be plotting 'to overthrow the Soviet power in the USSR and to restore capitalism ... to expedite the armed attack on the USSR' and to 'assist foreign aggressors [Nazi Germany and Japan] and to bring about the defeat of the USSR'. All this was absolute rubbish, but it served as a useful pretext for a new round of executions.

Despite such demonization, Trotsky little resembled the powerful political heavyweight pictured by Stalin. His influence waned with the years, and his overseas life was a decidedly precarious one. In 1932 the exile left Turkey to find a suitable European city from which he could operate, but within weeks he had been forced to return, since none of the governments he had approached had let him settle. Despite these initial set-backs, he was able to settle in France in 1933 but was forced to move to Norway in 1935. By the end of 1936 Trotsky was expelled, and this time he fled Europe for good, settling in Mexico in 1937.

Trotsky's close friend and the chief organizer of his anti-Stalin campaign was his son, Lev Sedov. Sedov had a large entourage of followers who helped the Trotsky movement keep in touch with dissident communists and whatever opposition remained behind in the USSR. Unknown to either father or son, however, the NKVD had successfully penetrated the entourage of both men. Agents of the organization had been sent abroad to win the confidence of Sedov and Trotsky, and they were rewarded with positions of some trust. Until the time of Sedov's death, his closest confidant had been Mark Zborowski, an NKVD agent to whom Sedov entrusted his father's most confidential files as well as the key to his letter-box. From December 1936 the head of the NKVD, Nikolai Yezhov, set in motion an assassination campaign to eliminate members of the Trotskyite leadership. Entitled the Administration of Special Tasks, the campaign sent out mobile groups to carry out the illegal killings. Their first operations took them to the battlefields of the Spanish Civil War, and one of the most fanatical of the killers was André Marty, a French anti-Trotskyite, who admitted to the murder of 500 members of the International Brigades. Ernest Hemingway was in Spain during the Civil War and had met Marty. He considered the NKVD hit man 'crazy as a bedbug. He has a mania for shooting people'.

The mobile groups were active across Europe in the late-1930s. Ignace Poretsky was one of their unfortunate victims. His bullet-ridden body was discovered by Swiss police on 4 September 1937 after his sealed dispatch to Moscow announcing his defection and his devotion to Trotsky's revolution was opened by an NKVD officer. A mobile group commanded by the short and rather rotund figure of Mikhail Shpigelglas was given the task of eliminating him. Shpigelglas recruited a friend of the family, Gertrude Schildbach, to meet with Poretsky and his wife at a café in Lausanne. She had been instructed to ask Poretsky's advice on some urgent matter, and in return hand over a box of chocolates that had been impregnated with strychnine poison. At the last minute the woman backed down and did not give the lethal present to Mrs Poretsky. Instead, Schildbach was able to lure Poretsky away and into an ambush down a side street. There an NKVD assassin with a sub-machinegun opened fire, killing Poretsky instantly. Poretsky tried to pull Gertrude Schildbach in front of him in that last second, and in his clenched fist was a clump of her distinctive grey hair. The Swiss police managed to locate the assassin's suitcase, and it contained a dark portent – a detailed plan of Trotsky's home in Mexico.

The Administration for Special Tasks reached even further afield. The former American NKVD agent Juliette Poyntz was kidnapped and murdered by the organization on 5 June 1937 after being lured to her death by an old flame (and NKVD agent) in New York. It later transpired that her lover, Schachno Epstein, had murdered her himself and entombed her body behind a brick wall in a Greenwich Village house. There were three principal targets for these mobile groups, and their attacks on the less important dissident Trotskyites were just preliminary affairs. Much of the wrath of the Administration for Special Tasks was being reserved for Lev Sedov (Trostky's son); for Rudolf Klement, the organizer of Trotsky's Fourth International Revolution; and for Leon Trotsky himself.

First to die was Sedov. The thirty two year old tried hard to live up to the exacting demands of his father, and he lived in poverty in Paris while publishing the Trotskyist magazine called the *Byulleten Oppozitsii*. Sedov was charming, friendly and able, but he was troubled by appendicitis. When he sought medical help in February 1938 his close friend Mark Zborowski convinced him that he should, for reasons of security, be seen in a private clinic run by exiled Russians. Zborowski was an NKVD agent and after first ordering the ambulance to take Sedov away, he called the NKVD to brief them on Sedov's situation and on the location of the clinic. Although the operation was successful, Sedov had a mysterious relapse on 13 February 1938, and his tearful wife told the surgeon that she suspected he had been poisoned by the NKVD. Despite efforts to save his life, Lev Sedov died in agony three days later. Although an inquest found no evidence of foul play, there were great discrepancies in the testimony of witnesses, and it is almost inconceivable that the NKVD did not poison the young man.

The NKVD had a section called the Kamera, which experimented in the various uses of drugs and poisons. It had been established by the previous head of the organization, Genrikh Yagoda, who was himself a trained pharmacist. By luring Sedov to a Russian-staffed clinic penetrated by agents, the NKVD surely guaranteed that the young revolutionary had little chance of survival. With Sedov out of the way, the agent Zborowski took over the running of the *Byulleten Oppozitsii* and used his position to stir up trouble between various Trotskyite factions.

Rudolph Klement was the next target on the Special Tasks hit list. Klement had been given the great responsibility of organizing Trotsky's Fourth International revolutionary meeting at the end of 1938. On 13 July, however, he mysteriously disappeared from his home in Paris. A letter was received by Trotsky and several of his French supporters that purported to come from Klement. The letter denounced the revolutionary leader and accused him of being in league with the Nazis. The letter was dismissed (probably correctly) as an NKVD forgery, and it was further undermined by the discovery of a headless corpse in the River Seine a few days later. Two of Klement's friends were able to identify the body from distinctive scars on the corpse's hands.

Klement's work, the Fourth International, was a resounding failure in his absence. Only twenty-one delegates attended the conference, and these represented tiny Trotskyite groups from eleven nations. Of particular interest were the Russian delegation (represented by the NKVD agent Zborowski) and the presence of one Ramón Mercader. The abject failure of the 'counter-revolutionaries' failed to convince the NKVD and Stalin that Trotsky and his dwindling band of supporters were no longer a threat to the Soviet Union. Stalin was convinced that the traitor posed more of a danger to his rule than the increasingly influential Adolf Hitler, even though at this time there were no more than thirty active supporters of Trotsky and despite the fact that, on May Day 1940, 20,000 Mexican communists marched through Mexico City demanding 'Out With Trotsky!'. Stalin was out of touch, but this did not prevent him from passing on his obsession to the new chief of the NKVD, the sexually depraved Lavrenti Beria (1899–1953), who was reputed to have had schoolgirls kidnapped from the streets of Moscow to satisfy the sick lusts of himself and his staff. It was during Beria's leadership that the assassination of Trotsky took place.

The NKVD agent in charge of the assassination was a Jewish operative called Leonid Eitingon, and he chose as his angel of death a member of the organization called Ramón Mercader. Mercader, who had attended the Fourth International, was a highly placed mole within Trotsky's entourage and well placed to carry out the intended assassination. He was the perfect assassin. Not only was he a skilled athlete with superb reactions, but he was also intelligent, with command of several languages. As well, he possessed a photographic memory, a remarkable ability to operate in the dark and a capacity for memorizing even the most complex of instructions. Tests indicated that Mercader could strip a Mauser rifle in the dark and reassemble it ready to fire within four minutes. Along with the self-control required of an assassin, Mercader had every advantage – he really was the perfect assassin. His mistress, Sylvia Ageloff, a loyal supporter of Trotsky, was persuaded by Mercader to follow him to Mexico City in January 1940. As expected, she made contact with Trotsky and found gainful employment as a secretary with him. Regularly arriving at the exile's villa to pick up and drop off his girlfriend, Mercader's face soon became well known to the guards at the estate. When Sylvia returned to New York in March 1940, Mercader was able to enter the Trotsky compound for the first time. His task was to provide the mobile group with enough intelligence to carry out the assassination. This attempt was carried out on 23 May by a veteran soldier of the International Brigades in Spain, Alfaro Siqueiros. With a force of over twenty men posing as soldiers and policemen, Siqueiros and his men overpowered the guards and led a machinegun and dynamite attack on the villa. Neither Trotsky nor his wife were harmed during the assault.

Although Siqueiros's attempt had failed, Mercader still enjoyed the limited confidence of Trotsky's staff. Only five days after the raid, the NKVD agent met the revolutionary for the first time. It was to be the first of several visits over the next three months, each one conducted with care. Mercader was at pains never to stay too long or to make any demands of the loyal villa staff. Neither did he ever try to question Trotsky, lest he rouse the exile's suspicions. On 20 August 1940 Mercader carried out the murder for which he had waited so long. In the pockets of his raincoat Mercader carried a revolver and an ice-pick, while in the coat's lining he had sewn a dagger (for use as a back-up weapon) in case the other two were discovered. The agent hoped to make an instant kill and be away from the villa before the alarm was raised. Unfortunately, things did not go quite as planned. Mercader had brought an article for Trotsky to read, and while the great revolutionary sat at his desk with the document, the agent brought out the ice-pick and approached the old man, blocking off his access to an alarm button. He brought the steel weapon down with ferocious force on the back of Trotsky's head, and his victim let out a strangled scream. Despite the bloody wound, he was able to grab Mercader's hand and bite into it in an attempt to force his assailant to drop the weapon. Then Trotsky staggered into the hallway to call for help. Guards were on the scene immediately and Mercader was apprehended and beaten mercilessly. Both men were rushed to the same hospital where Trotsky, the great bane of the Soviet Union, died from his head wound the following day.

Mercader was arrested and sentenced to twenty years inside a Mexican prison. Despite the offer of a reduced sentence if he would be willing to admit he had been working for the NKVD, Mercader refused and was not released until 1960. He remained loyal to the cause for which he had been imprisoned and considered himself a soldier of the world revolution. After his release he returned to the Soviet Union to rejoin his beloved Communist Party. Stalin had been dead seven years, however, and his terrible rule was not looked upon with much fondness. Mercader's crime was considered to be something of an embarrassment, one of many regrettable incidents from which the 1960s leadership was trying to distance itself. Mercader died in Havana, Cuba, on 18 October 1978.

That same year the Russian secret police (now reformed and renamed the KGB) assisted in one of the most bizarre assassinations of modern times. The death of Georgi Markov on the streets of London in 1978 at first looked natural, but it soon became apparent that foul play was to blame. Georgi Markov had made some powerful enemies. The Bulgarian defector worked in London for both the BBC and the CIA-backed Radio Free Europe. He had fled from his native country in the late 1960s after writing a play about a military assassination that angered the Bulgarian leader, Todor Zhivkov. From Bulgaria Markov travelled first to Italy and then to London, where he settled in 1969. He continued to write and broadcast material that the Bulgarian authorities considered offensive, and by the end of the 1970s became a target for assassination. This was no secret. Markov had already been given a warning that his life might be in danger from the Bulgarian secret service (the *Durzhavna Sigurnost*, DS), and that it planned to make his death look natural.

Other than fleeing London and escaping into anonymity, there was little that Markov could do but carry on with his work. On 7 September at half past six in the evening Markov left his car and walked to his night job commentating for the BBC World Service. As he made his way across Westminster Bridge, he felt a sharp pain in the back of his right leg and turned to see a man with a closed umbrella standing in a bus queue. 'I'm sorry,' said the stranger in a foreign accent, and as Markov continued to walk, the stranger stepped out of the queue and took a taxi. The broadcaster continued on his way to work and thought nothing more of the incident. Back at home several hours later, however, Markov began to feel seriously ill. His leg had stiffened up and he was wracked by nausea and fever. In hospital he told the doctors that he suspected he had been poisoned by an assassin and that the umbrella had been the weapon. Despite the skill of doctors in treating Markov, he died four days later.

The British secret services did not take his death lightly, and had his body thoroughly examined for traces of foul play. Skin samples taken from the dead man's thigh revealed a tiny pellet of platinum-iridium, almost invisible to the naked eye. The pellet still contained traces of a deadly poison that was identified as the killer toxin ricin. Even the minuscule amount injected was enough to kill, and there was no known antidote. From the moment he had been stabbed with the umbrella Georgi Markov was a dead man.

Few in the intelligence world doubted that the Bulgarian secret service had carried out the murder, probably with the official sanction of the KGB. The Bulgarian authorities denied any involvement, of course, and suggested that Bulgarian dissidents or even the British secret service had carried out the murder to embarrass the Bulgarian government. The truth later emerged, however, and was even stranger than had previously been thought.

Careful research in the years following the Markov assassination began to uncover other mysterious attacks. American intelligence reports seemed to indicate that several attacks in the US may have been connected to the Markov affair, two of which resulted in the death of two exiles, a Bulgarian and a Croatian. One Bulgarian defector on holiday in Europe from the UK became ill after the surfaces of the room in which he was staying were coated with an untraceable poison that could be absorbed through the skin. He survived, giving the killers further impetus to carry out more research on their delivery methods. These researchers were actually members of the Operational Technical Directorate (OTU) of the

KGB, the modern laboratory that had succeeded Stalin's Kamera. General Secretary Zhivkov had turned to the KGB during the 1970s for help in silencing the defectors that continued to criticize his regime from the safety of Western countries. KGB General Golubev was to liaise with the DS, and it was under his supervision that the Directorate OTU purchased a batch of innocuous umbrellas for conversion to poison-delivery weapons. The scientists adapted the metal tip to leave behind the toxin-filled pellet following an attack, and Golubev took the lethal umbrellas to Bulgaria with him. There he helped DS assassins to rehearse the attacks they would carry out.

Even before Markov's death, a poisoned-pellet attack had been made the previous summer on another Bulgarian exile, Vladimir Kostov. While he was travelling on a metro escalator in Paris, Kostov had been stabbed in the back 'accidentally'. Like Markov, he became ill and was rushed to hospital where he survived. After Markov's sinister murder, Kostov was X-rayed, and the authorities were able to remove from his back a tiny pellet similar to the one they had removed from Markov's leg. Why he hadn't been killed by the poison is not fully known, but the tiny pellet may not have contained enough ricin to do the job. The killers would not make that mistake again when they attempted to assassinate Markov the following year.

The KGB had operated a unique assassination bureau officially called the Ninth Division for Terror and Diversion. Its motto spoke volumes about the group's aims and attitudes: *Smert Shipionem* (Death to Spies). From this Russian motto came the more commonly known title of SMERSH. For many years the United States had suspected that Stalin's secret police ran some kind of international assassination agency, but only with the remarkable testimony of the SMERSH defector Captain Nicolai Khokhlov would Western intelligence agencies be able to create a picture of this terrifying organization.

Khokhlov, one of the KGB's star agents, had operated behind Nazi lines during the Second World War. In 1953 he was summoned to the offices of Colonel Lev Studnikov, the head of Stalin's SMERSH, and assigned the job of assassinating Igor Okolovich. Okolovich was head of the anti-communist National Unity (NTS) group in Frankfurt, West Germany. This group of dissidents opposed Soviet domination in East Germany and successfully spread anti-Soviet propaganda throughout that country, just over the border. Okolovich was identified as the mastermind behind the NTS propaganda machine, and SMERSH, in effect, signed his death warrant. Along with two East German assistants, Hans Kugovits and Kurt Weber, who had Russian sympathies, Khokhlov received special training in the assassination techniques they would employ against the West German. By Christmas 1953 the training had been completed, and the three men travelled by separate and circuitous routes, finally meeting up in Frankfurt in February 1954. However, although the three-man hit team had been well trained and had visited a secret SMERSH school in Baden, West Germany, Khokhlov was suddenly struck by a crisis of conscience. His wife, Yanina, in Moscow was a practising Christian and had asked Khokhlov not to kill Okolovich. Instead she urged him to try to prevent his death. In Frankfurt, with the SMERSH murder plan about to be put into practice, Khokhlov decided to tell Okolovich everything. He visited the target's flat on 18 February and told him exactly who he was and why he was there. A stunned Okolovich suggested that the KGB assassin defected to the United States. This Khokhlov did.

The Americans co-operated with Khokhlov, debriefing him as best they could without alerting any SMERSH surveillance teams (which Khokhlov had informed them were always present during an assassination mission – in order to ensure loyalty). They arranged to have his wife and her son extracted from Russia, which eased his worries and gave him confidence for the tasks ahead. At US insistence, Khokhlov arranged to have them intercept the weapons that had been delivered to Frankfurt especially for the assassination. On 25 February Khokhlov informed both of his colleagues about his plans to defect to the West and they immediately joined him. All three successfully sought political asylum in the West. Yanina Khokhlov and her son were not so lucky. Unfortunately the rescue attempt did not go as planned and both were captured and imprisoned.

Captain Khokhlov's defection exposed much of the KGB's spy network in one devastating blow, forcing it to recall a large number of agents, thus crippling its activities, but it was Khokhlov's revelations about SMERSH that took the Western intelligence agencies aback. Not only were they now able to fully debrief a leading light in the organization, but they had access to several purpose-built assassination weapons designed and manufactured in SMERSH laboratories. One unique pistol retrieved from the Okolovich's hit was actually disguised as a cigarette case, operated electrically to minimize the noise on firing. The bullet had a low muzzle velocity and would have inflicted little damage on a victim.

However, the bullet's deadly nature came from the poison that coated it. Revelations like these inspired non-Soviet intelligence agencies to create assassination tools and tactics of their own. The American CIA, a direct descendant of the wartime Office of Strategic Studies (OSS), reactivated many of the clandestine weapons that had been created for use in Nazi-occupied Europe. Similarly, the British Special Operations Executive had invented many ingenious weapons and techniques that would be used by military intelligence (MI6) after the war. One example was a CIA cigarette-gun, which fired a single .22 calibre bullet by pulling on the tiny weapon's spring-loaded end with fingers or even teeth. The gun's great surprise value easily compensated for its abysmal range (perhaps a metre at best). This obsession with political murder culminated in the farcical attempt by the CIA to murder the president of Cuba, Fidel Castro, in the early 1960s.

OPERATION MONGOOSE

The American Central Intelligence Agency (CIA) has long had an obsession with the communist leader of Cuba, Fidel Castro. It is an obsession that began in 1959 and continues unabated today. It is an obsession that has led the world's premier secret service to try any and every possible method of removing him, from propaganda, to military coup, to assassination. Yet Castro continues in power, untouched and unconcerned by the failures of CIA operatives to dislodge him. Known officially as Operation Mongoose, the assassination plot to kill Fidel Castro was a bizarre mix of desperation, optimism and fantasy.

Throughout the 1950s the Caribbean island of Cuba was held in the iron grip of the right-wing Batista regime. Fulgencio Batista had the backing of the CIA, and he allowed the American Mafia to profit from the island's position as a tourist destination with casinos, hotels and gambling houses. In 1959 the dictator faced a popular revolution, which was led by Fidel Castro and which successfully swept away the US influence on the island and established in its place a communist state. Castro immediately earned the enmity of the United States, and the CIA seriously discussed 'removing him'. Meetings held by the CIA in January and March 1960 advocated the assassination of Fidel Castro, as well as his brother, Raúl, and the communist leader's talented lieutenant, Che Guevara. Although several members of the CIA élite considered that they had been given a mandate to eliminate Castro, no evidence has arisen that can point to either President Eisenhower or President Kennedy having authorized the murder plot.

Once it was committed to the killing of Castro, the CIA had to formulate a way of carrying out the assassination. This proved remarkably difficult since the Agency had no way of gaining direct access either to Castro's entourage or to Cuban society at large. Several brainwashing programmes funded by the Agency were considered. Could the organization programme a deniable operative to get in close to the Cuban leader and assassinate him, with the killer afterwards remembering nothing of the deed itself or of the men who had sent him? The secret department co-ordinating this research was called MKULTRA. It was soon decided that a brainwashed assassin would not solve any of the basic problems. Brainwashing (if it could be done successfully) required not only 100 per cent control, but also 100 per cent dependability. Any deviation from the programming, any unforeseen event, could wreck the assassination attempt. The researchers also reasoned that any flexibility or choice programmed into the mind of a potential assassin had to be paid for with a certain lack of control. According to John Gittinger, a CIA agent involved with MKULTRA, the group eventually decided: 'You can get exactly the same thing from people who are hypnotizable by many other ways, and you can't get anything out of people who are not hypnotizable, so it has no use.' In the case of Castro, there were already many people who were willing to carry out the murder, and, according to Gittinger, 'A well-trained person could do it without all this mumbo-jumbo.' The Agency realized that it would have to go through a third party. Two options immediately suggested themselves: first, the highly motivated and well-connected Cuban exiles who had fled the communist revolution to settle in Florida; and second, the Mafia crime lords who had been unceremoniously booted off the island by the socialist leader but who combined a desire to return with a knowledge of Cuban society.

The Agency decided to explore both options, and while it gathered together a force of Cuban exiles to launch an amphibious offensive on Cuba, it also made overtures to the Mafia. CIA agents first needed a neutral go-between who could introduce them to members of the Mob. They chose Howard Hughes, the reclusive billionaire who had numerous connections with Las Vegas as well as with the Chicago Mob, which controlled much of the gambling there. Hughes's close friend and executive, Robert Maheu, was given the task of presenting suitable hit men to the

CIA operatives. Accordingly, a meeting was held between Johnny Roselli, the Mafia boss controlling Las Vegas, and the CIA's Jim O'Connell. In turn, Roselli introduced O'Connell to his boss, the Chicago godfather, Sam Giancana, and to the most important Mafia boss in Florida, Santos Trafficante. The two mobsters adopted pseudonyms as a cover: Giancana became Sam Gold, while Trafficante became Joe Pecora. The Mafia leaders agreed to assist the CIA in their murder attempt. Both men had suffered financially when Castro cut off their access to the gambling and drugs rackets from which they had profited during the 1950s. Should they succeed and American influence be re-established on the island, it was agreed that the Mob bosses would have the pick of the illicit businesses in Cuba.

Operation Mongoose got off to a flying start, and the CIA's Technical Services Division came up with a number of fantastic and deadly inventions designed to remove Castro. In February 1961 Roselli was handed a batch of botulinum toxin pills that had been successfully tested by the division on lab monkeys. They were to be dissolved in Castro's soup or coffee and were certain to be effective. Roselli passed them to Trafficante, who was to have them sent to his well-placed Cuban contact who worked on Castro's staff. Before the plan could go ahead, however, the Cuban mole lost his job. A second attempt was to take place at a restaurant frequented by the Cuban leader, and arrangements were made in April to have the poisoning take place there. Again the plan fell through at the last moment, when Castro changed his dining habits and stopped eating at that restaurant.

In April 1961 President Kennedy presided over the military disaster that was the Bay of Pigs. This poorly organized invasion by armed Cuban exiles failed because of a lack of air cover, that was promised but not delivered by the CIA. Hopes of the restoration of a friendly government in Cuba spearheaded by exiled Cubans vanished. The Agency decided to put all its trust in the second option for success in Cuba, the American Mafia. If the gangsters did actually murder Castro, the CIA could plausibly deny any involvement. After all, the Mob had its own reasons for getting rid of Castro as well as the means and motivation to do so. The Mob boss Meyer Lansky had even put a million-dollar bounty on Castro's head! What subsequently followed was a surreal series of deals and scams in which the gangsters discovered that they could bargain directly with secret elements within the US government and even, at times, hold the upper hand.

Sam Giancana and the 'dirty tricks' expert Maheu were no longer considered 'safe' assets and were dropped from Operation Mongoose. Now in full control of the audacious plot was William Harvey, a tough-talking, hard-drinking intelligence agent who managed the CIA's ultra-secret Executive Action capability. This capability involved the removal of foreign leaders – by assassination if necessary. Harvey forged links with some of the most powerful Mafia leaders in the country, and his 'gung-ho' attitude marked him out as a maverick. The next phase of the plan involved the procurement of explosives, sniper rifles, drugs and poisons, and their planned use in a series of murder attempts. None succeeded and many barely got off the drawing board. So many of the plans read like the flights of fancy of a deranged, third-rate script-writer.

The most famous assassination scam involved the doctoring of cigars, an indulgence that Castro was known to enjoy. The Agency acquired a box of the leader's favourite cigars and sprayed them with a deadly toxin, sure to kill within hours of use. The box was to be presented to Castro during his visit to the United Nations building in New York, but for reasons unknown, they were never received. According to one New York Police Department report the cigars had actually been rigged to explode in Castro's face!

Other plots were equally weird. It was known that Castro enjoyed scuba diving off the Cuban coast, and an ingenious murder plot was hatched that took advantage of this. Several Cuban exiles had been taken prisoner during the Bay of Pigs disaster, and an American lawyer was involved with negotiating their release. The plan involved this lawyer making a presentation of a diver's wet suit to the Cuban leader. This was to be no ordinary wet suit. The respirator had been contaminated with tuberculosis bacilli, and the inside of the suit with fungus spores that would result in the development of a rare skin disease. Unfortunately for the innovative Technical Services Division, the lawyer handed over an uncontaminated suit, foiling the plan.

The CIA did not stop at germ warfare, but also enthusiastically recruited the services of a popular CIA drug, LSD. This newly discovered drug had been secretly tested by the Agency for over a decade in the hope that it might lead to developments in brainwashing, interrogation and mind-control. Now the CIA planned to discredit Fidel Castro with its mind-bending effects. Again, the leader's cigars were to be laced, this time with LSD. It was hoped that this which would compromise the all too sober communist revolutionary, and a plan was envisaged that involved spraying his Havana broadcasting studio with the stuff. The idea was to trigger an on-air 'trip' that would discredit the leader, perhaps sparking a coup or battle for the leadership.

Another non-lethal plan designed to disgrace Castro and provoke some sort of leadership challenge involved the seeding of his shoes with thallium salts. This powerful depilatory chemical would cause the leader to lose hair at a prodigious rate. Once he was without hair, eyebrows and that famous beard, the CIA experts in the US were convinced that his machismo would disappear and his grip over the country would falter. Like the LSD plans, this plot never got any further than the fevered imaginations of the Agency's most inventive planners. It seemed as if they were so desperate to strike at Castro that they would try anything, whether or not it was likely to be lethal, effective or realistic.

Castro's love of diving inspired yet another far-fetched plan that could never have worked, even if it had been tried. A large explosive charge was to be disguised as a local conch shell. Left on the shallow seabed in the area frequented by Castro for his dives, it could be triggered as soon as he swam anywhere near it. It seemed as if the Agency would try anything as long as it didn't actually involve sending a man to Cuba to kill the communist leader. In fact, the CIA had earlier suggested to Roselli that he organize a 'Mob war'-style ambush on the Marxist leader, complete with blazing sub-machineguns. Roselli pointed out that the chances of making a successful escape under those circumstances were negligible, and that no Mafia hit man ever considered himself expendable.

In 1987, as part of the Iran-Contra hearings, the ex-CIA operative Felix Rodriguez publicly admitted that he had been involved in the attempts to kill Fidel Castro. And in his subsequent autobiography he even claimed that he had tried several times to enter Cuba with the aim of assassinating the Marxist leader. The Iran-Contra committee did ask Rodriguez if he had assisted in the plot to sabotage Castro's cigars. 'No, I did not,' the relaxed veteran replied. 'But I did volunteer to kill that son of a bitch in 1961 with a telescopic rifle.'

Throughout the 1960s Operation Mongoose continued to come up with ever more ingenious plans while increasing quantities of guns, powerboats, radios and poisons were passed on to Trafficante. The Mob boss took what was offered him and presented the CIA with one excuse after another: his men had been forced back; his agents in Cuba compromised. There is no record that any of the equipment and weaponry handed to Trafficante ever got to Cuba, and no evidence that the Mafia boss was ever seriously attempting an assassination. More likely, Trafficante had approached Castro with all the details of the plot on his life and found it more expedient to work for both sides in the dispute. Modern commentators point out that Trafficante only ever had a small piece of the Cuban gambling operation before the revolution, and that he may well have given the leader details of the Cuban exiles living in Florida. Perhaps he did this in the hope of being awarded a slice of the casino business if Castro ever decided to allow gambling back onto the island. This speculation on Santo Trafficante's motives is not especially important. What is important is that he used his position to great effect with the various US law enforcement agencies (especially the FBI). The Mob could effectively call on CIA protection, by claiming that some aspect of Operation Mongoose was in jeopardy of being exposed.

President Kennedy took office in January 1960 and presided over both the Bay of Pigs invasion and the greatest flurry of Castro murder attempts in the early 1960s. Meanwhile his attorney general (also his brother), Robert Kennedy, was busy pursuing prosecutions against the American Mafia. JFK had inherited Operation Mongoose from the previous Eisenhower administration, and it came as something of a shock to discover that an arm of government had recruited organized crime to carry out such a task. When Robert Kennedy was fully briefed on the plot by the CIA and discovered how Mafia bosses, whom he was trying to jail, were being paid by his own government, he was, according to a CIA lawyer, Lawrence Houston, 'mad as hell'. The attorney general went further: 'I trust that if you ever try to do business with organized crime again – with gangsters – you will let the attorney general know.'

At an undetermined point in the mid-1960s the CIA eventually realized that it was being fooled by Trafficante and his henchmen. Strange but true, Operation Mongoose was finally wrapped up, and plans to assassinate Castro were put on ice. The Agency attempted to cover its tracks but, by embroiling the Mafia in the conspiracy, it had guaranteed that this super-secret project ended up as anything but. Sam Giancana was murdered in 1975 just before he was due to testify to a Senate committee on the government's secret murder plots. Controversy still surrounds his death. Was he murdered by the Mob as tradition insists? Or did he have too many 'kill Castro' stories to tell? Did the CIA protect itself by assassinating Sam Giancana? Was it mere coincidence that Johnny Roselli was also murdered only a year later?

It wasn't so much the use of assassination as a tool of politics that had dismayed the Kennedys but such mercenary use of the Mafia – America's most feared and violent criminal society. CIA assassination plots were far from rare during the Kennedy years. In addition to Castro, names such as Patrice Lumumba (1925–61) of the Democratic Republic of Congo, Rafael Trujillo (1891–1961) of the Dominican Republic, Abdul Kassem (1914–63) of Iraq and Ngo Dinh Diem (1901–63) of South Vietnam were all to feature as targets for murder by the CIA during the three years that Kennedy was in power.

Shot and killed on 30 May 1961 by 'dissidents', President Trujillo was a CIA-backed dictator with all the faults of Batista, whom Castro had so embarrassingly deposed two years earlier. Trujillo ruled the island nation of the Dominican Republic with a totalitarian grip; his despotism was even compared to that of the insane Roman emperor Caligula. Repression, sadism, murder and torture were well-used, if unofficial, tools of government. The president's irresponsible behaviour seemed destined to court disaster – the Dominican Republic was a Cuba waiting to happen, and the United States could not face such a political disaster so soon after Cuba.

The State Department, with the aid of the CIA, realized that its 'best worst' option was to support some sort of local revolution. Luckily there was no shortage of Dominicans willing to have a go at killing Trujillo. Military leaders, left-wing activists and one of the country's most respected families, the de la Mazas, all became embroiled in the plot to murder their hated president. In late May a report to Washington stated bluntly that US officials in the Dominican Republic had been 'nurturing the effort to overthrow Trujillo and had assisted the dissidents in numerous ways, all of which were known to the [State] Department'. Supplies of American sub-machineguns and grenades were waiting within the country ready for the expected coup, but at the last minute Washington refused to sanction their use. The assassination went ahead regardless. Trujillo was ambushed in his limousine just outside the capital Santo Domingo, and he insisted on returning fire on the rebels, subsequently being cut down by automatic gunfire. The conspirators did not have absolute support for a coup, the US refused to step in, and the remnants of the Trujillo family mustered enough support to prevent a takeover. Those involved in the plot to kill the president were hunted down, mercilessly tortured and executed.

Exactly what role the CIA played in Trujillo's murder is still hotly contested. Was the Agency pulled out of the operation at the last minute, leaving the dissidents to fend for themselves as best they could? Or did it provide limited covert support for the assassination? One retired army colonel, Bill Bishop, actually boasted that he had been involved in CIA black operations. 'I made the hit on Trujillo,' he boldly admitted. 'That's one mission I'm kinda proud of, because a lot of my associates said it couldn't be done.'

Patrice Lumumba, the Democratic Republic of Congo's own dictator, was also at the receiving end of the unwelcome attentions of the CIA. When Lumumba was murdered on 17 January 1961 by rebel forces who had seized control of the country, the Agency was able to drop its own murder plans. In his bid to halt the rise of his enemies, the leader of the Congo had invited communist advisers from Czechoslovakia and the Soviet Union. Washington balked at this turn of events and ordered the CIA to act quickly. The CIA station chief in Kinshasa received a message from the Agency's director in Washington, which included the following message: 'Removal must be an urgent and prime objective and ... under existing conditions this should be a high priority of our covert action.' Several assassination plots were initiated, one of which was to involve the recruitment of a band of Western mercenaries. Another involved the use of a lethal poison, and the 'murder kit' to be used was handed to the local station chief ready for use. It included several doses of a deadly virus indigenous to that part of Africa. It was hoped that Lumumba's death could be made to appear natural. Included with the kit were several hypodermic needles and a pair of rubber gloves. The biological agent had been produced for the CIA's Technical Services Staff by the army's secret Special Operations Division (SOD) operating out of Fort Detrick in Maryland. This joint germ warfare programme, code-named MKNAOMI, supplied the Agency with all manner of lethal and non-lethal biological agents throughout the 1950s and well into the 1960s.

Obviously, the Agency seriously considered the use of biological agents as a method of assassination. The greatest problem with this mode of killing was identifying a suitable delivery method. MKNAOMI did not want to start an epidemic, it wanted to take out an individual. This was the thinking behind Castro's infected wet-suit. SOD had thought long and hard about the problem. The ideal system (according to one CIA document) was a weapon that could infect the target but that would not be 'easily detected upon a detailed autopsy'. Various types of aerosol delivery were experimented with, including a germ aerosol that was disguised as a cigarette lighter and a device within a sabotaged car engine, which would release a deadly agent into the passenger compartment. One ingenious device was silently activated by a fluorescent starter, which triggered the mechanism when a light was switched on in the room. SOD also developed aerosol sprays that could be activated by remote control. The development of a pointed delivery weapon always seemed to elude SOD, until its army researchers created the 'flechette' gun, a converted .45 pistol capable of firing low-velocity darts into targets. Individual darts could be treated with one of MKNAOMI's formidable array of germ weapons.

THE INTERNATIONAL CHE GUEVARA BRIGADE

Fidel Castro's reputation benefited immensely from his ability to evade the CIA's efforts to murder him. Ernesto 'Che' Guevara, Castro's loyal deputy, bathed in the reflected glory of his leader, but Guevara had cultivated a loyal following of his own. Some considered him a dedicated revolutionary with greater vision than Castro. Guevara's demise turned out to be a sad and dismal end to a promising future, and it sparked off a series of bloody, connected assassinations in South America.

Che Guevara was born into a wealthy Spanish-Irish family in 1928, and he proved a valuable asset in Castro's Cuban revolution of 1959. After only six years, however, the idealist fell out with Castro and left Cuba for good, renouncing his Cuban citizenship and announcing that he was about to begin a fresh revolutionary campaign. He travelled widely and was reported to have visited a number of far-flung locations, including North Vietnam and Algeria. Finally, Guevara settled in the poverty-stricken South American nation of Bolivia, which he considered was ready for armed revolution. He took to the jungle-clad hills with Bolivian rebels and helped them organize a guerrilla war against the government, although his attempts to enflame the desperate peasantry with revolutionary zeal were not entirely successful. As an outsider, Guevara never enjoyed the full confidence of the people with whom he was living, and the absolute poverty of the rebels soon began to tell on him. Guevara and his ragtag army were constantly on the run from government sweeps, and their ineffectual ambushes, followed by hasty retreats, far outnumbered their victories. To make things worse, Guevara was struggling with debilitating illnesses that frequently meant he had to be carried through the jungle by the rebels.

ABOVE Perhaps the most famous assassination of all time, Julius Caesar was murdered in 44 BC by his friends and colleagues. He sought to rule Rome alone, and so brought down upon himself the wrath of Rome's most powerful statesmen. *(Mary Evans Picture Library)*

RIGHT The dissolute Pope Alexander VI is better known as the father of Cesare Borgia, a young man considered to be one of history's most prolific assassins. Here, Alexander has invited fifty courtesans to the dine at the Vatican in celebration of his daughter Lucretia's wedding. *(Mary Evans Picture Library)*

ABOVE Adolf Hitler relaxes at Berchtesgaden, his mountain-top retreat, in the company of a hunting party. Hitler survived numerous assassination attempts by his own generals, and in 1944 the British concocted an abortive plan to murder him while he rested at Berchtesgaden. *(Mary Evans Picture Library)*

BELOW Stalin's arch enemy, Leon Trotsky, lies mortally wounded in a Mexican hospital in August 1940. His assassin was a communist agent named Mercader who had carried a revolver, a dagger and an ice-pick into Trotsky's room. Mercader's attack with the ice-pick was so sudden and so violent that Trotsky thought that he had been shot in the head. *(AKG Photo)*

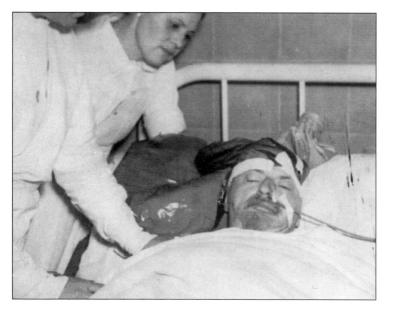

RIGHT Lee Harvey Oswald poses for the camera with the Mannlicher-Carcano rifle used to murder President Kennedy. No assassination in history has sparked as much debate, nor received as much media attention. This photograph, for example, was initially considered proof of Oswald's ownership of the rifle. It has since been dismissed by some sceptics as a clever government fake designed to frame him for the murder. *(Popperfoto)*

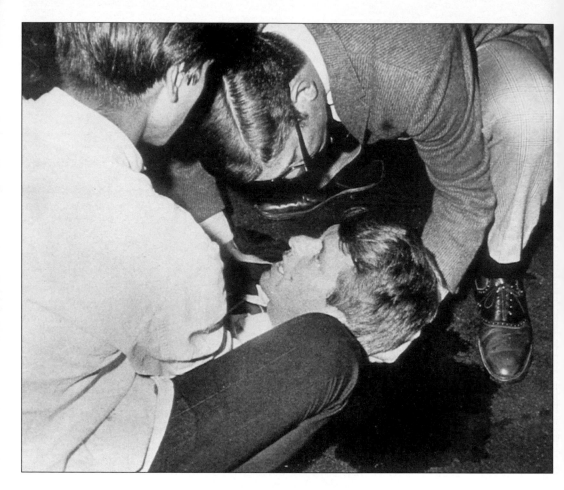

ABOVE Robert Kennedy lies dying at the Ambassador Hotel on 5 June 1968. His killer was Sirhan Sirhan, a disturbed and fanatical young Palestinian who later claimed to have no recollection of the murder. Some investigators have since tried to connect the two mysterious Kennedy assassinations. *(Popperfoto)*

RIGHT When Martin Luther King was shot by a sniper in 1968 the police apprehended this man, James Earl Ray, who was subsequently charged with the murder. In the three decades that followed evidence continued to come to light that cast doubt on Ray's guilt. *(AKG Photo)*

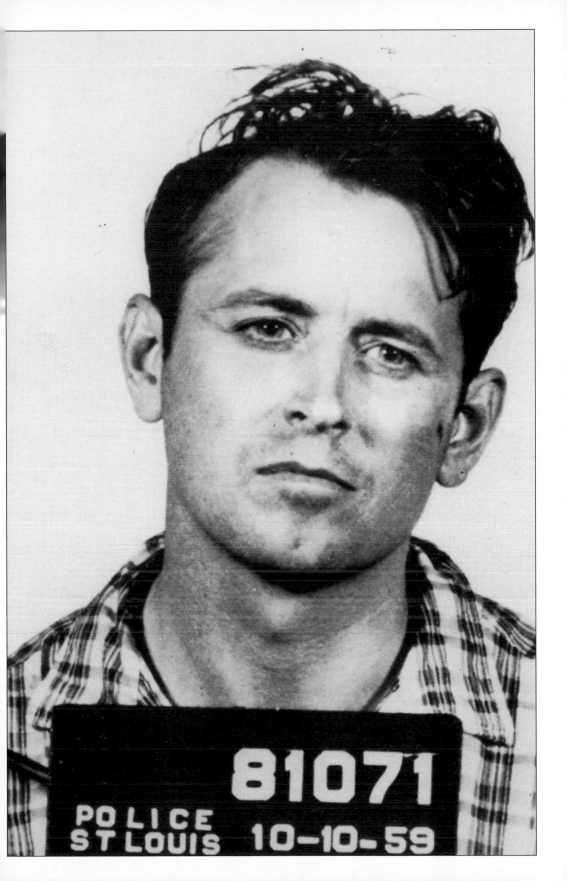

RIGHT Pope John Paul II being carried away to safety on 13 May 1981. As the pope greeted crowds that had gathered in St Peter's Square, the Turkish nationalist Ali Agca opened fire with a pistol, hitting his target twice. His motives are still not clear. *(AKG Photo)*

BELOW Sarajevo, 1914: a young man is bundled away by the authorities. He is Gavrilo Princip and minutes earlier he had shot to death Archduke Franz Ferdinand and his wife. No one could have foreseen the bloody carnage of the First World War that was the result of this assassination. *(AKG Photo)*

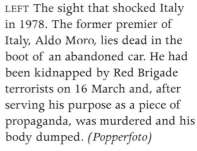

LEFT The sight that shocked Italy in 1978. The former premier of Italy, Aldo Moro, lies dead in the boot of an abandoned car. He had been kidnapped by Red Brigade terrorists on 16 March and, after serving his purpose as a piece of propaganda, was murdered and his body dumped. *(Popperfoto)*

LEFT The wrecked façade of the Grand Hotel in Brighton on 12 October 1984. The IRA had planted a sleeper bomb that successfully evaded detection, and exploded with devastating effect, injuring many members of the British cabinet. Prime Minister Margaret Thatcher narrowly avoided serious injury. *(Popperfoto)*

Dutch Schultz shortly before he appeared in court charged with income tax evasion. Schultz was assassinated in 1935 on the orders of the Mafia godfather 'Lucky' Luciano. Luciano had heard that Schultz was planning to have a government prosecutor murdered, an act that contravened the Mafia's own strict code. *(Popperfoto)*

It is thought that Guevara had been attempting to abandon the Bolivian rebels and leave the country altogether, but the government counter-terrorist campaign had cut off all the available escape routes. It was only a matter of time before one of the jungle engagements would prove fatal. Guevara and his rebel group were caught by an army unit on 8 October 1967 and Guevara was wounded by gunfire. Surrounded by soldiers he is reported to have confessed: 'My name is Che Guevara, and I have failed.'

Inspite of his wounds, the revolutionary is supposed to have survived until the following day. Later medical examiners, however, refused to believe that the terrible wounds inflicted on the corpse would not have been immediately fatal and therefore concluded that Guevara had been murdered by the army on the orders of the Bolivian government. Also controversial was the fact that the body of the martyred Marxist revolutionary was quickly consigned to a secret grave, which has only recently been located.

The death of the charismatic revolutionary caused outrage among Guevara's small band of international followers. Over the years this following was to expand, and Che Guevara became the focus for student activism around the globe.

On 11 May 1976, following the shooting on a Paris street of Bolivia's ambassador to France, a group of terrorists calling themselves the International Che Guevara Brigade claimed responsibility for the crime. The ambassador, General Joaquin Zenteno Anaya, had been the officer in charge of the operation that had cornered and killed the revolutionary nine years previously. The killers were never caught, and the death of Zenteno became entangled in controversy. Six days later a disgruntled Bolivian general, Luis Reque Teran, charged the Bolivian government, and in particular the Bolivian president, Hugo Banzer Suárez, with Zenteno's assassination. This created a storm of protests and counter-accusations. The commander of the army accused General Reque of revealing 'military secrets' and stated that Reque was guilty of treason. General Reque continued to accuse both the Bolivian president and army commander of the mass-murder of hundreds of innocent peasants and political prisoners of the Bolivian regime.

Despite these accusations and denials, the Zenteno murder was never solved, and it is still unclear whether the so-called International Che Guevara Brigade had anything whatsoever to do with it. The mysterious group did not entirely disappear following the Zenteno affair, however.

Within weeks another murder had been laid at the door of the Brigade, but again there is little doubt that the terror group was being used as a cover for the illegal actions of someone else. This time the victim was the retired Bolivian General Juan José Torres, who had fled his native country when President Suárez had seized power in August 1971. His body was discovered lying in a back-road outside Buenos Aires, Argentina, blindfolded and full of bullets. The Argentinian government, as well as Suárez's right-wing regime, denounced the murder. The Bolivians specifically charged the International Che Guevara Brigade with the terrible killing. Many saw in this finger-pointing the actions of a guilty party. Had the Bolivian president ordered the death of General Torres?

Torres's widow believed so, and she stated publicly that the Argentinian and Bolivian governments had conspired to murder her husband. Her statement also accused the Bolivian Colonel Raul Tejerina of threatening her husband. The Bolivian mineworkers had always been loyal to Torres, who had ruled Bolivia for several months in the early 1970s, and they went on strike to demonstrate their solidarity with the dead general. They were joined by students and left-wing activists as well as by workers from several Bolivian cities. The outcry demanded a response, but the offer of a state funeral for General Torres was not received warmly by his widow. In the tense period following Torres's funeral, President Suárez offered an amnesty to the many officials who had fled Bolivia over the years and who lived in constant fear of a Torres-style assassination. Several men took the president up on his offer and returned to their native land. Among them were several colleagues of General Torres, including Jorge Gallardo and Ciro Humboldt. All were immediately arrested and subsequently imprisoned, proving that their fears of retribution had been well founded.

The International Che Guevara Brigade may not have had any real substance, but the enigmatic figure of Guevara continued to fascinate and inspire beleaguered peasants across South and Central America. One such group was the tiny Guerrilla Army of the Poor, which fought for change in the jungles of Guatemala during this same period. The logo of these Marxist fighters was a picture of Che Guevara.

RELIGION VERSUS IDEOLOGY

Within St Peter's Square in the Vatican City, Rome, a man attempted to assassinate Pope John Paul II. The attempt was carried out on 13 May

1981, and the facts of the incident are not in doubt. A twenty-three-year-old Turk named Mehmet Ali Agca pushed through the mass of people trying to get a glimpse of the pope as he rode slowly in his open-topped vehicle. The white car stopped frequently to allow the pontiff to bless those nearby. Many hands were held out in greeting – Agca held out his 9mm pistol and fired, hitting two bystanders and twice wounding the pope. The wounds were not serious, however, and after emergency surgery and a period of recuperation, John Paul II returned to his duties. Ali Agca was tried and sentenced to life imprisonment for his crime. There the facts end and speculation begins. So little is known – so much has been theorized.

The attempted murder came at a time of increasing Cold War rhetoric when American sabres were being loudly rattled in the face of Soviet imperialism. Presidential candidate Ronald Reagan, who had made a virtue of hard-edged militarism, had secured his seat in the Oval Office on this ticket. Cold War paranoia swirled around the edges of the world's leading news stories, and the attempted murder of the pope, the pivot of Western Christianity, seemed to be the ultimate communist-atheist depravity. Had the Soviet Union engineered the murder plot? Or were the Soviet leaders taking the blame for the attempt in a propaganda battle waged by a ruthless CIA?

Initially, neither version seemed credible. Agca had little to do with communism. In fact, he was associated with the growing fascist underground movement in Turkey. Working with the Grey Wolves, a right-wing terror group, Agca first bloodied his hands on 1 February 1979 when he shot to death Abdi Ipckci, the editor of a left-wing newspaper, *Milliyet*. After his arrest and imprisonment, the Grey Wolves helped Agca to escape and continue his strange and bleak existence. In a letter he had raged about Pope Jean Paul II, calling him the 'Crusader Commander' and arguing that his imminent visit to Turkey was part of an imperialist plot to destroy the unity of the 'brotherly Islamic countries'. Agca, clearly, was a fanatic devoted to his cause. The fugitive from Turkish justice travelled widely, first to Iran and then back to Turkey. He journeyed to Bulgaria and on to Yugoslavia. From there he moved to West Germany, and he finally ended up in Italy. It was there that Mehmet Ali Agca tried to murder the pope.

Ten months into his sentence, Agca suddenly revealed that the Bulgarian authorities had actually offered him $1.25 million to kill Pope John Paul II. Investigators seemed able to verify a slew of minor details that appeared to corroborate his story. What was more, the notorious Bulgarian secret police, the DS, had already been implicated in the murder of Georgi Markov and were suspected by Western analysts of smuggling illegal arms as well as drugs. The Italian police decided to follow up Agca's remarkable testimony and arrested three Turks and a Bulgarian airline official (two other Bulgarians fled Italian justice). The trial began and Agca's evidence began to uncover details of the international conspiracy (the 'Bulgarian Connection') to murder the pope. He even implicated the KGB. But his testimony proved his own undoing: 'I am Jesus Christ!' he shouted in court. It soon became clear that Mehmet Ali Agca was not of sound mind, and all the defendants were released without charge. And yet his argument had seemed so convincing. The Bulgarians had indeed carried out international assassinations before 1981. The Soviet Union had previously worked with the DS and was greatly displeased at Pope John Paul II's vocal support for the Polish trade union Solidarity. The KGB had the motivation, the means and the opportunity to murder the pope.

The actual evidence of a Bulgarian connection (other than Agca's unreliable testimony) was slight and was promulgated by two key right-wing US journalists. One of these, Claire Sterling, had previously worked on a CIA newspaper and peppered her communist conspiracy theories with unadulterated CIA propaganda. The pressure to implicate the Eastern bloc steadily grew, and a number of articles appearing in American newspapers pushed the connection to its limit. Sterling and her associates (such as fellow journalist Paul Henze) are more likely to have been the unwitting messengers of a disinformation campaign carried out by the Italian secret service, SISMI. A tool of the ultra-right and the Mafia-connected masonic lodge known as P2 (Propaganda 2), SISMI has been accused of coaching Agca as he languished in prison, feeding him details of the Bulgarian connection. This 'left-right' disinformation was a tried and tested element of Italian terrorism. Neo-fascists were regularly planting bombs that were blamed on the communists and the Red Brigades. The sleight of hand was a calculated move to gain support for the right, and Agca's attempt on the pope's life was perhaps too good an opportunity to miss. His sudden confession was almost certainly inspired by Francesco Pazienza, an ex-SISMI agent, right-wing terrorist and P2 member. It seems that SISMI had seen in Mehmet Ali Agca a deniable asset that could be used to 'smear' the communists, whipping up fear and hatred among the Italian people.

Following the dismissal of the case against Agca's Bulgarian contact, one Italian newspaper commented, 'Only one thing is clear: Agca is a liar.' Whatever the reality might turn out to be, this much, at least, was true.

THE MIDDLE EAST HIT TEAMS

'State-sponsored terrorism' is a phrase that has gone hand-in-hand with the Reagan era of 'no deals' with hostages. This came in the aftermath of the disastrous Iranian hostage crisis of 1980. The United States had become embroiled in Middle Eastern power politics by choice. Its greatest ally and bulwark against communism in the region was Israel, a nation that relied on US support in the West for its often controversial actions, Such an interventionist approach earned the United States the enmity of the region's hardline terror groups. President Reagan's CIA advisers identified several key Arab governments that were specifically training, funding, supplying and protecting terrorists who struck against the West. Three Arab nations were at the top of the list: Iran, Syria and Libya. In the mid-1980s the Libyan leader Colonel Muammar Gaddafi incurred the full wrath of the United States.

The Arab leader was a committed supporter of the Palestinian cause and of the Palestinian Liberation Organization (PLO), which fought with bombs and bullets for the rights of Palestinians in Israel. Gaddafi was, in this respect, no different from many other leaders in the region. What made Gaddafi different was the way in which he perceived himself. In 1985 he claimed to have established a 'Pan-Arab Command for Leading the Arab Forces', an umbrella organization that was given the impossible task of uniting both the hardline Arab states and the militant terrorist factions and directing them in a war against the United States. Any Arab states that wavered or had a track record of 'liberalism' would also be targeted. This new move on Gaddafi's part was announced publicly, and the leader backed it up with generous offers of asylum, weaponry and the use of secret training facilities for PLO terrorists. All this antagonized the US, which began to focus more and more on Libya's true role within the international terrorist community. It seemed that, despite Gaddafi's self-aggrandizement and his failed attempts to style himself as a serious pan-Arab politician, the Libyan government did have links with terrorists. Rumours abounded of training camps that were being attended by West German Red Army faction (RAF), Italian Red Brigades and Irish Republican Army (IRA) members. In 1987 a 100-ton shipment of arms and ammunition was intercepted off the coast of Brittany, *en route* from Libya to Ireland. The rumours seemed to be true.

From the beginning of the Reagan administration, Gaddafi caused the CIA some concern. Intelligence indicated that he did have serious ambitions both within the Arab world and in the unstable region of Central Africa. The CIA was convinced of his territorial ambitions and, to that end, his desire to construct a nuclear weapon. A show of US strength in the Gulf of Sirte turned sour on 19 August 1981 when two F-14 fighters from a US aircraft carrier shot down two Libyan jet fighters, which were moving in to the attack. This incident heightened the tension between Gaddafi and Reagan, and the CIA soon discovered that Gaddafi did not intend to let the US push him around. Through a well-placed Ethiopian official the CIA learned that Gaddafi had privately declared that he was going to have President Reagan assassinated. Considering the leader's close ties with both the PLO and Black September (a radical Palestinian splinter group), his threat was not regarded as simply an empty gesture. Intelligence sources soon provided the CIA with a convincing picture of Libyan preparation for some kind of terrorist attack. One report received on 17 October stated that a five-man Libyan assassination squad had entered Italy. The Italian intelligence service later informed the CIA that it believed the group had left Italy for an unknown destination.

On 16 November an informant walked into an unidentified American embassy and claimed that he had recently left one of Gaddafi's terrorist training camps. He also claimed that one of the training routines that he had witnessed had been an attack on an American-style limousine motorcade. He also indicated that if Libyan gunmen could not get to President Reagan, they were instead to target Vice-President George Bush, Secretary of State Alexander Haig or Defence Secretary Caspar Weinberger. True or not, these reports created considerable anxiety within the highest levels of the CIA. When the White House was briefed on the scale of the emergency, the Secret Service began a programme of counter-measures. Surface-to-air Stinger missile teams were (and still are) placed on the White House roof, and decoy motorcades came and went in an effort to confuse a potential assassin. William Casey, the director of the CIA, warned Reagan of the dangers and reminded the president of recent shootings – Pope John Paul II, President Anwar Sadat and even Reagan's own wounding at the hand of John Hinckley in March.

Fear fed rumour. On 4 December it was reported in the *New York*

Times that a five-man Libyan assassination squad had arrived in the United States. Within days the five-man team had become a ten-man team. Composite sketches of the five assassins were compiled and distributed to TV stations across the country. Anyone connected with Reagan – his aides, advisers and friends – began to take precautions, for no one knew who would be the target of this Libyan commando team or when it would strike. Two days after the dramatic newspaper report, Gaddafi gave a live interview on American TV. In it he dismissed the reports of Libyan hit men: 'We refuse to assassinate any person,' he said. 'It is the behaviour of America, preparing to assassinate me, to poison my food. They tried many things to do this.' Gaddafi questioned the authenticity of the American reports and said he was keen 'to see this evidence, because we are sure we didn't send any people to kill Reagan or any other people in the world'.

President Reagan felt that the US had not pushed Libya enough, and dispatched a secret message for the Libyan leader's eyes only. In it the president stated emphatically: 'I have detailed and verified information about several Libyan-sponsored plans and attempts to assassinate US government officials.' He went further, invoking the United Nations article giving every nation the right to take military action in self-defence:

> Any acts of violence directed by Libya ... against officials of the US ... will be regarded by the US government as an armed attack upon the US and will be met by every means necessary to defend this nation in accordance with Article 51 of the United Nations Charter.

Within a week of receiving this communiqué, the Libyan government began to make overtures to the US government asking that diplomatic channels be opened, and it pledged that there would be no assassination attempts. By that time it was evident to the CIA that the murder attempt may not have been such a real threat after all. In every case but one, the intelligence came from questionable sources, and the Agency admitted in a memorandum on 18 December that 'some of the reporting may have been generated because informants are aware we are seeking this information'. Overall, the memorandum painted a picture of an assassination rumour that generated misinformation simply feeding off itself. Over twenty years later, few commentators take the story of Libyan-backed presidential hit squads seriously, and yet the reports almost brought the US and Libya to the brink of full-scale war.

While Gaddafi denied trying to assassinate the president of the United States, he was simultaneously waging a real campaign of overseas assassination that was to lead to the death of his own son. Gaddafi, like many dictators, ruled his people with a fierce and totalitarian grip. Those who had been able to escape from Libya considered themselves safe from government persecution, but now Gaddafi turned his attention to these exiles. Hit teams were dispatched to murder the 'enemies of the state', just as the NKVD had sent out mobile groups to slaughter innocent political activists who had also fled overseas. One of these murders, which numbered in the tens, not the hundreds, was carried out on American soil, which, as far as the CIA was concerned, provided further evidence of a plot to kill Reagan. Fisal Abulaze Zagalli, a Libyan dissident, was shot and killed at his Colorado home in 1981. His was to be the first of three murders the hit team had been sent to carry out, but they were fortunately forced to abandon the attempts without further bloodshed.

Libya has not been the only Middle Eastern nation to dispatch assassination squads in this way. Iran has become notorious for its reported use of terrorist murder teams. CIA agent Manucher Ghorbanifar informed the Agency that there was a three-man assassination squad operating in Europe that was engaged in tracking down and eliminating Iranian dissidents. The Iranian government had begun its fanatical persecution of supposed enemies following a bomb attack on the government's party headquarters on 28 June 1981. Rebel leaders of a left-wing group of the fundamentalist Iranian government detonated a car bomb that killed four cabinet ministers, thirty other officials and the party's secretary-general. A month later the new Iranian president, Mohammed Ali Rajai, was murdered. The backlash was bloody and brutal. Demonstrators, suspects and students were rounded up and executed, some being boys as young as twelve years old. This led the regime to seek out enemies abroad, or so Ghorbanifar would have the United States believe. There is some question as to his reliability in these matters, since he had unquestioningly circulated the rumours of a Libyan assassination squad. But there was no doubt that Iran was sponsoring terrorism in the Middle East, and there were hundreds of victims of Iranian-backed car bombs during the civil war that rocked Lebanon in the 1980s.

The CIA desperately wanted to strike back at the Iranian, Syrian and Libyan terrorists that were embarrassing the United States at every turn. Lieutenant Colonel Oliver North drafted an advisory document for President Reagan that suggested, in blunt language, taking the fight to the terrorists. His report called for CIA-backed and -trained squads of foreign agents to be sent out to eliminate known terrorists who targeted American citizens. When the deputy-director of the CIA, John McMahon, received a copy of North's report, he was incensed. Had North never heard of the executive order banning political assassination as a tool of the American government? This order had been signed by President Ford in 1976 and reaffirmed by President Carter. It was a reaction against the unregulated CIA attempts to eliminate foreign leaders of the 1960s. Within months, however, one particular assessment was circulated that suggested some sort of assassination attempt against Gaddafi, carried out by Libyan dissidents with CIA help, despite the Executive Order 12333 of President Reagan, which flatly stated: 'Prohibition on assassination. No person employed by or acting on behalf of the United States government shall engage in, or conspire to engage in, assassination.' McMahon successfully stifled any CIA attempt to try and overthrow Gaddafi with a CIA-backed revolution. This did not, however, prevent an assassination attempt from taking place on 14 April 1986.

Only one month previously, Libya and the United States had come to blows during a minor naval skirmish in the Gulf of Sirte. At the start of April a terrorist bomb exploded in a West Berlin bar, usually packed with American servicemen. One US soldier and a Turkish woman were killed – and the US announced that Libyan terrorists were to blame. Reagan ordered a 'retaliatory strike', which was to target a number of military sites in the Tripoli and Benghazi areas. The terror bombing did not just merit an airstrike against Libyan military installations, but also against Colonel Gaddafi's personal headquarters at the El Azziziya barracks. It looked as if the US were making an unashamed attempt to kill the Libyan dictator, although the Pentagon firmly denied this. Gaddafi survived the attack, although one of his children did not. Through a combination of his unpredictable behaviour and bellicose empire-building, Gaddafi has made a great number of enemies. Nonetheless, he has weathered several attempts on his life. The latest attempt is alleged to have taken place in February 1996.

According to David Shayler, a former member of Britain's counter-intelligence service, the government's foreign intelligence service (MI6), became intricately linked with a failed assassination attempt on the Libyan leader. Shayler alleges that an MI6 agent (code-named PT16B) controlled a Libyan agent code-named Tunworth. Tunworth, who had connections with a right-wing fundamentalist terror group, discovered that the group was plotting to kill Gaddafi. When Tunworth informed MI6 it seems that a large amount of money ($160,000) was allocated by the secret service to the plotters. MI6 now had a stake in the murder. It was unclear at the time of Shayler's allegations just how much official sanction the operation received. The Foreign Office denied all knowledge of it; sources at MI6 did not. The terrorists planted a bomb under a car in Gaddafi's motorcade. It was the wrong car, and when the device exploded it killed several bystanders. With Tunworth's links to right-wing fundamentalists in Libya, a suitable cover for the murder of the dictator had been provided. Otherwise, any one of Gaddafi's many enemies could have been held responsible. Only two months previously near Benghazi, gunmen had raked Gaddafi's entourage with gunfire in an attempt to kill him. Like Fidel Castro, Gaddafi has survived innumerable attempts on his life. Much to his enemies' annoyance, he will probably be around for some time to come.

Was the Gaddafi affair Britain's stab at international terrorism? It had a precedent. During Britain's bitter rivalries with Egypt's President Gamal Nasser, the secret services had tried to arrange for Nasser's assassination through an Arab hit team. The plan came to nothing, but the danger of such activity had been recognized. And as the British and American forces in Saudi Arabia prepared to liberate Kuwait in 1990, there was again much talk in the media of a plot to assassinate President Saddam Hussein. Military commanders controlling the aerial bombardment of Iraq were repeatedly asked if Saddam Hussein was being targeted by the attacks. These commanders repeatedly denied any such suggestion. In fact the CIA and MI6 did collaborate on a project to have Hussein murdered, but again, nothing concrete came of the plot. In the aftermath of the war, the CIA also made some attempts to assist the Shiite uprising in the south of Iraq. Attempts on Hussein's life by his own people have also been reported, but Saddam Hussein, like Adolf Hitler, changes his plans without warning, continually moves around to scotch murder attempts and surrounds himself with a huge armed bodyguard. Saddam Hussein stays alive by remembering that if he ever dropped his guard for one moment, he would without doubt fall victim to assassination.

The Iranian religious leader, Ayatollah Khomeni, startled the world in 1989 by declaring that the Indian-born British author Salman Rushdie should be executed for blasphemy following the publication of his controversial book *The Satanic Verses*. Scotland Yard detectives have since kept the writer under constant protection. Some British Muslims demonstrated in support of the Iranian ruling, and some bookshops that had agreed to stock Rushdie's novel were picketed. There have been no attempts on Rushdie's life as yet, but the author-in-hiding has heard confidential reports of Iranian hit squads that have tried to locate him. Those around him proved easier targets, however, and both the Japanese translator and Italian editor of *The Satanic Verses* have been murdered; only Rushdie's Swedish publisher survived a murder attempt. In June 1989 the Ayatollah who pronounced Rushdie's death sentence died without withdrawing the *fatwa*.

Until 1998 the Ayatollah Khomeni's successors showed no signs of lifting the death threat, and Rushdie continued to live in fear of his life for a decade. In 1998, however, the Iranian government formally distanced itself from any threat on the writer's life. This was an unashamed move by Iran to re-enter international politics - the *fatwa* had wrecked the country's relations with the West. Many Muslims have not been as forgiving as Iran, however, and the unofficial bounty on Rushdie has only increased. Moreover, because Khomeni died without revoking the *fatwa*, many Muslim hardliners consider that it remains in force. Rushdie can satisfy himself that Iran will not sponsor an official hit team, but he can never know how many individual Muslims have taken it upon themselves to carry out the *fatwa*, regardless of political developments.

6. JFK: Conspiracy and Confusion

onspiracy theorists and their theories have been around for quite some time (as we have already seen in previous chapters), but the 1960s bred an 'assassination cult' that continues unabated today. It began with the slaying of President John F. Kennedy on 22 November 1963 and has continued ever since. It was that killing, that quintessential assassination, that formed a baseline from which all further conspiratorial murders could be measured. In the light of President Kennedy's murder (and that of his brother, Robert, in 1968), the deaths of the rich and famous would always provoke scepticism and speculation. The tragic death of Marilyn Monroe from an overdose was an instance in point, and many later investigators have returned to the case to analyse the many discrepancies that her death had thrown up.

WHO MURDERED MARILYN?

The strange death of Marilyn Monroe in 1962 epitomizes an era in American history. Monroe, born Norma Jean Baker in 1926, had become the nation's most glamorous and most desirable star. In films such as *Gentlemen Prefer Blondes* (1953) and *Some Like It Hot* (1959) she captured the hearts of millions. The platinum blonde was already an icon, a symbol and a celebrity – and she had achieved cult status within her own lifetime. The world was stunned when Marilyn Monroe was discovered dead in her home on 4 August 1962 by Robert Greenson (who was both her psychiatrist and a close friend). The cause of death was quickly established – Marilyn Monroe had died of an overdose. This came as no surprise to those who knew her. Marilyn was suffering from quite severe bouts of depression at the time, and this quickly took a toll both on her personal life as well as her acting career (much to the chagrin of her fellow actors). According to her friends, Marilyn's love life was tearing her apart.

There is no doubt that Marilyn died in unusual circumstances, and many now believe that she was murdered to prevent a major political scandal. Marilyn Monroe had only recently ended an illicit affair with President John F. Kennedy and had then turned to his powerful brother, Robert, the attorney general, for comfort. These were dangerous liaisons indeed. If these affairs were to be made public, the political careers of both men would be placed in serious jeopardy. To make things worse, Marilyn was also reputed to have slept with the Chicago Mafia don, Sam Giancana.

Although the general public knew nothing of these sexual manoeuvres, the FBI certainly did. The Bureau's director, J. Edgar Hoover, had every room of her Malibu house bugged. Giancana is also supposed to have established a similar surveillance operation. The Mob boss saw this as an opportunity to keep the Kennedy brothers off his back for good. Between them, they had stepped up the war against organized crime to an unprecedented level, exasperating Giancana and causing some of his colleagues to consider returning to Italy. After Marilyn's death, Giancana even boasted that he had been the last man to sleep with her and that he had got one up on the Kennedys.

Was Marilyn murdered on the orders of Jack or Bobby Kennedy? Was she murdered at all? This type of speculation really sets the scene for the bloody and demoralizing events of the rest of the decade. Suggestion without evidence; theory without proof. Powerful figures in the underworld, in show business and in politics meet and begin to formulate sinister deals. The terrible shadow of conspiracy falls across the victim, and he (or she) is struck down. Half-hidden clues and tantalizingly revealed scraps of evidence lay down an indistinct trail that only the most diligent investigator can follow – and it leads directly to those who ordered the 'hit'. Marilyn's ambiguous death has all these ingredients, and it stands as one of the first in a series of murder mysteries that rocked the United States in the 1960s.

Tapes from Marilyn's home have since surfaced and have been carefully analysed by investigators eager to find out what happened on that warm August evening in 1962. The tapes are said by those who have listened to them to record lengthy liaisons between Marilyn and the president. The writers and private investigators who have had access to these explosive tapes claim that the answers are there. According to Anthony Summers (in his book *Goddess: The Secret Lives of Marilyn Monroe*), the conspiracy surrounding Marilyn's death involved Bobby

Kennedy. Milo Speriglio contends that it was, in fact, President Kennedy who ordered the star's murder and that he asked Giancana to provide a suitable team of hit men. The Mafia boss was supposed to have taken on the job of killing Marilyn on the understanding that he could expect a favour from the brothers at some time in the future.

By the summer of 1962 the situation had developed to such an extent that she needed silencing permanently. Rumours circulated of President Kennedy's affair with Marilyn, rumours fuelled by the star's constant barrage of telephone calls to the White House. Fears grew that she was about to call a press conference that would expose the affair and bring 'Camelot' crashing down. When the president was confronted with evidence that Marilyn was also sleeping with Sam Giancana, he ended the affair there and then. The story then has Bobby taking up the reins and beginning an intimate relationship with the star, who perhaps dreamed of taking Jackie Kennedy's place as the First Lady of the United States. Bobby continued this relationship into the summer of 1962. And there was more. If Speriglio is to be trusted, Bobby Kennedy had indulged in a little 'pillow-talk', which included details of Operation Mongoose and the CIA-Mafia assassination campaign. One story even suggests that at the time of her death Marilyn was carrying a child of one of the Kennedy brothers.

If the star did not commit suicide by taking an overdose of barbiturates, how did she die? According to the most common assassination theory, Marilyn was killed by a poisoned enema. The far-fetched theory is based on the fact that Marilyn (along with many other Hollywood stars of the time) took enemas regularly. Monroe is supposed to have taken them both to relieve constipation and to induce weight loss. The theory also hinges on the report that no drugs were ever found in Marilyn's stomach and that investigators could find no sign of the glass of water she must have used to take the deadly overdose. Strangely, there were no needle marks on her arms either. Sam Giancana's godson (also named Sam Giancana) is one of the main proponents of the lethal enema theory and, like Speriglio, provides a reconstructed account of the events of 4 August. Giancana's theory purports to place Robert Kennedy at the Malibu house that night. The Mafia killers overheard the attorney general attempt to subdue a distressed Marilyn and leave after having one of his men give her a sedative. The hit men are supposed to have crept in and administered the enema, a suppository that had been doctored with a lethal dose of barbiturates.

Another account has Johnny Roselli, the Las Vegas Mob boss, intimately involved in the murder. It was Roselli who waited outside the house until the coast was clear. He knocked on the door and provided a distraction for his comrades who crept around the back of the house and broke in there. Roselli is supposed to have used chloroform to have subdued Marilyn; once she was unconscious, the enema was administered. Roselli was a long-time friend of Giancana's and, like several other high-profile mafiosi, moved in fashionable Hollywood circles. Marilyn may have known her killer. Roselli was already involved in the attempt to kill Castro, and some conspiracy theorists also tie him into President Kennedy's assassination.

Anthony Summers has formulated a less sensational theory, moving away from direct assassination to a government cover-up meant to keep Robert Kennedy's name out of the headlines. Senator Kennedy was at Marilyn's house that night, but he arrived too late to prevent Marilyn dying from a barbiturate overdose. An ambulance was called, which duly arrived to ferry Marilyn's body to the hospital. *En route* a frantic Bobby realized that he could not go through with this – the attorney general could not appear at a hospital casualty department with the corpse of America's premier sex goddess. He had the ambulance return to her home, where a government cover-up began. She was laid on her bed, and the scene of her suicide was carefully and methodically recreated. Psychiatrist Greenson was called anonymously and as the police and medical units converged on the Malibu house, Robert Kennedy and his brother-in-law, Peter Lawford, quietly drove out of town.

DEATH OF A PRESIDENT

It is likely that more words have been written about the murder of President John F. Kennedy than any other murder in human history. For decades it has fascinated historians, writers, researchers, conspiracy theorists and investigators. There is something quite unreal about the assassination; the world's most powerful man with a beautiful woman by his side, shot to death in full view of the public. The drama of those immediate events was matched by the shock and pain of a nation and of the world at large. When the gunman, Lee Harvey Oswald, was himself shot within days of the assassination, the confusion and suspicion really began. People wanted answers, and everyone expected the official investigation, the Warren Commission, to provide them. When the report was finally released almost a year later, it seemed to raise as many questions as it answered.

President Kennedy was in Dallas, Texas, on 22 November, and was travelling in an open-topped limousine with his wife. At 12:30, as the motorcade passed through Dealey Plaza, several shots were fired at Kennedy from the Texas school book depository. Kennedy is generally thought to have been hit twice, and the governor of Texas, John B. Connally, who was sitting in front of Kennedy, was wounded by one of the shots. One bullet passed through the president's neck, while the second hit him in the head, causing almost instant death. The shots (numbering two or three, depending on the account) were fired from a high-velocity Mannlicher-Carcano rifle owned by Lee Harvey Oswald, an employee of the book depository. Oswald was himself captured within hours of the assassination.

Oswald had dumped the rifle behind crates in the depository and left the building amid the panic. He arrived home, picked up a revolver and left again. As he walked the streets, Oswald was stopped by a police officer named J.D. Tippit, whom Oswald shot and killed. The police converged on Oswald, finally cornering him in a movie theatre where he was arrested. The young man flatly denied having anything to do with the murder of either Kennedy or Tippit, but his palm print had been found on the Mannlicher-Carcano, and there had been several eyewitnesses to the murder of officer Tippit. It seemed the authorities had their man. An intense investigation into Oswald's past was immediately begun. Urgent questions needed answers. Above all, the murder investigators needed to find out why he had shot Kennedy and whether he was working for someone else. In the chaos following the president's death, Vice-President Lyndon B. Johnson was hurriedly inaugurated as president of the United States. The Secret Service had no way of knowing if the murder had been the first strike of some communist attack.

It soon became clear, however, that Lee Harvey Oswald had motives of his own for killing Kennedy. In 1959 Oswald had left the Marines and his communist sympathies led him to travel to the Soviet Union. He hoped to settle there permanently, but although he married a Russian woman named Marina, he soon found life dull and returned to the United States. Strangely, no questions were ever asked of his attempted defection, and he was allowed to live in New Orleans unmolested. There he became an on/off political activist for a number of diverse groups. His involvement with groups such as Fair Play for Cuba (which championed Castro's right to rule the island) and the local Communist Party sharply contrasted with his friendship with a number of people who had strong links with the CIA. After moving to Texas, Oswald became further involved in radical left-wing activities, and on 12 April 1963 he attempted to kill the controversial right-wing Major General Edwin Walker. Oswald used a newly acquired Mannlicher-Carcano rifle.

Although Oswald's background seemed to offer clues as to his real motive for murdering the president, only the killer himself could really say for sure why he had done so. Unfortunately, as Dallas police officers began to transfer Oswald to the county jail two days later, a bystander lunged forward and shot him at point-blank range. Killer Lee Harvey Oswald had himself been murdered by a shady Dallas night-club owner called Jack Ruby.

Ruby claimed to have murdered Oswald to avenge the president and to spare the feelings of Jackie Kennedy. Yet he was an unlikely avenging angel, a low-level hoodlum in the Dallas underworld who revelled in both his Mob and police connections. That he could so easily gain access to the president's murderer amazed everyone. The ineptness of the Dallas police in protecting their only suspect in the greatest murder of the century was later seen by some theorists as proof of a government plot to have Oswald eliminated. Doubts were also raised by the poor conduct of Kennedy's rushed autopsy. The resultant lack of professionalism seriously damaged the gathering of forensic evidence in a way that was to hamper any future inquiry into the murder. Inevitably, the rushed examination is branded a cover-up by conspiracy writers, some of whom insist that the president's body was tampered with, either to remove or conceal vital evidence that would have discredited the 'lone gunman' theory. The 'lone gunman' hypothesis was the government's authorized version of events, as described in the Warren Commission report of 1964. In it, Oswald is said to have acted alone. He fired all the shots in Dealey Plaza that day and had no support, before, during or after the assassination.

With the release of the celebrated Zapruder film, the home movie taken by Abraham Zapruder of the motorcade at the time of the assassination, the speculation really began to pick up momentum. Governor Connally had been hit by the same bullet that was supposed to have pierced Kennedy's throat, but he seemed, in the film, to react much later than Kennedy (and the bullet initially must have been travelling faster than the speed of sound). The two men could not have been hit by separate bullets, theorists argued, since no one could fire three times in 5.6 seconds with an old Second World War rifle and still hit a moving target at over 200 metres. A CBS-sponsored test using expert gunsmiths and marksmen in 1967, however, did show that Oswald could have fired three shots from his bolt-action rifle during that short period of time. One of these weapons experts was Howard Donahue, a gunsmith who participated in the experiment and who equalled Oswald's performance of three shots in under 5.6 seconds.

Other information gleaned from the film seemed to back up the argument of those trying to prove that some kind of conspiracy had been responsible for Kennedy's murder. Scraps of evidence and the testimony of important witnesses seemed to argue a different case – the case for the existence of multiple gunmen in Dealey Plaza on 22 November. The role of a fleeting and mysterious figure on the so-called 'grassy knoll', somewhat ahead of the motorcade, was also raised. His existence was posited as proof of a conspiracy to assassinate Kennedy, for he was the 'second gunman'. Poor quality recordings taken from the microphone of one of the motorcycle outriders seemed to have picked up the sound of another shot, confirming this suspicion. And the Zapruder film also seemed to substantiate these assertions. The final killing shot that blew apart Kennedy's head seemed to throw him back in his seat, proof the unqualified weapons experts said, of a shot from the front – a crossfire! The conspiracy seemed to grow and grow, and no evidence to the contrary, no matter how rational or logical, could halt it.

The imagination of theorists was able to conjure up a disconcerting number of alternative assassination theories, each one backed by a degree of solid enough argument. Some thought that the assassin Oswald had been a puppet of the KGB, others that he had murdered Kennedy at the behest of Castro, in retaliation for Operation Mongoose. Alternatively, he had been killed by anti-Castro elements who blamed the president for the failure of the Bay of Pigs adventure and who considered the president to have 'gone soft on communism'. Others argued that the Mafia wanted Kennedy dead in order to cripple his crusade against organized crime, or that Jimmy Hoffa, the corrupt head of the powerful Teamsters' Union, wanted him dead for the same reason. Then again, the CIA may have wanted to murder the president to keep their kill-Castro operation out of the public domain. What of the Secret Service who sanctioned the president's open-topped drive through Dallas without adequate back-up? Had the Secret Service some role to play in the assassination? There seemed no end to the plots, counter-plots and conspiracies that one could attribute to the murder. Conjecture turned to speculation, speculation to fantasy, and any worthwhile argument advanced for a second gunman or for a governmental cover-up, seemed to be lost in a sea of speculation. The New Orleans district attorney, Jim Garrison, rode the crest of this wave of conspiratorial complexity.

Garrison's investigation and the subsequent bringing to trial of one Clay Shaw formed the basis for Oliver Stone's ground-breaking movie *JFK* (1991). In February 1967 Garrison revealed that a conspiracy to murder President Kennedy had been organized and initiated in Louisiana. Clay Shaw, a prominent local businessman, David Ferrie, a former pilot and private investigator, and Oswald himself were all named as co-conspirators in the probe. But Garrison lacked the evidence he needed to secure any arrests and convictions. Indeed, with Oswald already dead, and David Ferrie dying in mysterious circumstances within days of the story hitting the headlines, only Clay Shaw remained to take the heat. Garrison became something of a media celebrity during that period, but the public – and the media itself – soon tired of Garrison's sensational allegations, allegations that failed to live up to close scrutiny. In fact, many of his claims were quite bizarre. He once even claimed that a Kennedy gunman had popped out of a manhole cover to use a .45 pistol, but eventually settled on a now well-known scenario – that multiple gunmen, 'guerrilla fighters shooting in a crossfire', shot and killed the president.

Garrison was convinced the president had been assassinated by a secret cabal of right-wing industrialists, a number of officers of the Dallas police department, the Mafia, anti-Castro activists and members of the US intelligence services. This mixed bag of murderers wanted revenge for the botched invasion at the Bay of Pigs, and it wanted to stall any attempt that Kennedy was making to begin amicable relations with both communist Cuba and the Soviet Union. The trial eventually opened on 29 January 1969, but the poor quality of the witnesses and the testimony they gave left the jury with only one verdict to give – on 1 March 1969, Clay Shaw was pronounced not guilty.

This verdict did not mean that the official Warren Commission inquiry was now automatically accepted by its strongest critics. In fact, the report had come under such pressure by the mid-1970s that the House Select Committee on Assassinations was established to resolve, once and for all, the anomalies in the report. A number of controversial political murders were also to be looked at, murders that had suffered from the same conspiratorial speculation as the John F. Kennedy case, including the murders of Robert Kennedy and Martin Luther King. It was the committee's unenviable task to sort speculation from rumour and to try to discover whether any government cover-ups had taken place. These investigations were conducted in the light of startling new information that the CIA had actually conspired with the Mafia to assassinate Fidel Castro. Suddenly, high-level government murder plots and conspiracies did not seem so far-fetched any more.

The House Committee received some new evidence and eventually came to the conclusion that President Kennedy's murder had been the result of a conspiracy. It ruled out any Cuban involvement – at one point a member of the committee even travelled to Cuba to talk with Fidel Castro personally. What clinched the argument for a conspiracy theory was not the evidence of witnesses or the activities of possible suspects, it was a sound recording taken from the radio of one of the motorcade's motorcycle outriders. An expert claimed to be able to pick out the sound of gunshots normally indiscernible to the human ear. Without really being able to provide hard forensic evidence to tie in named individuals, the committee declared that Kennedy had been shot by two gunmen, Oswald in the book depository and a second assassin (possibly a Mafia killer) on the 'grassy knoll'.

This acoustic evidence was always going to be controversial and could not stand up to the detailed analysis of the Committee of Ballistic Acoustics that later analysed and unanimously discredited it. But a remarkable amount of material had been uncovered to link the Mafia into the murder of Kennedy. Today, the American Mafia is often popularly associated with the killing of John F. Kennedy, as is some form of government cover-up. Was there any evidence to implicate the Mafia in the plot to kill the president? Could the powerful Mob bosses that we have already met in Chapter 5 have murdered Kennedy to protect their secret involvement in Operation Mongoose? Without the identification of a strong suspect who has the motive, opportunity and ability to carry out a killing like this, little can be gained from establishing that two (or more) gunmen were present at Dealey Plaza that afternoon. Homicide detectives routinely investigate suspicious deaths, which could be interpreted either as accidental or natural but which on another level, raise questions that must be answered. The most obvious of these is: who had most to gain from the victim's death? The second is: who had the opportunity and the skills needed to carry out this murder? The third is: is there any evidence that can tie this suspicious death with the chief suspect in the inquiry?

Many did not accept the 'lone gunman' theory and pursued the only other credible alternative – that the Mafia was deeply involved in the plot to kill the president. Throughout the 1980s this theory gained a considerable following and today ranks as the most popular Kennedy conspiracy theory, championed by books such as *The Kennedy Conspiracy* (1981), *Crossfire: The Plot That Killed Kennedy* (1989) and the *Mafia Kingfish – Carlos Marcello and the Assassination of John F. Kennedy* (1989).

DID THE MAFIA KILL JFK?

We have already seen how the Kennedy administration had inherited a shadowy CIA-Mafia assassination pact and may even have worked with the gangsters to murder Marilyn Monroe. But the links went further than that, or so important witnesses have claimed. Joseph Kennedy, the president's double-dealing father, has been accused of forming an unholy alliance with the Chicago Mob (and that meant Sam Giancana) on behalf of his sons. The story goes that Joe convinced the Chicago don to help rig the elections in Illinois, a state that could swing one way or the other on election day. The Mafia rarely did anything for free. It not only wanted concessions once the Kennedys were in power but expected them. What they got was quite the opposite. Once JFK was elected, both he and his brother turned on organized crime with some ferocity. As attorney general and the head of the American justice system, Robert Kennedy was given the task of bringing to trial as many Mafia hoodlums as possible. He became a crusader, with the complete backing of the president, and the Mob quickly grew to hate the both of them. But did it resort to murder?

The Kennedys first locked horns with organized crime in the mid-1950s when both men, as senators, were involved in the Senate Sub-committee on Investigations, and one of their main targets had been the Teamsters' Union. With its membership involved in trucking and warehousing, the union was the largest and most powerful labour organization in the United States. It was also the most corrupt. Jimmy Hoffa (1913–c.1975), the president of the union in the latter part of the decade, proved to be a cunning, vicious and violent opponent of the brothers. He made no secret of his hatred for the Kennedys, and for Robert in particular. Hoffa was investigated for bribery, corruption, vote-rigging, perjury, wiretapping and a host of other offences, but always seemed to avoid prosecution. Years later he boasted that he had 'seamy' information that could have seriously damaged the Kennedys. Perhaps he was referring to the Marilyn tapes and so could use the recordings as a stick with which to beat off the attorney general if he seemed likely to secure a conviction.

Alternatively, Hoffa may have been referring to the fact that he knew that Sam Giancana's girlfriend, Judith Exner, was having an affair with the president. This is unlikely to have been mere coincidence – she was introduced to both men in Las Vegas by Frank Sinatra, the entertainer, who always enjoyed the friendship of some powerful Mob bosses. The White House telephone log shows that Exner repeatedly made calls to the president, calls that ended suddenly in March 1962 when J. Edgar Hoover, director of the FBI, confronted Kennedy about the affair and threw light on her relationship with Giancana. Exner later told investigators that she had passed sealed packages between Kennedy and Giancana, and she speculated that they contained information pertaining to the attempts on Castro's life.

Giancana, like Hoffa, was forced to testify in front of one senate committee after another, and he was often questioned by Bobby Kennedy in person. The hearings amounted to a public humiliation for the mobsters concerned. This kind of treatment did not endear John Kennedy to either man. To a cheering crowd of Nixon supporters before Kennedy's election as president, Hoffa is reported to have said: 'If it is a question, as Kennedy has said, that he will break Hoffa, then I say to him, he should live so long.' Giancana, too, talked idly of having Kennedy killed. Out on the golf course, the crime boss was picked up on an FBI surveillance tape. The FBI report states: 'They discuss golf. Somebody asks if Bobby Kennedy plays golf; they know that John Kennedy does. Suggest putting a bomb in his golf bag. (They all laugh.)'

Other members of the Mafia hated the Kennedys almost as much as Sam Giancana and Jimmy Hoffa did. At times men like Santos Traff[-]cante and Carlos Marcello talked of having one or other of the Kennedy brothers assassinated. Trafficante was the most powerful and ruthless mafioso in Florida. According to one Cuban exile who knew the mobster well, Trafficante was blunt about President Kennedy's chances in the next (1964) election: 'You don't understand me. Kennedy's not going to make it to the election. He is going to be hit.' In New Orleans the diminutive Mob boss Carlos 'Little Man' Marcello made a similar boast. He likened the brothers to a single dog, with John, the head, wagging Bobby, the tail. 'You know what they say in Sicily: if you want to kill a dog, you don't cut off the tail, you cut off the head.'

John Roselli, the Las Vegas gangster who had played an important role in the CIA's plot to murder Castro, was the victim of a Mob-style killing in 1976, shortly after meeting with Trafficante. Cut up into pieces and stuffed inside an oil drum, his body was found in the sea ten days after his disappearance. Roselli had been about to testify to the Senate Intelligence Committee, and there was some speculation that he had been murdered on the orders of the Florida gang boss. His testimony, had he given it, would have been startling. Before his death he is said to have told a government agent that he believed his former associates from Operation Mongoose had actually gone on to assassinate President Kennedy. The name of William Harvey, the unorthodox CIA agent who organized the anti-Castro operations, has re-appeared in connection with the Kennedy killing. He is suspected by Anthony Summers, one of the most notable 'assassinologists', of being the single most important individual in the orchestration of Kennedy's murder. His motive? Harvey had a freewheeling attitude to the anti-Castro job, to such an extent that he is reported to have sent commando teams into Cuba during the delicate knife-edge negotiations of the Cuban Missile Crisis in 1962. For that he earned the undying wrath of Robert Kennedy. In addition, the blame for the Bay of Pigs debacle may have been foisted on President Kennedy by the CIA. The Agency had even told the Cuban exiles involved in the operation to continue with the raid, even if the president pulled the plug. When he discovered the degree to which he had been duped by the CIA, Kennedy seethed with rage, and vowed to 'splinter the CIA into a thousand pieces and scatter it to the winds'. Instead, he cut off the Agency's head, forcing a round of impromptu resignations.

When President Kennedy stepped up his crusade against organized crime on entering office in 1960, the CIA must certainly have felt that he was reneging on a promise made by Eisenhower the year before. Even as Robert Kennedy organized face-to-face confrontations with Mafia bosses who were still in the Agency's pay (Summers argues convincingly), a diabolical plan was being hatched to get even. The CIA maverick and the bitter mafiosi decided to 'hit' the president – the man who was the source of so many of their woes. By using his extensive intelligence connections, Harvey was able to procure a suitable 'patsy' in Lee Harvey Oswald, an individual who was a perfectly unstable contradiction, a man tainted by the suspicious colours of communism and Trotskyism.

In keeping with the previous co-operative effort, low-level Mafia men would do the actual killing, and in this case they were recruited from the emerging French Mafia. The actual murder is thought to have been carried out by three members of the Corsican Mafia (the Union Corse). Led by Lucien Sarti, they are believed to have entered the US via the Mexican border and been given the full support of the Chicago Mafia while in the country. On 22 November the three French gangsters set up a crossfire in Dealey Plaza after having first taken reconnaissance photographs of the intended 'killing zone'. And Oswald? The theory contends that Oswald really was the patsy that he claimed to have been.

William Harvey (who died without furore in 1976) could not have guessed how utterly impenetrable this particular 'executive action' would be. Almost forty years later the world is still haunted and obsessed by both the fact and the fiction of the assassination. So much argument has raged over this single murder, that historians discussing its motivations and its possible perpetrators will never come to an agreement. With such a vast amount of written material in existence, so much conflicting evidence and so much testimony and hearsay, no single theory could ever be contrived to thoroughly satisfy every interested researcher.

The theories of Summers and others are lucid and persuasive arguments for a Mafia assassination of President Kennedy. The wealth of detail used to back up the arguments, and the careful sifting of evidence that accompanies them are impressive, and a book this size cannot do justice to the mountain of research that has already been conducted on this single subject. But there remain the seeds of doubt. There is no concrete proof for one of the theories. There is no clear ballistic evidence for the second or third gunman. Third, and most importantly, the Mafia in America has observed a strict code of practice. This code prohibits any mafioso, whether a lowly gunman or the most powerful of dons, from murdering a member of the government. Since the foundation of the modern American Mafia at the start of the 1930s, there has been a traditional ban on the killing of law enforcement officers (both cops and federal agents), on newspaper men and district attorneys and also on the men in power – the politicians. The aim has always been to keep these elements 'on side' if possible, most often through the liberal application of bribes. Every attempt has been made to avoid direct confrontation with the establishment.

The result of this successful policy was virtual anonymity for the state-wide Mafia organization (the National Commission) until 1957. It is a code of conduct that has, for the most part, been rigidly enforced up to the end of the century. The murder of a cop or an attempt to murder a politician of any stature (let alone the president of the United States) would have forced the family's don to discipline the men involved. If the family boss himself had been involved, the National Commission, the 'ruling council' of America's Mafia families, would have dispatched enforcers to eliminate the rogue individual. Carlo Gambino, the head of the country's most powerful crime family and the ruling head (the 'godfather') of the National Commission, would, without doubt, have dealt severely with Trafficante, Marcello or Giancana. He was not a man to be trifled with. One mafioso who murdered a New York cop was immediately ordered to surrender to the authorities in order to prevent a more rigorous investigation. And back in 1935, the Mob boss Dutch Schultz had been planning to murder a prosecutor named Thomas Dewey. The newly formed commission, led by founding member Lucky Luciano, voted to prohibit the murder. Schultz foolishly continued with his plans, and Luciano and the other members of the commission had no alternative but to pass a death sentence on the errant boss. He was ambushed by gunmen in a New York restaurant on 23 October 1935. Unbeknown to the criminal prosecutor, Dewey's life had been saved by the Mob, and Dewey went on to wage an unrelenting campaign against organized crime that would eventually earn him the governorship of New York. With this kind of rigorous self-discipline, how could Mafia heavyweights such as Sam Giancana and Santo Trafficante plan and execute such a high-profile assassination? Despite the convincing Mafia conspiracy theories, this single prohibition seems to preclude the involvement of organized crime in the most famous murder in American history.

Today the theorists and investigators continue to speculate, but the recent release of government papers pertaining to the murder enquiry should at last end this debate. Many of the documents, when looked at together, seem to rule out any government involvement in Kennedy's murder. Of course, the speculation will continue almost unabated. Falsification and misinformation are well-worn techniques of organizations like the CIA, the conspiracy theorists will argue. But had Lee Harvey Oswald acted alone after all? The lone gunman theory is disputed on only one or two pieces of erroneous ballistic evidence. Conspiracy theorists unacquainted with the realities of firearms use have argued the case for a Dealey Plaza crossfire since the 1960s. The arguments *against* a lone gunman revolve around:

1. The speed at which a good marksman can get off three shots on the Mannlicher-Carcano rifle is outside of Oswald's 5.6 second firing time.

2. The so-called 'magic' or 'pristine' bullet, which the Commission claims hit Kennedy in the neck and went on to hit Governor Connally, despite problems with that supposed trajectory. Left in a 'pristine' condition, it is supposed to have hit both men for a total of *seven* wounds.

3. Kennedy was killed by a head-shot, which propelled him back in his seat and therefore came from the front. Oswald, however, was firing from behind.

4. Witnesses at the scene claim to have heard a shot coming from a grassy knoll to the front and right of the president's car. People who ran in that direction in the confusing aftermath of the shooting were turned away by a man claiming to be a Secret Service agent. At least one other witness also saw a man running from the scene.

Together, these four points seem to point irrevocably to a second gunman, and a second gunman therefore meant that Kennedy had been murdered by a conspiracy. However, apart from some confusing eyewitness testimony given in the last point, all these arguments are based on ballistic evidence, poorly carried out by researchers unfamiliar with the exacting techniques required. The subject can be likened to 'ballistic' pathology – determining the origins and trajectories of bullets and producing detailed analyses of their actions after striking a target.

Only one man, Howard Donahue, has applied his expertise in ballistic analyses to the problems associated with the Kennedy shooting. Donahue first became involved in the case when CBS asked him to participate in trial firings of a Mannlicher-Carcano in a private re-enactment. The test, held in 1967, was designed to answer the question: could Oswald have fired all three shots in 5.6 seconds? The Warren report had said 'yes'. Donahue was able to hit the moving target three times, first in 4.8 seconds and again in 5.2 seconds. Walter Midgley, a CBS executive producer, congratulated Donahue in a letter thanking him for his help in dispelling the myth of 'multiple assassins', but because it supported rather than contradicted the conclusions of the Warren report the CBS report aroused little comment.

Donahue's career as a gunsmith has run parallel to his role as an expert witness in and around Baltimore. For two decades he has studied a vast number of shooting incidents and his findings have been used as evidence in court. Donahue has lived and breathed guns. His investigation into the ballistic evidence from Dallas was carried out over twenty-five years and was finally published by the professional writer Bonar Menninger in 1992 as *Mortal Error: The Shot that Killed JFK*. Both his exacting evidence and his contentious argument have received little popular attention, in the main because they dispel forever the myth of multiple gunmen. Lee Harvey Oswald acted alone – almost.

In a step-by-step fashion, uncovering information and then creating a workable hypotheses based on that information, Donahue, who originally supported the Warren Commission's findings, found that there were a small number of odd inconsistencies in the ballistic evidence. Using all the skills of an expert courtroom witness, Donahue was able to lay these inconsistencies to rest. Trying to prove nothing, he continued to ponder the ballistics of the Kennedy case, sorting out the greatest shooting incident of all time for himself. As he considered the probable trajectories with freshly released autopsy data, spoke to someone who had helped perform the autopsy and re-appraised the commission's decision on the trajectory of that last, fatal, head-shot, Donahue came to a startling and unexpected conclusion.

Of the main four arguments for the supposed existence of a second gunman on the grassy knoll, the first had already been flatly disproved. The 'magic' bullet theory did not hold water. Careful examination of the bullet showed clear distortion, and the tests originally conducted did not account for the round's dramatic dropping off in speed after passing through Kennedy and Connally. The greatest revelations came when the details of Kennedy's head-shot were re-examined. First, the bullet that struck Kennedy had come from the rear, despite evidence that seemed to conflict with this hypothesis. There was no exit wound at the back of Kennedy's head, and the backward movement observed of the president's body has been noted many times before in shooting incidents that have involved high-velocity rounds. What puzzled Donahue, however, was that the trajectory seemed to be all wrong. Unlike the neck wound, the huge head wound had been made by a bullet that was travelling nearly horizontally, yet Oswald was firing from a sixth-storey window. Tracing the trajectory backwards, it seemed to pass directly through the Secret Service bodyguards who sat upright in the car that trailed behind the presidential limousine. What was more, the evidence seemed to point to two different types of bullet in use. The Carcano bullet had without doubt been responsible for both Connally's wounds and the president's neck wound. But the head-shot had been explosive, the bullet disintegrating on impact, much as the bullet of a modern high-velocity rifle (such as the M16) would do. Donahue's inevitable conclusion? Oswald had fired two shots, one of which was the neck wound. The third dramatic head-shot was caused by an accidental discharge by one of the Secret Servicemen in the follow-up car.

This unbelievable conclusion seemed to be backed up by testimony from witnesses who say they saw one agent, George Hickey, pull out an M16 as the first shot rang out. As the car picked up speed, one eyewitness even saw Hickey tumble backwards. Only one photograph exists that shows Hickey sitting bolt upright on the back seat of the follow-up car as it trails Kennedy's limousine on its mad dash to Parkland Hospital. The fourth argument for a second gunman actually reinforced Donahue's remarkable conclusions. Witnesses on the south side of Elm Street did hear the M16's report, but thought it had come from the grassy knoll on the opposite side of the presidential motorcade. The Commission itself noted that: 'If a bullet travels faster than the speed of sound, the acoustics are such that an observer at right angles to the path of the bullet may perceive the shot to have been fired from a site somewhere opposite to him.'

Hickey, still alive today, denies Donahue's allegations, but neither he nor the Secret Service has attempted to challenge the findings. As Dr Russell Fisher, the Maryland state examiner, who studied the Kennedy autopsy for the Garrison case, observed: 'That would certainly explain the strange antics of the government.' The official cover-up that seemed to take place following Kennedy's death, the hurried (and botched) autopsy, the fact that John F. Kennedy's brain has since been misplaced, the apparent whitewash, can be put into some kind of perspective. The death of its president was a great trauma for the country, Donahue mused. How much greater would be the trauma if it were known that the death had been accidental? The US government had good reasons for concealing the incriminating evidence, but in doing so had unleashed a monster. Conspiracy theories, Mafia plots and apparent government complicity in the assassination ushered into American politics a dark and portentous chapter.

The American Dream that had galvanized the nation in the immediate post-war period proved to be nothing more than a hollow nightmare – a nightmare of political corruption, terrorism, foreign warfare and scandal. Writers and historians have argued long and hard in an attempt to try and identify the exact incident that triggered the wave of pessimism and scepticism that still continues to dog both American politics and American society in general. Was it the death of Kennedy? Was it the start of the Vietnam War in 1965? Was it the Cuban Missile Crisis in 1962? A period of social and cultural unrest was triggered in the mid-1960s that rapidly transformed American society and, by extension, the attitudes and expectations of much of the Western world. The first thing to vanish without trace was trust. No one seemed to trust the American government any more; and even the 'system' itself was brought into question. Suspicion of some sort of cover-up concerning the Kennedy assassination had a certain currency in the aftermath of the killing, and this uncertainty and suspicion continued to grow in strength over the years. The publication of the Warren Commission report in September 1964 failed to allay these fears. The assassination cult was born and now refused to die. From that moment any discrepancy, no matter how small, could be identified and used as evidence of a government conspiracy surrounding the death of any famous individual. The legacy of this 'cult' is a long one. Its victims include the deaths of Robert Kennedy, Marilyn Monroe, Martin Luther King, Elvis Presley, Princess Grace, John Lennon, Jim Morrison and Princess Diana and the attempted murders of President Ronald Reagan and Pope John Paul II in 1981.

The heartfelt grief and disbelief experienced by Americans in the wake of Kennedy's assassination was accompanied by a familiar set of human responses: why him?, why now?, and how? Kennedy's youth and charm engendered a tangible sense of disbelief in the wake of the killing. JFK may not have been swept into power with a landslide victory and he may not have been the most popular president in American history (contrary to modern popular opinion), but he held a certain allure for the American public. His charisma captured the hearts and imaginations of the public in a way that had never been seen before. It is easy to compare President Bill Clinton and Prime Minister Tony Blair to Kennedy in this respect, and in many ways the analogy is a good one. Kennedy was undeniably the first 'TV president', who combined an easy manner with good looks to produce a smooth and effective performance. People found great difficulty in believing that a rogue madman with a sniper rifle could have murdered their president. Many looked to the theories being offered by the alternative investigators. They looked for meaning behind the murder. They wanted the death of Kennedy to have some kind of relevance. Surely he could not have died at the hands of a lone gunman?

It is said that everyone who is old enough can remember where they were at the moment they heard the news of Kennedy's assassination. Such events are rare indeed. The unexpected destruction of the space shuttle *Challenger* and the death of Princess Diana are perhaps more modern examples of this phenomenon. Again, the first reaction of disbelief is followed by questions. Death must have meaning, and the death of a 'personality' must have more meaning than most. Someone must be to blame – the death must have some significance for someone. Surely the death must have been for a reason. Within minutes of hearing the news of Princes Diana's death in a car crash on 31 August 1997, a friend of the author commented idly on the probability that the car crash had been arranged by the British secret service, MI6, in order to protect the royal family from future embarrassment. It was idle speculation, not intended to be taken seriously, yet his words were repeated within days of the tragedy. Today, a concerted group of 'assassination cultists' (encouraged by the speculation of Mohamed Al Fayed, Dodi Fayed's millionaire father) insist that Diana was murdered by the British secret service in a carefully arranged hit-and-run accident using another (untraced) car as the murder weapon or by sabotaging the limousine – the theories vary enormously. Diana's relationship with the Muslim Dodi Fayed (and speculation that she might have been pregnant and/or planning marriage) and her influential campaign to ban the manufacture of land-mines are cited as the two most likeliest reasons for her murder.

THE LINCOLN CONSPIRACY

President Kennedy was not the first American president to be assassinated while in office. During the first 217 years of American history, four US presidents have fallen to the assassin's bullet – Abraham Lincoln (in 1865), James Garfield (in 1881), William McKinley (in 1901) and John Kennedy (in 1963). Seven other presidents have been stalked by potential assassins, and some, such as Gerald Ford, have even survived more than one assassination attempt.

Almost a century before Kennedy's death, the murder of Abraham Lincoln had similarly thrown the nation into shocked turmoil. Within days of the assassination, theories were expounded that charged the US government with far more knowledge of the killing and of John Wilkes Booth, the killer, than they were ready to admit. It remains one of the most perplexing mysteries of modern history, and it is remarkable for the bizarre number of odd coincidences with some aspects of the Kennedy assassination.

Lincoln was due to attend the Ford Theatre in Washington on 14 April 1865 with his wife. The couple were to be accompanied by the daughter of Senator Ira Harris, who was in the company of her fiancé, Major Henry Rathbone. Their original partners were to have been General Ulysses S. Grant and his wife, who cancelled at the last minute. Only four days earlier Lincoln had presided over the surrender of the Confederate South – the hard fought-for goal of the Union Army in the American Civil War. John Wilkes Booth, an actor from Maryland, had long nursed an intense hatred of Lincoln. The defeat of the South spurred Booth into action, and he decided to assassinate the president. On 11 April the would-be killer attended a White House celebration at which Lincoln spoke of freeing the Black slaves of the freshly conquered South. Booth vowed that it would be the last speech that Lincoln would ever make. On the day of the president's visit to the Ford Theatre, Booth had spent the day drinking in a nearby bar, a common pastime for the actor who, over the past few weeks, had regularly boasted of kidnapping Lincoln and dragging him in chains to the Confederate capital of Richmond, where he would be held hostage. This dream of winning the war faded when Richmond was captured. Now John Wilkes Booth thought only of revenge. He would murder Abraham Lincoln and General Grant together while they watched the comedy *Our American Cousin*.

At ten o'clock that evening, his plan was put into action. After he entered the theatre he purchased tobacco from the ticket-taker and made his way to Lincoln's flag-draped box. The single police officer assigned to protect the president had left the theatre during the performance to enjoy a drink at a nearby tavern, and the president was unguarded. Stepping into the box behind the president, Booth pulled out a .44 Derringer pistol, placed it behind Lincoln's left ear and pulled the trigger. Lincoln was killed instantly. Major Rathbone jumped up to grab Booth, but the assassin dropped the gun and drew a knife with which he slashed at the officer. In an attempt to flee, Booth leapt from the box to the stage, but one of his spurs caught in the flag that was draped over the presidential box, and he almost lost his footing completely. As it was, he had broken his leg, but he regained his composure on the stage, shouting out: 'Sic semper tyrannis!' ('Thus always to tyrants!'). He limped painfully from the stage, out of the theatre and after mounting his horse, rode away into the night.

Booth's murder of Lincoln was only one part of a wider conspiracy. His friends had agreed to murder both Vice-President Andrew Johnson and Secretary of State William Seward. Neither succeeded, but Booth did meet up with one of his co-conspirators, David Herold. Together they located a doctor, Samuel Mudd, who could treat Booth's broken leg. Once this had been set, the two men fled across the Potomac River into Virginia. They remained at large until 26 April, when Union soldiers surrounded the two men at a farm outside Port Royal, Virginia. The commanding officer ordered the fugitives to come out, and although David Herold surrendered, Booth remained defiant. The farm was set alight. The soldiers could see Booth hobbling about inside – suddenly there was a shot. They rushed forward to drag the dying man out of the fire. It was uncertain whether Booth had shot himself or had been shot accidentally by one of the soldiers at the scene. His last words were: 'Tell Mother I die for my country.'

Altogether nine people involved in the conspiracy to murder President Lincoln were specifically named by the government. Booth had died, but the others were tried in May and June of 1865. In the hysterical post-war atmosphere that surrounded the assassination trial the defendants became implicated in a number of other (totally unconnected) events. When the trial had drawn to a close one of the defendants faced a six-year prison sentence, three others faced life sentences, and the remaining four (including Mary Surratt, owner of the lodging house in which the plot was conceived) were condemned to death. They were hanged on 7 July 1865. Surratt was considered by many people at the time to have been wholly innocent, a judgement with which historians today concur.

The suspicion and paranoia of America at that time, newly emerged from the most savage of civil wars, bred a number of conspiracy theories, the like of which were not seen again until the assassination of President Kennedy in 1963. Was Booth in the pay of the Confederacy? The actor seems to have had dealings with a man named Jacob Thompson, head of the Confederate secret service. Booth had already given him details of his plot to kidnap Lincoln. Historian Theodore Roscoe believes that the southern spy-master may have suggested that John Wilkes Booth should attempt to murder Lincoln rather than kidnap him.

In the 1930s a new candidate for conspiracy emerged. This suspect was Edwin Stanton, Lincoln's Secretary of War, who stood to gain from the president's death. He was one of several 'Radical Republicans' who wanted to see Lincoln take a much tougher line with the reconstruction of the defeated Confederacy. Stanton would clearly have profited (at least politically) from a military occupation of the South. Minor coincidences were seen by some to point to Edwin Stanton's tacit complicity. Before the assassination, for example, Stanton refused to allow his assistant, Major Thomas Eckert, to accompany Mr and Mrs Lincoln to the theatre. Why? And why was the president allocated only one police bodyguard when a number of death threats had been made against him? When Booth's diary emerged from Stanton's safe several years after the assassination and trial, eighteen pages were missing. Lafayette Baker, chief of the National Detective Police, testified that all the diary's pages were intact when his men handed the book over to Stanton. Of course, it might just be that the government risked being embarrassed by the content of the missing pages, which may have detailed Booth's failed kidnap attempts. Coupled with the dire lack of personal protection and the suspicion of some that the government was actually aware of the plot, it seems only natural that the US government should try to cover up its own failings after the event.

A more recent theory contends that John Wilkes Booth murdered Lincoln on behalf of a secret alliance of Northern industrialists, mainly cotton and gold speculators. There has even been speculation that a second 'Booth', a man named Boyd, was hired in place of John Wilkes Booth to carry out the assassination on his behalf. This J.W. Boyd was thought to be more reliable than Booth, and it was Boyd who was supposed to have died from the fatal gunshot wound in Port Royal. Without the Boyd conspiracy, there was still the matter of Booth's death at the farm in Port Royal. Was it suicide or murder? And why was Booth's body so hastily disposed of? It was even said that Booth's own doctor had some trouble identifying the body.

Apart from the enduring popularity of associated conspiracy theories, there have been other ways in which conspiracy theorists have been able to compare notes on the two most famous assassinations in American history. Hardly relevant to the how, why and wherefore of either murder has been a large number of astonishing coincidences that seem (on the surface) to tie the two assassinations together. When considered together, they may give some pause for thought:

1. The first public proposal that Lincoln should run for president
(a letter to the Cincinnati *Gazette* in November 1858) also endorsed a man
named John Kennedy, formerly secretary of the navy, as his vice-president.
2. The first name of Abraham Lincoln's private secretary was John,
while the last name of John Kennedy's private secretary was Lincoln.
3. John Wilkes Booth shot Lincoln in a theatre and was apprehended in
a barn; Lee Harvey Oswald shot Kennedy from a warehouse and was
eventually arrested in a movie theatre.
4. Both of the presidential assassins were themselves murdered before
they could be brought to trial.
5. Lincoln was elected president in 1860, exactly 100 years before
Kennedy was elected president in 1960.
6. Both Lincoln and Kennedy were succeeded by vice-presidents called
Johnson. Both Johnsons were former senators and southern Democrats.
7. Andrew Johnson, Lincoln's vice-president, was born in 1808 while
Lyndon Johnson, Kennedy's vice-president, was born in 1908, exactly
one hundred years later.
8. According to some sources, John Wilkes Booth was born in 1839. Lee
Harvey Oswald was born in 1939, exactly 100 years later.
9. Both Oswald and Booth were southerners who held extremist views.
10. President Lincoln was shot in Ford's Theatre while President Kennedy
was shot while travelling in a Lincoln car, manufactured by the Ford
Motor Company.
11. Both Lincoln and Kennedy made the fight for racial equality a major
part of their administrations.
12. Both men were shot in the presence of their wives, on a Friday, in
the back of the head.
13. Each presidential wife had lost a son while in residence at the White
House.
14. The names Lincoln and Kennedy each has seven letters.
15. The names Andrew Johnson and Lyndon Johnson each have thirteen
letters.
16. The names John Wilkes Booth and Lee Harvey Oswald each have
fifteen letters.

Obviously, these facts are mere coincidence and no conspiracy theorists,
no matter how hard they might try, could use them credibly to link the
two assassinations. Yet coincidences like these, trivial though they are,
provide many conspiracy researchers with their material. If anything,

these incidences of coincidences show how apparent 'clues' might, in fact, be no more than pure chance. We should not wonder at the incidence of coincidences. We should, instead, wonder at a world where there was never any incidence of coincidences.

One Kennedy 'assassinologist' has taken the incidence of coincidences to its ultimate extreme. In James Shelby Downard's words: 'The JFK assassination encounters [the science of names] in a decisive way, and contains a veritable nightmare of symbol-complexes having to do with violence, perversion, conspiracy, death and degradation.' It is Downard's contention, based on sophisticated research to analyse the numerous coincidences of names and titles, that a cabal of American Freemasons was behind the murder of John F. Kennedy. Not only did it plan and execute this plot using masonic sorcery but in doing so it left dozens of obscure clues that point to a Masonic involvement. For example: 'The Kennedy administration was referred to as Camelot ... The site of King Arthur's castle was not far from Tintagel, the Camel River and Camelford ... The officer in charge of the first camel corps in the US army was a certain Lt. Edward F. Beale. JFK was born on Beals Street and Jacqueline Kennedy's poor aunt ... was a Beale by marriage'. Downard's articles are littered with connections of this kind. He points out: 'The term "Jack Ruby" was once used by pawn brokers to indicate a fake ruby. In iconography, a ruby or carbuncle symbolizes blood, suffering and death.' Downard uses magical symbolism to identify Vice-President Lyndon Johnson (a Free Mason) as the real architect of the assassination plot to kill the Catholic Kennedy (since Catholics have traditionally opposed Freemasonry).

Investigators like James Shelby Downard create conspiracy out of coincidence and contradiction. Although legitimate research into the mysterious death of a state official can only be applauded, the work of these fringe conspiracy theorists has done nothing but harm to such work. A number of shocking political murders took place in the United States during the 1960s. At every turn, incident and coincidences were woven together to create new and ever more fanciful plots. After Kennedy's murder, the death of a famous individual could never be taken at face value ever again.

SIRHAN SIRHAN

Only a matter of five years separate the murder of John F. Kennedy from that of his brother Robert in 1968. To some, the incredible personal magnetism and political astuteness of the Kennedys made them prime targets for lone gunmen, individuals with a grievance who were determined to take out that deadly grudge on one important and very public figure. To others, it seemed improbable that both Kennedy brothers could be gunned down within five years of one another without there being some sort of conspiracy linking the killings together.

Robert had continued to pursue a political career after his brother's sudden death, and by 1968 was in the running for nomination as the Democratic candidate in the forthcoming presidential election. Ill-health and a growing tide of public resentment against the Vietnam War had forced the current Democratic president, Lyndon Johnson (who had been sworn in after John Kennedy's murder in 1963) to step down. The Republicans were fielding Richard Nixon, who stood a good chance of winning the election at the end of the year. Johnson's vice-president was just as encumbered by the situation in Vietnam as the president, and this gave Robert Kennedy and a handful of other rising Democrats a chance to make it to the White House. After defeating Senator Eugene McCarthy in the California primary, Robert Kennedy seemed likely to win, and there was every likelihood that America would vote another Kennedy into the White House in late 1968. But history seemed to rebound on the Kennedy name.

After giving a celebratory speech to Democratic party workers at Los Angeles' Ambassador Hotel on 5 June, the senator made his way out of the auditorium through the cheering crowds and through a serving pantry to avoid the crush of enthusiastic supporters. As he strode through the pantry, lined with onlookers, he came face to face with a Palestinian youth named Sirhan Sirhan who had concealed a low-calibre, .22 Iver-Johnson revolver behind a campaign poster. The twenty-four-year-old shouted, 'Kennedy, you son of a bitch,' and fired a volley of shots, hitting Robert three times. The first two shots struck an armpit and would not have been fatal. The third shot, which hit him in the head, behind the right ear, most definitely was. The hollow-point round penetrated the skull and both shattered, sending fragments of bone and lead into the delicate tissue of Kennedy's brain and brain-stem. A post mortem later revealed that the senator had sustained massive trauma; memory, thought processes and balance would all have been irreparably damaged. As Robert Kennedy's bodyguards frantically grappled with the gunman in an attempt to wrestle him to the ground, he fired off shots at random, wounding five bystanders.

Sprawled on the ground, blood oozing from the wound behind his ear, Kennedy's head was cradled by a young kitchen worker. The dying senator murmured to his aides, his left eye opened and closed. But it was evident to everyone that he had little chance of survival. Robert Kennedy died in the early hours of the following morning, less than two hours after being shot. There had been plenty of witnesses to the tragic event in the hotel pantry, and the unrepentant Sirhan Sirhan had openly boasted to police about his actions. He spoke about the evils of American society and later of his burning hatred for Israel and for Kennedy's support for that nation. His bail was set at $250,000. Sirhan Sirhan was not another Lee Harvey Oswald. Having fully admitted responsibility for murdering Robert Kennedy, the Palestinian youth was eventually found guilty of first degree murder and given the death sentence. In 1972 the sentence was repealed and Sirhan Sirhan has languished in prison ever since.

Even as news of the murder began to circulate, however, conspiracy theories were taking shape. Some of the details surrounding the assassination were called into question, as were Sirhan Sirhan's motives. Who was he? Why would he murder a Democratic candidate? Did he have an accomplice? Who sanctioned Robert Kennedy's murder? Reports were soon circulated that more than eight shots had been fired (Sirhan Sirhan used an eight-shot revolver), leading to speculation that there had been a second gunman. In addition, according to eyewitness testimony, the youth had not got closer than a metre from Kennedy before pulling the trigger, yet there were powder burns around the fatal head wound. Powder burns are always associated with the discharge of a firearm at very close (practically contact) range, which seemed to contradict the testimony of those who saw the shooting.

A second gunman surely pointed to a conspiracy to kill Robert Kennedy – and some strange reports seemed to back this up. Sandra Serrano, who had stepped out onto a balcony for a quick break, told investigators that two men in the company of a woman in a white polka-dot dress passed by her as they entered the hotel. They rushed out shortly after the shooting, and Serrano remembered the woman shouting triumphantly: 'We shot him!' According to Serrano, she asked who they had shot, and the woman replied: 'We shot Kennedy!' Despite lengthy follow-up investigations, no trace was ever found of this mysterious trio, and the Los Angeles police could not take Serrano's allegations seriously.

Suspicion soon fell on Kennedy's security guards, who were not only armed at the time of the assassination but were at all times within killing distance of their charge. Some witnesses claim to have seen one body-guard, Thane Eugene Cesar, draw his gun and fire it. When it was revealed that Cesar carried a rather more substantial .38 calibre revolver, and that no bullets (or bullet tracks) from this gun were ever found, some con-spiracy theorists speculated that Cesar might have carried a concealed .22 pistol in his sock and after shooting the president in the head, might have disposed of it by secretly handing it over to another accomplice.

Alternatively, some of the bullets fired by Sirhan Sirhan may have ricocheted around the pantry as he continued to wave the gun around indiscriminately. This would account for more than eight traces of bul-let strikes. In any event, no trace of bullets fired by a second gun was ever discovered. In explaining the close proximity of Kennedy's head to the gun that killed him, investigators have tried to show that he could have fallen towards Sirhan's gun as the first two shots hit him.

Sirhan Sirhan's motives for killing Robert Kennedy were also called into question. The gunman had openly admitted his guilt, but was he really a crazed psychopath? The Palestinian youth had initially admired the senator, but when Kennedy made clear his support for the sale of fifty Phantom fighter-bombers to Israel, Sirhan considered this a betrayal. In January 1968 Sirhan scribbled down his discordant, confused thoughts in a notebook:

RFK RFK RFK RFK RFK
Robert F. Kennedy Robert F. Kennedy
RFK RFK RFK RFK RFK must die RFK must die ...

On 18 May his obsession had become all consuming as he wrote:

Robert F. Kennedy must be assassinated RFK must be assassinated
RFK must be assassinated ... RFK must be assassinated before 5 June 68 ...

The selection of that particular date added further weight to Sirhan Sirhan's own admission that by striking against Robert Kennedy he was striking against Israel – for the date was the first anniversary of the Six Day War. To the young man 5 June meant more than his own birthday, he later told an investigator. His notebook ramblings were later used by psychologists to look inside the mind of the killer. He was a loner, a student with a chip on his shoulder, an inadequate failure who had turned to the bizarre world of psychic phenomena for consolation. Sirhan believed he could see 'mystical bodies', that he could transmit mental messages and that he could inflict psychic wounds on distant targets. At the start of 1968 Robert Kennedy had become a focus for Sirhan's isolation and frustration; from that point on, the disaffected student began to consider the assassination campaign, which ended so dramatically on 5 June.

In custody after the murder, Sirhan Sirhan claimed that he remembered nothing of the tragic event and that the last thing that he did remember was downing several drinks at a Democrat party elsewhere in the Ambassador Hotel. He realized that to admit premeditated murder would probably earn him the death penalty. Unfortunately, several comments about killing Kennedy that he had made prior to the shooting, and page after page of his obsessive hatred for Kennedy that he had described in notebooks seemed to point clearly to premeditation. Sirhan's incoherent ramblings were analysed by psychiatrists who deemed the youth a 'borderline psychotic' and a 'schizophrenic of the paranoid type'.

Conspiracy theorists who believe that the CIA wanted to silence Robert Kennedy claim that Sirhan Sirhan was brainwashed by Agency scientists working with Project MKULTRA. They claim that both his sudden memory loss and the disjointed and repetitious phrases in his notes point to some kind of mental indoctrination, as if the message 'RFK must die' had been a single omnipresent message burning its way out of Sirhan's troubled brain. William Turner and Jonn Christian argue quite strongly in their book *The Assassination of Robert F. Kennedy: The Conspiracy and Coverup*, that the CIA orchestrated Robert's death in this way. After the murder of the singer and ex-Beatle John Lennon on 8 December 1980, a similar theory arose in order to give his motiveless killer, Mark David Chapman, a motive. According to Fenton Bresler, in his book *Who Killed John Lennon?*, ultra-right wing elements connected with the newly elected Reagan camp had wanted Lennon removed. As a 'dangerous extremist', Bresler argues, John Lennon represented the forces of liberalism and anti-government activism. He possessed the ability to inflame the anti-establishment and anti-war passions of America's youth in the early 1970s (although it is debatable whether that was still the case in 1980). But would Reagan's supporters in the CIA have gone to such alarming lengths to remove him? Was Lennon that much of a danger? And where was the evidence linking Chapman to an individual or group that was able to 'programme' potential assassins? Evidence that could prove either Chapman or Sirhan Sirhan were brainwashed by some rogue department of the CIA has yet to be discovered.

The powerful Mob bosses who had already been implicated in the killing of President Kennedy were also named as suspects in both the organization and prosecution of his brother's death. After all, as attorney general, Robert ruthlessly pursued the Mafia bosses for years, and the president's death had not meant the end of Robert's career. At the beginning of 1968 it seemed as if he were destined to take up his brother's place in the White House. Finding some connection between the lone Palestinian and the powerful Mob bosses who had endured Robert Kennedy's unwanted attentions proved most difficult, however. It has been claimed that Carlos Marcello had connections in California (namely a racketeer called Mickey Cohen). Both men had previously been investigated by the then attorney general. Sirhan Sirhan had previously worked at Cohen's Santa Anita racetrack as a groom and had got into debt betting on the races. Had Cohen approached Sirhan Sirhan and forced him to carry out the murder of Robert Kennedy? In fact, throughout the 1960s, Cohen was languishing in an Atlanta prison, partially paralysed and fighting to cope with both his crippled condition and the immediate dangers of prison life. It seems highly unlikely that Sirhan Sirhan had been manipulated by Carlos Marcello in a Mafia conspiracy to murder Robert Kennedy via the crippled and incarcerated Mickey Cohen.

ENEMIES OF THE STATE

There were other casualties of the 1960s. The noted Black activists Malcolm X (1925–65) and Martin Luther King Jr (1929–68) were both gunned down while at the height of their (very considerable) influence. Some doubt remains today as to the identity of their actual killers. Assassinologists have even suggested that the government agency that had organized a campaign of surveillance and harassment around Martin Luther King had gone one step further – and had him murdered.

Malcolm X fought passionately for the rights of Black Americans, and he operated from a number of Muslim ministries in the ghettos of Boston and New York. Born Malcolm Little, he had undergone conversion to the Nation of Islam (the Black Muslims) while serving time in prison. In the late 1950s Malcolm X began his controversial struggle for racial equality in New York. It was not to be an easy struggle. The charismatic activist argued with other members of the Nation of Islam, which led him to establish his own pressure group, the Organization of Afro-

American Unity. His friends became his enemies, and in February 1965 he and his family narrowly escaped death when three petrol bombs were tossed through the windows of their apartment. His old allies, the Black Muslims, might have been to blame; alternatively, the ultra-violent Ku Klux Klan might have made the attempt. This ambiguity says much about the precarious position of Malcolm X.

On 21 February, exactly a week after the firebomb attack, Malcolm X addressed an audience of 400 Black Muslims at the Audubon Ballroom in Harlem. He had only just greeted the crowd that had gathered to hear him speak, when someone at the back (one of the conspirators) began shouting loudly, momentarily distracting the activist's bodyguards. In that moment an assassin stood up in the second row, pulled out a pump-action shotgun from beneath his trench coat and blasted Malcolm X in the chest, fatally wounding him. Talmadge Hayer, a young Black Muslim from New Jersey, then pulled out a .45 pistol, while an accomplice drew a 9mm Luger handgun. Both fired a deadly volley of shots into Malcolm as he lay bleeding on the stage. Only Hayer was captured at the scene – after being shot in the leg he had attempted to limp out through a doorway, but had been grappled to the floor by the crowd. Two men, members of the militant Fruits of Islam group, were later arrested for their part in the murder and served twenty years in prison. However, today it is thought likely that the New York police had arrested innocent men. Hayer later admitted committing the crime out of loyalty to Malcolm's former mentor and later rival, Elijah Muhammad, the leader of the Nation of Islam.

Malcolm X was in many ways the opposite of Martin Luther King. While both men fought tirelessly for the rights of the Black minority, Malcolm urged his followers to take up arms against their oppressors, while King urged non-violence. Malcolm X worked for separate equality, while King campaigned for racial integration. Malcolm was a Muslim, King was a Christian. Undoubtedly, Martin Luther King was considered to be a highly dangerous individual by the FBI, part of whose job it was to monitor any 'subversives' who might threaten the government of the United States. His authority and charisma, his great personal conviction and his total condemnation of violent protest earned him a huge and loyal following. By the mid-1960s King represented the Black civil rights movement in America at the highest level. He had even been awarded the Nobel Peace Prize in 1964. But he had also earned the hatred of the FBI's powerful director, J. Edgar Hoover.

In 1968 King and his entourage arrived in Memphis, Tennessee, to speak in support of the city's striking sanitation workers. Rioting had already broken out in March, and King had returned to show that non-violence could work. But the local law enforcement authorities, as well as the FBI, considered King a dangerous man, an agitator who stirred up racial hatred and sparked off the violence and chaos that he claimed to abhor. King's group was to have checked in at a white-owned hotel in Memphis, but a news story hinting at possible violence forced King to switch to the Lorraine Motel on Mulberry Street. King had a second-floor room, which was reached by an iron stairway and walkway that served as a common balcony for the residents on that floor. It was there that an assassin's bullet found Martin Luther King. At about six o'clock in the evening on 4 April the civil rights campaigner leant against the balcony railing and chatted with fellow activists, including Jesse Jackson and Ralph Abernathy. Suddenly a single, high-velocity rifle bullet hit King in the face, smashing into his jaw, his neck and causing tremendous damage to his spinal cord. The energy of the bullet kicked King back against the wall and completely ripped off his tie.

Within moments policemen were running into the courtyard, and King's friends pointed desperately to where they all believed the shot had come from – the back of Bessie Brewer's boarding-house across Mulberry Street. Inside that rooming house several tenants had heard a shot fired and thought it might have come from the bathroom at the back of the house. Soon after, another witness spotted a white man drop a bundle in a shop doorway at the front of Brewer's place and drive away in a white Mustang. Inside the bundle police discovered the Remington .30-06 rifle that had been used to shoot Martin Luther King, a pair of binoculars, US road maps and a host of personal effects, all of which pointed to the identity of one man, James Earl Ray.

Ray owned the missing white Mustang and had checked into the rooming house that afternoon, using the alias John Willard. It was not the first alias Ray had ever used. His life had been dominated by petty crime, time in prison, prison escapes and life on the run. Ray had last escaped from prison a year before and he had remained on the run until he was arrested for the murder of Martin Luther King at London's Heathrow airport. Following the assassination, Ray immediately fled to Canada and there acquired a false passport. From Canada he travelled to London and to Lisbon, before being apprehended at Heathrow. Never before had Ray gone to such sophisticated lengths to avoid capture. At his trial, James Earl Ray pleaded guilty to the murder of King and was sentenced to ninety-nine years. Almost immediately afterwards he pleaded innocence and changed his defence attorney. Now Ray insisted that he knew nothing about the killing of King, and that the trail of evidence connecting him to Memphis, to the gun and to the white Mustang was the result of a botched gun-smuggling job for a shadowy figure named 'Raoul'. Despite these claims, the absence of any clearly defined motive and an inability properly to account for the resources used by Ray in preparing for and fleeing the assassination, James Earl Ray was the only man to be convicted of the murder.

Ten years after the assassination, enough doubt still existed for another investigation to be held, this time by the House Select Committee on Assassinations. This was convened to try and sort rumour from fact in the murders of President Kennedy and Martin Luther King. During these investigations evidence came to light of the CIA conspiracy to have Fidel Castro assassinated, and this only fuelled the suspicions of a growing number of assassinologists. The investigation also uncovered a number of startling revelations that revolved around a man called Russell Byers.

Byers came forward to testify that in the late-1960s he had been approached by two men who wanted Martin Luther King assassinated. These men Byers identified as John Sutherland, an up-market attorney, and John Kauffmann. When Byers arrived at Sutherland's home he claimed to have come face to face with Sutherland in the full military regalia of a Confederate officer. Confederate flags covered the walls. If Byers agreed to arrange an attempt on King's life, the two men were prepared to pay him $50,000. During the 1978 investigations, Byers told the committee that he believed Sutherland and Kauffmann were, in fact, setting him up to take the blame for the murder. He did not accept their proposal and later went to the authorities with the sinister information. The FBI had received Byers's story in 1973, but the evidence was never acted upon, either through negligence (as the Bureau today claims) or deceit. The Committee was also fascinated to hear that James Earl Ray had killed King in the hope of receiving a $50,000 bounty. Had he accepted the offer that Russell Byers had refused?

By 1978 both John Sutherland and John Kauffmann had died of natural causes, and their widows strongly defended the innocence of their late husbands. Nevertheless, based primarily on the intriguing evidence of Russell Byers, the Committee decided that there may well have been some sort of conspiracy at work in the assassination of Martin Luther King. The long shadow of suspicion that still remained over the FBI and some of the Memphis law enforcement agencies was not dispelled, however. The Committee absolved all federal, state and city authorities of any participation in King's assassination, but it was on record that the Bureau had relentlessly harried the civil rights leader and his supporters throughout the 1960s. Not only was the Bureau responsible for the false story of trouble at the white-owned hotel in Memphis (causing King to switch to the Lorraine), but FBI agents also bugged his phones and even sent anonymous (and defamatory) letters to his wife. The Committee fully recognized the abuse of power that the FBI had perpetrated in the 1960s, and it condemned that part of the Bureau responsible for monitoring King's activities.

As the war in Vietnam heated up during the latter half of the decade (coincidentally reaching its violent peak in the month of King's assassination), the civil rights campaigner was beginning to speak out against it – and against the way in which it exploited the nation's poorest and least educated young men. It may have been King's growing opposition to the war that led the 111th Military Intelligence Group to send officers to Memphis before King's arrival. They shadowed his movements and wire-tapped all the telephone lines used by members of his entourage. Just how paranoid the authorities had become was recently illustrated by the testimony of a US Army intelligence officer who, in 1993, told of a Special Forces mobilization throughout the South. According to this officer, many Vietnam veterans of the Special Operations Group (a wartime assassination and reconnaissance unit) were now in the Alabama-based 20th Special Forces Group, and this unit is alleged to have sent reconnaissance teams into several major cities in the South, scouting for troop landing sites, sniper vantage points and assessing street layouts. This measure was supposed to be a precaution against the race riots that the authorities feared would break out following King's appearance in these cities.

According to a recent report in the *Memphis Commercial Appeal* 'eight Green Beret soldiers from an "Operational Detachment Alpha 184 Team" [a Special Forces A-Team] were also in Memphis carrying out an unknown mission'. Some conspiracy theorists consider the reports of military activity in Memphis during King's visit to be a signpost to the true killers, and that the Green Berets themselves (using skills and techniques honed in Vietnam) assassinated the civil rights leader. The military might have feared that his anti-war oratory was having some effect and decided to silence him with a bullet – or perhaps it was some element of the FBI, which a number of theorists believe could have stepped up its harassment operation to the ultimate level. Then again, there were numerous White supremacist groups around at the time that openly called for King's murder. Another theory suggests that James Earl Ray's slick getaway from the scene of the assassination bore all the hallmarks of CIA operation. The CIA is supposed to have flown a specialist killer in to do the job, and to have set up Ray as an Oswald-like patsy. The Agency did, in fact, have a limited interest in Martin Luther King because of unsubstantiated rumours that the Black activist had actually received funds from communist China. To top it all, a White Memphis businessman named Loyd Jowers claimed, in 1993, that *he* had arranged to have King assassinated back in 1968. He also claimed to have been paid $100,000 by two men to carry out the crime.

James Earl Ray continued to deny any involvement in the assassination of Martin Luther King and always claimed that he had been the victim of an elaborate conspiracy. Exactly which conspiracy he was a victim of, Ray could not say. Perhaps only the murder of President Kennedy has spawned a greater number of conspiracy theories than the slaying of Martin Luther King. What separates the basket of plots to kill the president from the King assassination theories, however, is the fact that James Earl Ray clearly did have some help. His aliases, his passport, his funds and his purpose all seem to have been provided for him. Few will argue with the findings of the 1978 House Select Committee on Assassinations that announced that there was indeed the 'likelihood' of a conspiracy to murder King. Discovering who masterminded that conspiracy may prove to be an impossible task. Mrs Coretta King, for one, will not rest until she has uncovered the truth, and she recently began attempts to have a US court of law reinvestigate her husband's murder. She, like many others, is dissatisfied with the previous attempts of the government to identify and bring to justice his killer. She intends to find out the truth, this time *without* the government's help.

REAGAN–HINKLEY–BUSH

The House Select Committee on Assassinations certainly piqued the interest of the general public for the murky underworld of political assassination and assassination conspiracy. By the end of the 1970s few

murders or murder attempts seemed to be taken at face value by a sceptical public. There were always a few dedicated conspiracy theorists who
continued to suspect that members of the government were pulling the
strings. Perhaps justifiably, it was the CIA that seemed to take the brunt
of these unfounded conspiracy allegations.

On 30 March 1981 John Hinckley Jr shot President Reagan, seriously
wounding him. In Chapter 1 we looked at Hinckley's actions and at his
motivations, but an odd coincidence connected with the murder attempt
forced various conspiracy 'trackers' to dig a little deeper into the story.
Their conclusion was a startling (and, one must admit, highly unlikely)
one, and of course it involved the CIA. The bizarre twist of fate that set
fevered minds racing was the little-known fact that on 30 March John
Hinckley's older brother, Scott Hinckley, was dining with Vice-President
George Bush's son, Neil. Neil Bush was an old family friend of the
Hinckleys – both families were in the oil business. In Texas in the 1960s,
John Hinckley Sr had been a distant acquaintance of George Bush. Both
men had made their fortunes in the lucrative oil industry and moved
within the same élite Texan social circles. Had the vice-president tried
to engineer the death of Ronald Reagan using a family acquaintance to
pull the trigger and thus take the blame? Was the shooting in reality a
coup d'état?

The questions began at the scene of the crime, Washington's Hilton
Hotel, and radiated away through ballistic reports, family histories and
police files. Almost immediately after the shooting, an NBC correspondent reported the existence of a second gunman, thought perhaps to be
a police marksman on the hotel overhang. Had he shot by accident, on
purpose or was he even seen at all? The existence of a second gunman
seems to explain the fact that a bullet hit the president, even though
there was an armoured limousine door between him and Hinckley.
Almost as if fully briefed on the impending shooting, the president's
Secret Service entourage seemed to give their charge a suspiciously wide
berth as they emerged from the hotel. Had they known?

How might George Bush have gone about masterminding his superior's sudden and violent demise? Bush had many connections to draw
upon, not the least of which was his close relationship with the CIA.
Late in his political career George Bush had been able to gain the
Agency's top job, becoming the director of the CIA and thereby beating
a number of professional intelligence officers to the post. Some believe
that Bush had been rewarded with the directorship for past favours to

the Agency. Decades earlier he had helped to establish the Zapata Offshore Oil Company, which was rumoured to have been used as a front for CIA special operations in the 1960s. What is more, the disastrous Bay of Pigs invasion that foundered on the shores of Cuba in 1961 is reported to have been christened Operation Zapata. Coincidence? And is it coincidence that the two US Navy vessels assigned to the invasion were named *Houston* (George Bush's adopted home) and *Barbara* (the name of his future wife)?

Prescott Bush, the vice-president's father, had also been heavily involved in espionage. During the First World War Prescott Bush had served as an intelligence officer with the US Army, and like the son destined to follow him, was a member of the super-élite Skull and Bones fraternal society. Members of this organization kept in touch in later life, forming almost masonic-like links.

As the threads of the conspiracy began to be discerned a complete reappraisal was made of John Hinckley Jr. Doubt was thrown on the assertion that Hinckley was a psychotic loner, a violent loser harbouring a grudge. To some, he appeared to be more of a Sirhan Sirhan than a Travis Bickle. It was well known (at least by the early 1980s) that the CIA had been experimenting with mind-control techniques since the 1950s. Hinckley, like Sirhan Sirhan, could have been 'programmed' to murder Reagan, with his motivation then fabricated by the fanciful references in his letters to Jodie Foster. He apparently read all he could on Arthur Bremer and the enigmatic Sirhan Sirhan. The assertion that John Hinckley was a misguided loner and misfit was also challenged by the theorists. He certainly had links with the American Nazi Party, and according to one reporter, also had some contact with an Islamic faction based in the United States. That same reporter had allegedly been informed by a member of the Islamic group that it had warned the Secret Service of Hinckley's intention to kill Reagan – a full two months before the event.

Suspicion that the authorities were conspiring to kill President Reagan seemed to be validated by reports of Hinckley's sudden release after his arrest at Nashville airport on 9 October 1980. He had been picked up for carrying three handguns concealed in his suitcase across state lines and into a city about to be visited by the then-president Jimmy Carter. Later researchers have also considered Hinckley's small fine and sudden release suspicious.

Writers like Barbara Honegger and Joseph McBride ask probing questions on the nature of political assassination, but continually fail to

175

provide answers that adequately satisfy the sceptical. Lacking 'hard' evidence, the conspiracy theorists resort to tenuous connections, to coincidence and to allegations made by people whose identity and authenticity is usually difficult to verify. One can read half a dozen different theories on the John F. Kennedy assassination, each lucidly and convincingly written, but in the end, only one (if any) of these grandly created theories can be correct. What does this say about those that remain? That they are fabrications? That individual testimony has been exaggerated or misrepresented? Or that connections made between one individual and another, one organization and another, have been given more weight than they deserve?

The Kennedy killing spawned a monster. The conspiracy cult has yet to reach its apogee, and it is unclear what its effects in the future are likely to be. As we have seen, the conspiracy theory is far from being simply harmless speculation. By implicating entire branches of government, even the government itself, the conspiracy theories surrounding the assassination of Kennedy dealt a grievous blow to the confidence and national pride of the American people. Vietnam kept the wound open, allowing it to fester, and Nixon's Watergate finished the job. The assassination conspiracy plots that have followed build on the public's acceptance of the Kennedy conspiracy. Everyone 'knows' the Mafia killed Kennedy, yet few can say why or how. Such a fundamental rewriting of history has had a remarkable consequence. Individual writers can continue to weave ever more insubstantial and improbable webs of deceit and conspiracy, unhindered by withering cross-examination and analysis. Built on foundations of supposition and conjecture, the theories are often impossible to prove conclusively. By the same token, however, they are just as impossible to disprove.

7. The Mafia Hit Man

From 1900 onwards the Five Points Gang had a monopoly on brutality, greed and criminal activity in the poverty-stricken Five Points district of New York. Tenements and slums jammed this area, stretching from Broadway to Canal Street and from the Bowery to Park Row. The gang had many notorious members who went on to carve niches for themselves in America's criminal underworld. Most successful of these nasty and violent thugs were Al 'Scarface' Capone, John Torrio and Frankie Yale. Capone and Torrio moved to Chicago during the lucrative years of Prohibition (1920–33), in which the manufacture and sale of alcohol were outlawed by Congress. This legislation enabled those with cunning, bravado and a penchant for violence to supply an entire black market economy in smuggled ('bootleg') or home-brewed booze. Competition for the immense profits enjoyed by the successful bootleg gangs was stiff, and many gangs made a killing – quite literally, for routes, markets and leadership were all contested in bloody gang wars. The murky politics of the underworld were driven by assassination – of treacherous upstarts, of rival bootleggers and of vulnerable bosses who hung on to power.

Frankie Yale did not follow Torrio and Capone to Chicago. During Prohibition he emerged as a powerful force in the New York bootlegging business, and he backed this up with a brutal extortion racket. Yale used a cigar-manufacturing business as a legitimate cover for his illegal operations, which mainly involved intimidation and outright violence to force cheap and nasty cigars onto frightened tobacco dealers. Any second-rate item, cheap or badly made, was soon labelled a 'Frankie Yale'. But it was the trade in bootleg liquor that was responsible for much of Yale's illicit wealth. Al Capone, the former Five Pointer, acted as Yale's main buyer, and the two co-operated successfully throughout the 1920s.

In November 1924 Yale and two accomplices agreed to carry out a gangland assassination for Capone. The Mob boss needed out-of-town killers – men he could trust – to do the job, and he turned to Yale, since the New Yorker had just as much to lose as Capone. The three killers surprised Capone's main rival, a powerful gang boss by the name of Dion O'Bannion, at his flower shop in Chicago. The murder involved a deception: Yale smiled, introduced himself and reached out to shake O'Bannion's hand. With his hand grasped firmly, the accomplices emptied their guns into O'Bannion's body. At such close range the shots could not miss and proved fatal. The treacherous assassination quickly became known as the 'handshake' murder. Despite this brutal show of loyalty, the two bosses eventually quarrelled, and Capone began to suspect that Frankie Yale was hijacking his own beer trucks as they left New York in order to hurt Capone. Capone decided to send one of his men, James F. DeAmato, to see if there was any truth in the rumours of Yale's treachery. Yale had the man quietly killed, but Capone was not fooled. He warned Yale: 'Some day you'll get an answer to DeAmato.'

Almost a year later, Capone had his revenge. He got together his four most ruthless and efficient killers – John Scalise, Albert Anselmi, 'Machinegun' Jack McGurn and Fred 'Killer' Burke – who travelled by rail from the Chicago mobster's Florida retreat to Knoxville, Tennessee. There they bought themselves a cheap car and drove the rest of the way to New York. The men had suitcases packed with weapons and ammunition. On 1 July 1928 Frankie Yale was relaxing with his friend Jimmy Caponi in an illegal drinking den, a 'speakeasy', on Fourteenth Avenue. While the nattily dressed Yale chatted to Caponi about his new 1928 Lincoln convertible, the telephone rang. The anonymous call was for Yale, and the mysterious caller told the New York Mob boss to go home immediately – the life of his wife, Lucy, was in danger. Desperate to find out what had happened to her, Yale dashed outside and jumped into his Lincoln. At a set of traffic lights on the way home, Yale spotted a black Buick behind him that carried four ominous-looking men. Quickly putting two and two together, Yale sped away, trying to put some distance between his car and that of his pursuer. His attempts at escape proved fruitless, however, and on Forty-fourth Street the Buick carrying Capone's team of professional killers pulled alongside the speeding Lincoln. Firearms stuck out from the Buick's side windows. A shotgun suddenly blasted Frankie Yale, who slumped forward against the wheel. From the rear window a Thompson machinegun opened fire, its bullets smashing the Lincoln's windows and ripping holes in Yale's body. The car careered out of control, mounted the curb and smashed into the side of a house. Yale's bloody body was tossed out into the gutter by the ferocious impact. The Buick accelerated away and turned the corner of the street.

At Yale's spectacular and ostentatious funeral, which was attended by almost 10,000 mourners, five men seemed particularly upset by the sudden death of the powerful New York boss. These men, who were all dressed impeccably in black, were Al Capone, 'Machinegun' Jack McGurn, John Scalise, Albert Anselmi and Fred 'Killer' Burke. The use of the Thompson machinegun in Yale's murder was the first such incident in New York's history, and it was one of incidents that helped earn Jack McGurn his nickname.

As a weapon of violent and bloody murder, the tommy-gun had come into its own. Designed too late for use in the trenches of the First World War, the weapon was snapped up by commercial wholesalers in the United States and purchased (at first legitimately) by Chicago's gangsters. Al Capone spearheaded the use of the gun and, indeed, owed something of his rise to prominence to its awesome firepower. Before the Thompson made its spectacular impact on the Chicago and New York crime scenes, the weapons of choice had been the revolver, pistol and shotgun (often sawn-off). The Thompson's high rate of fire and huge, fifty-round circular ammunition drum gave individual gunmen the firepower of a squad of riflemen. Mafia assassinations using this new weapon were now far more likely to succeed because the volume of fire increased both the chance of hitting the victim and the amount of damage done. Unfortunately, it also increased the chance of wounding or killing innocent bystanders.

Although the brutality of Yale's murder by machinegun had shocked the city, it was not the last time the tommy-gun was put to such grim use by Mafia enforcers. And back in Chicago, the weapon was about to perform its bloodiest job to date.

THE ST VALENTINE'S DAY MASSACRE

In Chicago by the end of the 1920s Al Capone had murdered and beaten his way to the pinnacle of organized crime. The fierce competition for domination of the bootleg trade had thinned out the opposition, and by 1929 Capone's vast criminal empire faced only a single rival. The thorn in Capone's side was Charles Dion O'Bannion's old gang, which continued to dominate the North Side. O'Bannion had been assassinated on

Capone's orders in 1924 by Frankie Yale, and O'Bannion's successor had met a similar fate in 1926. Now the North Side gang was led by George 'Bugs' Moran, a tall, well-built mobster, who habitually carried two revolvers. The gang war that dominated life in Chicago was controlled by these two violent and powerful individuals. Moran's organization was at a disadvantage, being heavily outnumbered by the 'Outfit', as Capone styled his all-encompassing, multi-faceted empire of rackets, yet the war continued, with hijackings, raids and murders. Moran vowed to have Capone killed, if only to avenge O'Bannion, who had been a close friend of 'Bugs' Moran.

Moran made several attempts to have Capone assassinated. He tried to bribe members of Capone's own bodyguard to do the job for him. He tried to have prussic acid secretly dropped into the mobster's soup to poison him. And he also resorted to a classic ambush, guns blazing, on Capone's armoured, chauffeur-driven limousine. The North Siders failed to kill their intended victim, but the ferocity of the murder attempts eventually forced Capone out of Chicago. From the safety of his Florida estate, the Mob boss continued to direct his lucrative operations further north. The future of these operations depended on a bold and bloody plan to have Moran murdered and the North Side gang closed down permanently.

It was decided to catch Moran and his men at one of their headquarters on North Clark Street. The large garage used by the gang had a truck entrance at the rear and a single door at the front that opened out onto the street. The place was a useful meeting point and an ideal location for daily briefings. The gang could also off-load shipments of bootleg liquor directly into the garage without fear of being seen. Capone knew that Moran's operations (much like his own) were constantly plagued by minor raids by the local police, which were usually designed to show the public that something was being done about organized crime. Typically, though, the gangs simply paid off the police and had all their men quickly released. This minor police harassment was an accepted, if annoying, aspect of Mob life in Chicago. Capone, looking for some way to catch the North Siders off guard, settled on this everyday event as a cover for his assassination. By the time Moran knew what had hit him, it would be too late.

On 14 February 1929 (St Valentine's Day) 'Bugs' Moran and his two bodyguards, Willie Marks and Ted Newbury, walked along North Clark Street towards a rendezvous at the garage with seven members of the gang. It was half past ten in the morning, and Moran was late. As the trio approached the gang's hideout, a police car pulled up at the curb and two uniformed officers stepped out and entered the garage. 'Bugs' Moran and his bodyguards ducked out of sight, disappearing into a coffee shop where they waited for the inevitable arrests. Moran expected to have to bail the seven men out. It was a predictable and frustrating routine. Or it should have been. St Valentine's Day 1929 was to be different and would radically change the face of organized crime in the decades that followed.

'Machinegun' Jack McGurn, the Thompson-wielding gunman who had so recently murdered Frankie Yale, had been put in command of the St Valentine operation. The son of an Italian grocer, McGurn was born James DeMora. He had a talent for boxing, which at the time was domi-nated by Irish fighters, and his promoter urged him to adopt the Irish-sounding name of McGurn. When his father, Angelo, was murdered by gunmen outside his Chicago store in 1923, the teenager vowed to avenge his death. He gave up his interest in boxing and joined Capone's gang, and within only a few years, McGurn's deadly skill with the Thompson machinegun made him the most feared killer in Chicago.

It seemed McGurn was born to kill and that he was ever eager to carry out hit after hit for Capone. When a $50,000 bounty was placed on Capone's head by a rival in 1927, four out-of-town killers stepped off the train to collect. Within hours Jack McGurn had hunted them down and murdered each one of them with his trademark Thompson machinegun. All the corpses were discovered with a nickel clasped in their lifeless hands, McGurn's personal signature. The machinegun killer did get to avenge his father in 1928 when he murdered several influential members of the powerful and murderous Genna gang from Sicily. It had been Genna hit men who had shot down his father, and Jack McGurn had heard that the Genna killers had derisively called his father a 'nickel and dimer' before they had murdered him. As an act of vengeful irony, he had placed nickels in the hands of the Genna hit men once he had shot them down. Now it became habit – the sinister trademark of America's most notorious hit man.

McGurn prospered from his association with Capone and indulged in the high life of chorus girls and night-clubs. His growing influence in the underworld made him a target for other gangs, and on one occasion he was ambushed while making a call in a hotel phone booth. The would-be assassins, Frank and Peter Gusenburg (who worked for the North Side gang), hosed down the booth with bullets from their Thompsons, seriously wounding McGurn, who nevertheless survived and made a full recovery. Capone turned to McGurn to clear up the North Side problem once and for all. He needed 'Bugs' Moran murdered, and 'Machinegun' Jack McGurn was the only man for the job.

McGurn had arranged for two out-of-town mobsters, Fred 'Killer' Burke and perhaps (no one is exactly sure) Leo Vincent Brothers, to dress as uniformed policemen for the deception. As the two men entered the garage and challenged Moran's startled gang, three men remained in the car and prepared for their part in the grisly murder. McGurn was probably at the wheel and would remain there throughout the bloodbath that followed. The other two – John Scalise and Albert Anselmi – were professional killers in the pay of Capone. Both men were dressed as plainclothes police officers. Giving the two uniformed men a minute or two to get Moran's men up against the back wall of the garage, their hands in the air, the two killers walked into the place, machineguns ready. They found six of Moran's gang lined up facing the back wall of the garage, all wearing tailored suits, felt fedora hats, long coats and expensive silk shirts. The immaculately turned out gangsters were James Clark, an enforcer; Frank and Peter Gusenberg, both gunmen; Adam Heyer, the garage owner; John May, a safecracker; and Albert Weinshank, Moran's trusted book-keeper. One other man stood with them, Dr Rheinardt H. Schwimmer. This professional optometrist had many friends in the Chicago underworld and spent much of his free time 'hanging out' with Moran's men. The thrill-seeker was about to meet the same terrible fate as the doomed men he idly consorted with.

Scalise and Anselmi cocked their Thompson sub-machineguns and opened fire on the seven gangsters, spraying powerful .45 bullets into their bodies and into the plaster wall behind them. The gunmen swept their guns back and forth, creating a lethal crossfire. Even before the echoes of the gunfire had faded with the gun smoke, the two 'uniformed cops' stepped forward and blasted anyone who moved, moaned or twitched with 12-gauge shotguns. And then it was over. The final phase of the plan was put smoothly into action. Scalise and Anselmi concealed the machineguns inside their overcoats and put their hands over their heads. The 'cops' pulled out revolvers and marched the grim executioners out of the front door of the garage and into the waiting car. McGurn pulled slowly into the traffic on North Clark Street and headed south. Behind them lay a scene of utter devastation.

From the window of her apartment across the road from the North

Clark Street garage, Mrs Jeanette Landesman had heard the sound of gunfire. She phoned the police and hurried downstairs to the garage door. Over the shoulders of Sergeants Loftus and O'Neill, she glimpsed something of the macabre scene in the darkened garage. Four well-dressed men lay face-up near the back wall, dark pools of blood oozing around them. Each one was shot full of bloody holes, and several of the unfortunate victims had portions of their heads blown away. These four corpses stared, eyes-wide, up at the garage ceiling. Another victim had fallen against a blood-soaked chair and had died in a kneeling position, and another lay face-down along the wall in a thick puddle of his own blood. The policemen realized, unbelievably, that the seventh victim was still alive, despite at least seven major gunshot wounds. This mortally wounded man was Frank Gusenberg, the mobster who had once been audacious enough to try and murder McGurn. Now McGurn had had the last laugh on Gusenberg and his brother, but when he was pressed for information by Sergeant O'Neill, the dying Gusenberg refused to name his killers. The law of the underworld applied even to the dead.

With the death of Frank Gusenberg, the authorities realized that the greatest bloodbath in Chicago's sordid history would probably remain unsolved. Al Capone had been behind the massacre, that was certain, and his real target, 'Bugs' Moran, had escaped assassination by a whisker. Despite that fact, the North Siders had effectively been shut down by McGurn's cleverly planned murder. Machinegun Jack McGurn soon became a liability to Al Capone, however, and the Depression began to run McGurn's own nightclub out of business. Without the protection of Capone, McGurn was almost as vulnerable as the man on the street. On 13 February 1936, on the eve of the seventh anniversary of the massacre, McGurn was shot dead in a Chicago bowling alley. One of the gunmen was 'Bugs' Moran, finally avenging himself for the terrible events seven years earlier.

Although Moran continued to operate in Chicago, he no longer offered Capone's vast crime syndicate any real competition. Al 'Scarface' Capone ruled supreme in Chicago, but the staggering success of the St Valentine's Day Massacre was surprisingly short-lived. The public had become desensitized to much of the violence that had been luridly recounted in their newspapers during the 1920s. Despite this, the events of 14 February focused the attention of the entire nation on the horror of gang warfare and the effects of Prohibition. Al Capone achieved an instant notoriety that brought down the full force of the US government on his head. The president himself called for Capone's arrest, no matter the cost or the time involved. The Mob boss was well used to the media attention and regularly courted the press, seeming at times to revel in his notoriety. After the St Valentine's Day Massacre, however, the heat became unbearable, and Capone was eventually jailed for income tax evasion, the only one of his many crimes for which the Federal investigators could actually find any hard evidence.

The lesson of the St Valentine's Day Massacre was not lost on the remaining crime-lords, many of whom were members of the Sicilian Mafia. As the 1930s slipped by, they disappeared into the woodwork and began pooling their resources. No one flaunted their wealth in front of the press, and no one operated without some kind of 'front' company or job that could reasonably account for their earnings. The memory of the violent gang wars that had characterized the 'Age of Capone' quickly receded in the minds of both the FBI and the public. Meanwhile, the Mafia gangs grew and prospered in the darkness, turning to bloodshed only when some danger threatened to endanger their organization. Chicago was soon eclipsed as the main focus for organized crime, since the Italian Mafia families were strongest in New York. Consequently the new power struggles began to take place there.

BOSS OF BOSSES

In the Roaring Twenties one man had dominated the crime scene in New York. That man was Joe 'The Boss' Masseria, a short, squat Sicilian who loved his food. He also happened to be the most powerful Mafia boss in America at that time. Prohibition, the nationwide ban on the production and sale of alcohol, proved to be a lucrative time for Masseria, whose Lower East side bootlegging operation raked in a fortune. With wealth came expansion, and the Mafia moved into a number of other profitable rackets, including prostitution, extortion and gambling. To run these illegal operations Masseria's New York Mafia began to recruit men who were smart and ruthless enough to turn a decent profit. One new recruit was Charles 'Lucky' Luciano, a talented gambler and gunman who needed to prove himself. He soon got his chance.

Masseria teamed Lucky Luciano with a womanizing street enforcer called Joe Adonis, and the two were given the task of 'rubbing out' a rival named Umberto Valenti. The two men approached Valenti and told him that the Mob boss wanted to organize a truce.

The meeting was to take place at a restaurant on East Twelfth Street, and Valenti arrived in the company of three armed bodyguards. As they entered the restaurant, both Luciano and Adonis rose from their seats and pulled out their guns, chopping down the three bodyguards in a hail of gunfire. Valenti fled in terror out into the street and scrambled onto the running board of a passing car. As it continued down the street, Masseria's two hit men dashed out into the street. Valenti was firing furiously as he clung to the car, but both Adonis and Luciano returned fire. Before it vanished out of sight, a lucky shot struck Valenti and he fell lifeless onto the street.

This and other successful jobs earned Luciano a place in Masseria's organization as his top lieutenant, and this gave him responsibility for a whole range of illegal and murderous activities. To strengthen both his own and Masseria's position, the able enforcer recruited most of New York's toughest and most experienced mafiosi, including Carlo Gambino, Albert Anastasia, Thomas Lucchese, Vito Genovese and Frank Costello, who were soon to hold the most powerful positions within the nation-wide Mafia syndicate. In the late 1920s Masseria's criminal empire came under fire from a new Sicilian boss in town, Salvatore Maranzano. Brooklyn-based Maranzano had one aim – to take over all Masseria's operations in New York and win formal recognition as the 'boss of bosses'. Masseria refused, and the two men began a violent power struggle. Maranzano understood, however, that although the reigning 'boss of bosses' was indeed powerful and commanded the loyalty of an army of thugs across the Lower East Side, much of his strength rested on his lieutenants and that the most dangerous of these was 'Lucky' Luciano. In October 1929 Maranzano had some of his hit men 'take care' of Luciano. It was sloppily done, and despite being slashed and stabbed with a knife and then dumped out of a moving car, 'Lucky' Luciano survived. Like all hardened mafiosi, he stuck rigidly to the *omerta*, the Mafia code of silence, and refused to tell the cops at his hospital bedside who had tried to kill him.

The inevitable Mafia war that followed was a bloody conflict that raged back and forth between Maranzano's gangsters and the forces of Masseria. Later known as the Castellammarese War, it culminated in the violent deaths of both Joe 'the Boss' Masseria and Salvatore Maranzano. While they fought to destroy one another in order to seize the rich criminal pickings of New York, their attention shifted from the real danger. The rising star of the Mafia world, the predatory 'Lucky' Luciano, was about to make his play. His first priority was Masseria. In the spring of 1931 he met secretly with Maranzano and offered to kill Masseria for him, on condition that Maranzano would then allow Luciano, who would owe him allegiance, to take over the running of Masseria's old operations. He also asked that Maranzano take no action against any of Masseria's men. Maranzano, who of course had plans of his own, agreed to Luciano's proposal.

Luciano did not rate the chances of an open attack on Masseria, who lived in a veritable fortress on Second Avenue, its floors and hallways guarded around the clock by thoroughly loyal and trustworthy Mafia 'soldiers'. A hit man lucky enough to get in close to Masseria would never get out alive. Luciano considered an alternative. He had to lure out his boss – preferably to a location that the old Sicilian don considered 'safe'. Luciano knew the perfect spot, a little restaurant on Coney Island called the Nuova Villa Tammaro. The place was owned by Gerado Scarpato, a trusted friend of Masseria's, and there was every chance that the old-fashioned mobster might relax his guard there. Using a pretext, Luciano convinced Masseria to visit the restaurant with him, and had Scarpato prepare a sumptuous Italian meal for them both. While the greedy Masseria ate and drank his fill, Luciano dined with a little more restraint. He had prepared an extra course for the stout mobster, one definitely not on the menu.

After the meal the two men began a game of cards, but Luciano soon made his excuses and disappeared to the toilet. This was the cue Luciano's men had been waiting for. A car sat outside the Nuova Villa Tammaro, Ciro Terranova at the wheel. At the agreed time its passengers stepped out and strode into the empty restaurant. They were Albert Anastasia, Benjamin 'Bugsy' Siegel, Joe Adonis and Vito Genovese, all Mafia men from a number of different gangs. Joe Masseria sat alone at his table drinking coffee, and initially he didn't know what to make of the group of men who surrounded him. He realized in an instant, however, as the four killers pulled out revolvers and opened fire on him. In seconds it was all over, and the powerful crime lord who had held much of the New York crime scene in his hand slumped forward onto the table in a bloody heap.

Maranzano immediately took over Masseria's criminal empire and soon began to expand its reach to other cities across the United States. His ambition was to rule the quarrelling Mafia clans just as the Roman emperors had ruled their many provinces. In fact, Maranzano had made a study of Roman history, and what he had read profoundly impressed him. Now he sought to realize his dream. With the death of Joe 'the Boss' Masseria, he had gained control of all Mafia operations in New York – and, due to the scale of Mafia activity there, that effectively meant the whole of the United States. Within weeks of his predecessor's death, Maranzano had convened a sumptuous banquet in the Bronx to which he invited the most influential Mafia gangsters from across the country. They came from Kansas City, Chicago, Cleveland and Detroit to listen to Maranzano's proposal. In his speech to the Mafia bosses, Maranzano proposed that the Mafia should unite to become a single associated entity. Each boss (and his lieutenant) would enjoy the freedom to run his own operations in his own territory, but ultimately he owed allegiance to a 'super-boss', the 'boss of bosses', known in Italian as the *capo di tutti capi*. Don Salvatore Maranzano would, of course, occupy that privileged position. He clearly defined for the assembled mafiosi the leadership of the five New York factions, or families, naming both their bosses and their under-bosses. One of these New York bosses was to be 'Lucky' Luciano, with his under-boss Vito Genovese.

The Mafia bosses welcomed this grand alliance, and it set the scene for an America-wide, city-by-city takeover. In principle it seemed to eliminate the Mafia's greatest rival – itself – but there were some who were not happy with Maranzano's undisguised self-promotion. To some he seemed to be more harsh and dictatorial even than Masseria, and a small number of mafiosi began to talk about deposing him. Maranzano, like the paranoid Roman emperors he so admired, heard rumours of a plot to have him killed and in retaliation compiled a 'hit list' of potential conspirators. Both Luciano and Genovese were on that list. He told his chauffeur: 'I'm not hitting it off with that bastard Luciano and his under-boss Genovese. We gotta get rid of them before we can control anything.' The 'boss of bosses', godfather Maranzano, concocted a plot to have both men murdered, and he hired a professional, Vincent 'Mad Dog' Coll, to do the job. This psychopathic killer would, and could, eliminate anyone for a fee. Maranzano arranged for 'Mad Dog' Coll to ambush the two bosses at a meeting in the office of his Park Avenue real estate firm. On 9 September 1931 the newly installed Mafia godfather privately boasted: 'I'm having one last meeting with Luciano and Genovese tomorrow around three o'clock.'

Maranzano arrived at the Park Avenue offices in good time, his normally large armed escort notably absent. He had heard rumours that there was going to be a police visit to check on the legitimacy of his real estate business any day now, and he did not want to give the officers any reasons for suspicion. By a coincidence, a five-man team of police officers arrived at two o'clock, the very afternoon that 'Mad Dog' Coll had planned to surprise and murder Luciano and Genovese. The five police officers flashed their NYPD badges and were invited into Maranzano's offices, where he greeted them. Three remained in an outer room while two others entered his private office. The godfather must have realized, too late, that these men were not bona fide cops, and he made a desperate grab for the .38 Colt pistol hidden in a drawer. The two killers were faster than the Mafia boss, however, and the first, Sammy 'Red' Levine, grabbed Maranzano and pinned his arms behind his back. The second, Abe 'Bo' Weinberg, pulled out a knife and thrust it into the don's body again and again. Grievously wounded, Maranzano made one final effort to reach his handgun, but was cut short by a salvo of .38 bullets from Levine's own handgun. America's first godfather, the 'boss of bosses' was dead.

The two killers rushed into the outer office to team up with the three anxiously waiting there. Together the gang fled from the building, using the stairs for speed and security. No one relished the slow and vulnerable ride down in an elevator. In the lobby the team of assassins passed a man going the other way into the building – it was 'Mad Dog' Coll, on his way to meet Maranzano and prepare for the killing of Luciano and Genovese. Coll took one look at the bloody spectacle in Maranzano's office and got himself out of there as fast as he could. 'Lucky' Luciano had pre-empted Maranzano's own assassination attempt. Like a seasoned Western gunslinger, the Sicilian boss had pulled a faster, slicker move – and got there first. He still had an immense task ahead of him, however, for many of the nation's Mafia bosses had already pledged allegiance to the dead 'boss of bosses', and Luciano now rightly feared that they would ally against him to defend Maranzano's legacy. Luciano, understanding the danger of passivity, went on the offensive – and committed mass murder.

The 'Moustache Petes', the old Sicilian Mafia bosses who had come to America and brought with them the ancient Mafia traditions and customs, were Luciano's greatest threat. Salvatore Maranzano had been one of these 'Moustache Petes', and within only a matter of days, over fifty others were dead, assassinated by Mafia enforcers loyal only to Luciano and his under-boss Vito Genovese. This unexpected bloodbath had the

THE MAFIA HIT MAN

effect of preventing an all-out Mafia war and secured for decades Luciano's position as the new *capo di tutti capi*. The American Mafia had a new godfather. For the bosses who remained alive, Luciano's astonishing murder spree in the twenty-four hours that followed the murder of Maranzano became known as 'the Night of the Sicilian Vespers'. The success of his murder campaign taught the new godfather a valuable lesson. It was a lesson he would rework in order to fashion a terrifying assassination agency, Murder, Inc.

MURDER, INC.

'Lucky' Luciano presided over the formation of the National Commission, the Mafia syndicate that united the scattered Mafia families across America. At its heart was a New York-based 'board of directors', made up of the country's top bosses, including Joe Adonis, Meyer Lansky and Louis 'Lepke' Buchalter. These bosses paid homage to Luciano as the new 'boss of bosses' – the Mafia's supreme godfather. The decisions made by this syndicate became law. To back up this awesome power, the syndicate even had its own Brooklyn-based enforcement arm, nicknamed Murder, Inc. The two Mafia chiefs entrusted with control of this dreaded new organization were Benjamin 'Bugsy' Siegel and Meyer Lansky. These men recruited prospective killers from their old 'Bug and Meyer' gang which had flourished during Prohibition (the amendment banning the manufacture and sale of alcohol was eventually repealed in 1933).

Within a few years the running of Murder, Inc. was taken over by 'Lepke' Buchalter and his under-boss, Albert Anastasia. Both men were ruthless killers in their own rights, and, indeed, such was the preponderance of Jewish mafiosi in the organization that it was occasionally (and jokingly) referred to as the 'Kosher Nostra', a play on the Mafia's own name for itself, La Cosa Nostra ('this thing of ours'). There was nothing humorous about the cartel's activities, however. Recruits were specifically picked for their skills and experience in untraceable murder. The United States had never seen anything quite like it before – a secret society of professional assassins that sent its members to any city in America with the sole objective of murdering some unsuspecting victim. Most recruits in the 1930s came from the Jewish gangs in eastern towns like Ocean City and Brownsville, as well as from the street gangs of New York.

189

The professionals were treated well by the organization. They enjoyed salaries that rivalled some of the country's top executives, they had medical plans, retirement plans and even life insurance! Each killer knew that his family would be well looked after by the syndicate should he be unfortunate (or sloppy) enough to be arrested or killed in the line of duty. Even arrest did not automatically mean an end to the hit man's career, since Murder, Inc. could pull a number of strings to get its man free. Expensive lawyers would often be put onto the case, and judges, attorneys and policemen who were in the pay of the Mob were 'asked' to release the killer. This not only boosted the confidence and morale of Murder, Inc.'s troops, but it also ensured that no hit man caught in a jail cell would need to betray the group to save his own skin. Murder, Inc. looked after its own. Members of an assassination team were rich enough to drive the best cars, wear the best suits and eat in the best restaurants.

A typical victim might be a mafioso who had turned informant, a 'loose cannon' Mafia enforcer who was beginning to attract unwanted police attention or a boss who refused to comply with the dictates of Luciano's Mafia syndicate. The Murder, Inc. assassins arrived in town from New York. They were total strangers to the victim and had no physical or social ties to him. The victim himself would usually have no inkling of the killers' identity or mission. It was inevitable that most investigations carried out in the wake of a Murder, Inc. hit never made any headway. One or two (sometimes more) strangers arrived from out of town in a hired or stolen car. They located the victim, and then savagely and effectively murdered him. No link could ever be discerned, no evidence was ever left behind and no motivation for the murder could ever be found. Such random killings were nearly always unsolvable.

The culture of killing that Murder, Inc. created and sustained had its own dark terminology. Words were often euphemisms used to fool investigators who might be listening in on phone lines. Many have since passed into popular usage. A 'contract' was a murder assignment. A 'hit' or a 'pop' referred to an actual killing. A 'bum' was the victim to be targeted. Outside the organization, a Mafia killer was often known as a 'torpedo'. Every city that the Mafia controlled had its Murder, Inc. 'troop' in residence. Each 'troop' was an autonomous team of hand-picked killers, led by a single experienced Mafia chief. The 'troop' from Brownsville had the toughest reputation among those who knew of the organization's existence. Its most notable killers were Albert 'Tick Tock'

Tannenbaum, Abe 'Kid Twist' Reles, Harry 'Happy' Maione and Harry 'Pittsburgh Phil' Strauss. For ten years the Brownsville troop selectively assassinated men totally unknown to them, and estimates of the total number of victims range from fifty to a hundred.

'Kid Twist' Reles later turned informer and gave several graphic and disturbing accounts of the grisly murders carried out by his fellows. A typical Mafia Inc. hit was carried out in 1937 by Strauss (also known as 'Pep' Strauss) and Maione. The two men had located the unsuspecting victim, Harry Millman, in a Detroit restaurant and walked straight in off the street. They strode purposefully past innocent diners and approached Millman's crowded table. There the two men promptly pulled out concealed revolvers and blasted away at Millman until the guns were empty. Several of Millman's dinner guests were wounded in the fusillade, while the intended victim himself was killed outright – his body riddled with bullets. The immediate reaction of the other customers was predictable. Screams and shouts rang out and people dashed for safety. Amid the chaos and confusion, the killers holstered their revolvers and strode back out of the restaurant. Maione picked up speed as they left; his natural reaction was to run before the cops arrived. Strauss, more experienced, grabbed his arm, holding him back. He told him never to run from a murder scene: 'You run and somebody runs after you, Happy … We don't want that guy back there. He didn't know us.'

The syndicate, like any successful business concern, demanded regular reports on any outstanding contracts, and 'Bugsy' Siegel and Albert Anastasia also had the responsibility of giving a weekly 'body count' of assassinations committed by the organization. Talented individuals from Mafia families in the northeast continued to be recruited throughout the 1930s. The 'talent-spotters' looked for an absolute lack of remorse in potential candidates, as well as an ability to kill quickly and efficiently. They had to be men who would be unlikely to boast about their bloody careers and who could dispose of a body without leaving any incriminating evidence for the police to find. No one cared whether the murderer had an ability to make a 'clean' kill or not. Some members resorted to the most primitive and brutish of weaponry available, including axes, ice-picks and meat cleavers. If it worked, it was used.

One unfortunate victim of the cartel was Walter Sage who had been marked for death by the top bosses in New York for taking an unauthorized cut from the Mafia's slot machine operations. Sage found himself bundled into a car with four Murder, Inc. members, each of whom was a pathological killer. At an isolated spot one of the killers, Jack Drucker, grabbed Sage from behind, lifting him up in his seat. Then he stabbed Sage in the back thirty-two times. Each blow penetrated the back of the seat and impaled the screaming victim. The authorities later found his body floating in a remote lake. Gasses inside Sage's body had pulled it free of the heavy pinball machine it had been tied too, forcing it to the surface. A lesson was learned there: always puncture the dead man's stomach before tossing him into the water.

'Bugsy' Siegel had once said to a frightened businessman that the Mafia only 'kill each other', and he was more or less correct. One of the most dramatic examples of this was the murder of 'Dutch' Schultz, the only syndicate boss to be targeted by Murder, Inc. This powerful Mafia boss had become an uncontrollable and unstable man, who so hated the New York district attorney, Thomas E. Dewey, that he plotted to have him killed. This flouted a basic law of the National Commission: that no mafiosi may murder a politician or justice official. It didn't matter whether they were low-ranking thugs, *capos* or bosses. Three members of Murder, Inc. led by Mendy Weiss ambushed Schultz in the men's room of a Newark restaurant in 1937. He later died in hospital.

It seems paradoxical that an organization created to assassinate individuals known to have betrayed the secrets of the Mafia to the authorities should have been destroyed when several of its own members became police informants. One killer in the murder cartel, Harry Rudolph, had been exploited by his superiors, and frustration drove him in 1940 to turn to New York's assistant district attorney for help. He implicated 'Kid Twist' Reles, Dukey Maffetore and Martin 'Bugsy' Goldstein in the murder of his friend some years previously. When Reles and Maffetore learned that the syndicate had put out a contract on them to prevent them from revealing the secrets of Murder, Inc., both men turned informant. The testimony gathered from Reles alone was enough to break Murder, Inc. for good. He explained how the organization recruited its members, how it worked and who its leaders were. As a direct result of this information, Louis 'Lepke' Buchalter, who sat on the National Commission, was arrested, convicted and executed for the part that he had played in ordering the murders of dozens of his enemies. Through his loyal follower Albert Anastasia, Buchalter (known in the underworld as 'Judge Louis') had deployed Murder, Inc. like a private army.

The resourceful Anastasia was able to avoid arrest, despite the damning testimony of Reles. His eventual promotion to the head of a New

York Mafia family in 1951 led to conflict with some of the city's other bosses. Despite having risen through the ranks like many other American mafiosi, Anastasia proved to be a poor Mob boss, and he was executed on the orders of Frank Costello. Anastasia had ruled Murder, Inc. for over a decade, and was greatly feared. He had been responsible for organizing the deaths of hundreds (perhaps thousands) of Mafia informers and thieves throughout the 1930s, and in his younger days had personally murdered fifty or more people. Such was Anastasia's grisly and fanatical reputation that he began to go by names such as the 'Lord High Executioner' and the 'Mad Hatter'. But the murder chief lacked the essential vision required to rise to the top of the Mafia and instead doggedly followed the orders of his idol Buchalter.

In the wake of the investigations that broke Murder, Inc. in the 1940s, the Mafia changed the way it meted out justice. Instead of employing a single group of assassins assigned to carry out murders on the order of the National Commission, individual families would send one or more enforcers to do the job. The assassination of a Mafia informer in Chicago (for example) would be handled by a Mob family from out-of-town, who would send a couple of men out to Chicago. As strangers, anonymous and unaffiliated with the organized crime scene in Chicago, the murder that they were about to commit would be a difficult crime to solve. Who were these strangers? Why was this man murdered? What was the motive? Reliance on a single organization to do this work had proved risky. Not only did it give the authorities more chance to 'crack' it, but it also placed immense power in the hands of the cartel's bosses. The system of using hit men from different families to carry out underworld murders is one that is still in place today.

Following the 1940s the Mafia became ever larger and ever greedier, until it penetrated many aspects of life in America. The move to adopt legitimate businesses as fronts created an 'invisible' Mafia of corruption, kickbacks and blackmail. Old-style gun battles in the street and the notorious drive-by shootings became a rarity within the world of organized crime. With the relentless persecution of Mafia *capos*, bosses and under-bosses throughout the 1990s, much of the traditional power of the American Mafia has been broken. John Gotti, leader of the Gambino family and perhaps the most powerful Mafia boss of the 1980s, was arrested in 1990 on multiple counts, none of them involving murder. This was ironic, since Gotti (known as the 'Teflon Don' since the FBI could not find any charges strong enough to stick) had clawed his way to the top of the Gambino family by assassinating his rivals.

The Gambino leadership had previously passed from Carlo Gambino to his brother-in-law Paul Castellano in 1976. Nine years later Castellano's under-boss died of natural causes, and the Mob boss made preparations to name Thomas Bilotti as his successor, passing over the arrogant and ambitious Gotti. John Gotti, resentful of being bypassed, decided to make a play for the leadership of the Gambino clan. He plotted to have both Castellano and Bilotti assassinated. On the evening of 16 December 1985 Castellano and his soon-to-be under-boss arrived at the Sparks Steak House on New York's East Forty-sixth Street. Three men suddenly emerged out of the shadows, and as Castellano and Bilotti stepped from their limousine, they were shot down, dying soon after from their wounds. The three killers escaped in a waiting car. Although no one knew who had actually pulled the triggers, everyone knew who the beneficiary had been. With the boss and under-boss now out of the way, John Gotti stepped up to take command of the Gambino family. His reign, however, was short-lived.

8. Target for Terror

Assassination has never changed the history of the world.

Benjamin Disraeli

The traditional definition of an 'assassin' is perfectly summarized by Collins dictionary, which describes that individual as the 'murderer of a prominent political figure'. The crucial word here is 'political' – a politician, a political activist. Our definition of politics is, as already discussed, far wider than this, however, encompassing as it does the human obsession with the acquisition of power. Assassins use murder to subvert or pervert the course of power politics. Nevertheless, the dictionary definition is a valuable one and gives us an insight into the general perception of assassination. The word is popularly associated with the murder of well-known political leaders, whatever their national origins. Names and faces have flashed across the newsreels and TV news broadcasts for the better part of a century. Many have been etched deep onto the global psyche. The Gandhis, mother and son; the tragic Kennedy brothers; Archduke Franz Ferdinand, whose death sparked the carnage of the First World War; Egypt's Anwar Sadat; Yitzhak Rabin, murdered in 1995 by an Israeli patriot determined to prevent peace by committing murder. And then there are the survivors. Men like Pope John Paul II and Ronald Reagan, and women like Princess Anne and Margaret Thatcher. The violent attack on legitimate heads of state has been global in scope and relentless in tempo.

There are countless political leaders who have fallen to the guns and bombs of politically motivated terror groups. These factions typically operate outside a nation's official political structure as terrorist groups or even government-sponsored 'death squads'. They believe their cause to be strengthened by the assassination of a prominent political figure who is opposed to them. This belief is usually erroneous. Western leaders also face the less deadly yet far more unpredictable threat from a lone assassin, hellbent on murder in the pursuit of some highly personal and sometimes unfathomable goal. The death of his or her intended victim may have many wider repercussions, but the assassin is oblivious to, or uncaring of, them all.

Why are politicians popular targets for assassination? The simple answer is found in their perceived role as a controller or director of human affairs. Politics is all about the organization of society, and, rightly or wrongly, the politician is often seen as the scapegoat for some aspect of an assassin's life. If things aren't going well, someone must be doing something wrong. Of course, it isn't the assassin who is responsible – it's the political figure who is about to become his victim. Generally, the harsher or more underhand the 'control' that a leader enjoys, the greater the danger to which he expects to be exposed. Winston Churchill, for example, was universally highly thought of and had only a single body-guard. Julius Caesar fought his way to the dictatorship of Rome by every trick in the book, and he depended on 2000 armed men to keep him there.

MADMEN AND ROYALTY

Factions and terror groups who use assassination as a tool are trying to subvert the workings of the political machine. The victim is murdered because the terror group wishes to prevent him or her from exercising political power. This contrasts with the murderous actions of disturbed killers, those loners acting on an impulse or a grievance. Here, the politicians are murdered because the killers feel that they are in some way to blame for the state of affairs that have pushed the killers 'over the edge'. Or, more radically, the assassins murder politicians, those who are 'in control', because the assassins have no control. Both parties are caught in vortices of jealousy, rage and revenge.

Although the history of British politics is littered with violent incidents, a small number has been perpetrated by psychopaths, unbalanced individuals driven to commit a violent and irrational act. The shocking assassination in 1812 of the British prime minister, Spencer Perceval, is one of the most celebrated of these cases.

Perceval governed Britain at a time of intense social hardship. The *laisser-faire* economics promoted by the Tory Party of the day reduced many hundreds of thousands of workers to abject poverty. In addition, skilled textile workers saw their industry becoming ever more mecha-nized and standards falling. Lace-makers were the first to revolt against the system, smashing their frames in 1811. Other textile workers in the north of England began to follow suit, and Spencer Perceval realized that he had a small-scale revolution on his hands. The name of a mysterious and heroic leader, General Ned Ludd, began to circulate, and popular songs were even composed in his honour. The activities of the machine-breakers, known as Luddites after the movement's leader, became increasingly violent, culminating in murder and attempted murder in 1812. Some members of the government suspected the complicity in the Luddite violence of Napoleon Bonaparte, who was feared at the time to be planning an invasion.

Spencer Perceval was shot and killed as he walked through the lobby of the House of Commons on 11 May 1812. The gunman stepped out in front of the prime minister and fired his revolver into him at point-blank range. The bullet wounds were severe, and while his killer was being apprehended and bundled away Perceval died. Suspicion fell immediately on the Luddite movement. The government had taken a hard-line against these desperate and down-trodden men and dispatched soldiers and undercover agents to root them out. The truth, however, proved to be far less sinister and yet far more bizarre. The identity of the assassin proved to be one John Bellingham, a merchant who travelled and traded abroad. It soon became clear that he was no Luddite assassin or, for that matter, an Irish assassin, whom others had suspected to be behind the murder. He had killed the prime minister out of pure frustration. Bellingham had travelled to tsarist Russia where he had been unjustly arrested and thrown into an Archangel prison. His business interests collapsed, and Bellingham was financially ruined. The painful experience cut deep, and Bellingham was determined to seek redress. He blamed not just the Russian authorities but also in some way the British government, both for its lack of sympathy and its refusal to offer some sort of compensation. The officials with whom he corresponded stubbornly refused to accept any responsibility for Bellingham's predicament.

Rage and resentment burned fiercely within him, finally leading him to the House of Commons and the deadly encounter with Perceval. Bellingham did nothing to hide his motives from those holding him, for his desire for official recognition of his plight had at last been achieved. At his trial shortly afterwards, the nature of Bellingham's state of mind at the time of the assassination was examined. Had he murdered the prime minister with a clear head and full knowledge of the implications of his actions? Or was he mentally disturbed and unable to distinguish right from wrong? The trial ended on 15 May, just four days after the assassination, and Bellingham was found guilty and hanged only three days later. In 1812 British justice had no legal precedents for the murder of a prime minister and the trial of his killer. The trial of John Bellingham provided that precedent. It was not until 1843 that the state of mind of an assassin could be formally called into question.

The assassin who sparked off this next debate, three decades later, was one Daniel McNaughten. It was believed that McNaughten had tried to assassinate the prime minister, Sir Robert Peel, but had mistaken Edward Drummond, Peel's private secretary, for the prime minister. Drummond was shot and killed by McNaughten on 20 January 1843. It seemed the killer would be destined for a speedy, Bellingham-style trial and execution, but questions raised at the 1812 trial were asked again here. McNaughten had no legitimate grievance against either Peel or Drummond, and his defence counsel insisted that he was criminally insane. The trial judges studied the matter exhaustively and the level of interest in the case grew to such proportions that they were even quizzed by the House of Lords. McNaughten was eventually found to be insane and utterly incapable of distinguishing between right and wrong. Thus he avoided the death penalty and was admitted to a mental asylum. The McNaughten Rules have since been invoked in British and American courts many times. One of the most famous cases in modern history, the murder of Robert Kennedy by the Palestinian student Sirhan Sirhan, also hinged on the mental state of the killer at the time. As we have seen in Chapter 6, Sirhan Sirhan did not lack for motive, despite both his claims of amnesia and the hate-filled scrawlings in his notebooks. The jury did not find Sirhan Sirhan criminally insane, despite the lengthy testimony of numerous psychiatrists and psychologists.

Only the year before McNaughten's attack on Drummond, Queen Victoria had been the target of a failed assassination. A young chemist's assistant, John Bean, had decided to kill either the queen or her husband, Albert, the Prince Consort, in a fit of despair after quarrelling with his brothers. Bean left a note with his father in which he stated that he wanted to be remembered by his brothers, who openly scorned John and his hunch-back. The would-be-assassin signed himself 'Your Unhappy, but Disobedient Son'. As the queen and prince emerged from Buckingham Palace, Bean, standing amid a crowd of bystanders, drew his cheap pistol and tried to fire at the couple. Bean's weapon misfired and a boy called Basset jumped on him, wrestling the gun away. Prince Albert, not understanding the scene he was witnessing, laughed at the struggle and thought it all a big practical joke. Worse still, the police arrested young Basset. Only later did they become aware of the mistake. Bean was tracked down and arrested. Until that time the courts could only charge a would-be royal assassin with high treason. When the defendant was later found to be insane, the charge had to be dropped and the prisoner eventually released.

Two previous murder attempts had already resulted in the arrest and conviction of the gunmen involved. Edward Oxford shot at the queen in 1840, was found insane and spent twenty-seven years in an asylum. John Francis fired on the royal couple two years later, was convicted of treason in 1842 and transported to Tasmania. With the law as it stood in the summer of 1842, the queen was only too aware of the inadequacies of the judicial system that seemed to offer a loophole to potential killers. John Bean was charged with, and convicted of, 'shooting at Her Majesty', technically a misdemeanour for which he received eighteen months' hard labour. The judge was able to see Bean's tragi-comic attempt on the queen's life for what it was, an attention-grabbing stunt that luckily went wrong. The trial of Daniel McNaughten the following year might have changed the law to remedy the situation. Instead however, the McNaughten Rules enshrined the plea of 'not guilty by reason of insanity' in law. And Queen Victoria soon faced more attempts on her life than ever before.

On 19 May 1849 an Irish labourer named William Hamilton fired at the royal coach but failed to hit either Queen Victoria or Prince Albert. It soon transpired that Hamilton had actually fired a blank cartridge. This attack was almost certainly politically motivated (the authorities at the time made no mention of the fact), although Hamilton had acted alone and out of frustration. In a little over a year another attempt was made on the queen's life. This time the assailant was a former army officer named Robert Pate, who held a grudge against the British monarchy. Pate waited with a crowd outside the palace, and as the queen's carriage passed through the gate he lunged forward and tried to hit her with a baton. Although bruised and shocked, she was not badly injured.

The royal household seemed almost oblivious to the dangers of open-topped carriages, pre-announced trips and the lack of any real bodyguard. Things slowly began to change, however, and the cumulative shock of these attempts on her life began to weigh heavily on the queen, who became increasingly aware of the risks. The greatest threat to her life was the Fenian Brotherhood, an Irish secret society that was engaged in a terrorist campaign to free Ireland from British rule. Fortunately, the rise of the Fenians coincided with Queen Victoria's retreat from public life following the death of Prince Albert in 1861. Although her advisers and the police Special Branch, which had been established to guard against Irish terrorism, feared a Fenian assassination attempt, it never came. The Fenians did, however, succeed in shooting and wounding one of her sons, Prince Alfred, the Duke of Edinburgh.

The controversial issue of an insane assassin came again to the fore in 1872 during the trial of an Irish youth called Arthur O'Conner. In February O'Conner had hidden inside St Paul's Cathedral to await the arrival of the queen who was to attend a service later that afternoon. Discovered and ejected, he spent two days procuring a cheap pistol and composing a fanciful letter demanding that the queen release all Fenian prisoners. He intended to put his little pistol to the queen's head and force her to sign his petition. Armed with gun and letter, O'Conner climbed the railings around the palace and approached the royal carriage as it rolled to a stop. As the door opened, the seventeen-year-old suddenly appeared out of nowhere. The queen screamed in terror and her close companion, John Brown, grabbed the boy and held on. O'Conner was convicted of treason and forced to emigrate to Australia, despite convincing testimony given in the boy's defence. The doctors who had been able to study O'Conner were sure that the boy was mad and not responsible for his actions, but doubt was cast on the credibility of these experts by the prosecutor. It soon transpired that O'Conner was indeed mad. During his forced exile he sent a series of letters to Queen Victoria, each one containing bizarre requests and statements.

Within three years O'Conner was back in London, and it was clear that he still intended to inflict some injury on the queen. As O'Conner's psychosis matured, police detectives kept a careful watch over him. When the Irishman made his way back to Buckingham Palace, the scene of his previous attempt, the police immediately arrested him. He was found to be insane and committed to a mental asylum.

The final attempt on Queen Victoria's life came on 2 March 1882. A clerk, hungry and desperate, shot at the queen's carriage as it left Windsor railway station for the castle. The man's actions, like those of previous attackers, seemed to be a cry for attention and not a terrorist act full of political meaning. Again, the wretched motivation for the would-be assassin proved to have a direct bearing on his fate. The assailant, Roderick McLean, was found to be found criminally insane under the

McNaughten Rules and was acquitted. Like his predecessors, McLean was not let off, but incarcerated within a mental asylum. The queen was outraged that McLean would not have to face the hangman for his attempt to gun her down. A plea was made to the prime minister, William Gladstone, and changes to the law were again introduced. What the queen sought was a deterrent for mad men as well as sane men. With her quite considerable backing, the House of Lords introduced a new bill that specifically prohibited the courts from acquitting a criminal who was thought to have been insane when he committed his crime. The criminal would still be convicted of the offence with which he was initially charged.

Attacks on the royal family by disturbed individuals did not end with the death (from natural causes) of Queen Victoria. One of the most notable, and most recent, examples was the strange attempted kidnapping of Princess Anne in the Mall, London, in 1974. The princess was travelling in the company of her first husband, Captain Mark Phillips, their bodyguard, Jim Beaton, and the princess's lady-in-waiting, Rowena Brassey. The four were being driven in a chauffeured limousine towards Buckingham Palace on the evening of 20 March when, without warning, another car pulled over in front of the limousine, and its driver, Ian Ball, approached as if to have an altercation with the princess's chauffeur. As soon as the car stopped, Beaton got out and walked around the back of the vehicle to provide some security for its passengers. As he emerged from behind the limousine, Ball shot him. Beaton took cover behind the limousine and drew his Walther PPK pistol. He tried to fire back, but the wound he had suffered spoiled his aim. He tried desperately to fire again, but his gun jammed. As Beaton ducked back behind the car to try to free the mechanism of his weapon, Ball walked forward and tried to pull open the passenger door. Despite the attempts of Princess Anne and her husband to keep the door closed, Ball forced it open and tried to drag out the princess. Captain Phillips held her tightly, and as the sleeve of her dress gave way, she was pulled back into the car by her husband. The two slammed the door shut, and as they did so Inspector Beaton re-emerged to confront Ball. The man pointed his pistol at the bodyguard and told him to drop his gun. Beaton did so, then climbed into the car to try to defend the princess.

The situation rapidly began to deteriorate. The lady-in-waiting got out of the car and tried in vain to get to Beaton's (jammed) pistol. Meanwhile, a journalist stopped his cab and got out to try and help. Ball drew another gun, a .22 revolver, and shot him. The gunman turned once more to the limousine and ordered Beaton to open the door, threatening him with a gun. As Beaton held up his hands, Ball fired, blowing a hole in the officer's right hand. A uniformed policeman arrived, after having just reported the incident on radio. He moved to intercept Ball but was also shot by the crazed gunman. He spotted the Walther on the ground and, like Rowena Brassey, tried to get to it. The shock and pain of his wound overtook him, however, and he collapsed. Ball then turned on the chauffeur, shooting him once. Next he grabbed the passenger door handle and tried to get at the princess again. In the confusion, Beaton was shot for a third time. He slumped out of the car, totally incapacitated.

Passers-by continued to get involved. Another chauffeur blocked off Ball's car and tried to get close to the fracas on foot but was warned off by the gunman. Then a taxi driver moved in to confront Ball, and was able to punch him, before being shot at in retaliation. The shot missed. As the two men struggled with one another, police cars arrived *en masse*. Ball attempted to flee towards St James's Park but was brought to the floor by the police.

If anything, the Ian Ball kidnap incident clearly illustrated that the royal family was just as much at risk in 1974 as it ever was. It was also a damning indictment of royal protection. The limousine hadn't been armoured (a feature that had been available since the 1920s – Frankie Yale's 1928 Lincoln had been armour-plated) and the chauffeur had received no special training. Firearms were an optional extra for bodyguards. There were no back-up cars, and no direct radio contact with the police was available. The attack galvanized Scotland Yard into a radical rethink of its protection strategies. It was no longer good enough to maintain traditional methods of close protection when it was now obvious that these methods were wholly out of date. Ball's first volley on the Mall had been a warning shot.

Investigators quickly discovered that Ball had written a letter he had planned that the princess would sign. This was to give him a pardon for the crime and authorize a ransom of £3 million. When police discovered that Ball had made arrangements to rent a house in Fleet, Hampshire, for use as a hideaway after the kidnap it became clear that he had not acted on impulse. Nevertheless, Ball (again like O'Conner) was incarcerated for an indefinite period within a mental institution. Is an individual who carries out a shocking and bizarre attack with little if any chance of success actually insane, however? The amount of forethought and planning that Ian Ball had put into the attack clearly showed that he had not acted spontaneously or was unaware of what he was doing. He obviously did. The law remains ambiguous and will continue to confuse and bewilder courts for many years to come. There is no empirical method to determine a criminal's sanity (or insanity). Are serial killers or paedophiles the victims of mental illness? Or are they criminals, knowingly committing crimes and fully aware of the gravity of their actions?

This argument applies with equal measure to the study of assassins on trial. Assassination is not a crime of opportunity, it requires a (sometimes considerable) degree of planning. Where can the target be accessed? What method can be used to murder the target? When should the assassination take place? These questions are asked by every professional assassin, and must of necessity also be answered by any 'insane' killer wanting to assassinate a celebrity or politician.

THE WHITE HOUSE UNDER SIEGE

The shadow of sudden death has fallen across American politics for a century. John F. Kennedy became the most famous American president of all time due, in some large measure, to his shocking assassination in 1963. He was not, of course, the first US president to have been removed from the White House by a gunman's bullets – Presidents Lincoln, Garfield and McKinley were all murdered while in office – and a peculiarly large number of other presidents have been the victims of botched assassination attempts.

The first attempt to assassinate an American president occurred on 30 January 1835. President Andrew Jackson (1767–1845) had just attended the funeral of a congressman and was passing through the rotunda of the Capitol in Washington with his entourage. It was there that the house-painter Richard Lawrence was lying in wait, with two percussion cap pistols in his pockets. As the president passed within 3 metres (10 feet) of him, Lawrence drew one of the guns and pulled the trigger. The percussion cap exploded, but the shot did not leave the barrel. As he hastily drew the second pistol, Jackson, who had flinched at the sound of the first shot, lunged at the gunman with his cane. The second pistol went off – but again it did not discharge any shot, leaving the president unharmed. Lawrence was grabbed and Jackson, enraged, shouted out that he knew who was really behind the attempt to kill him.

Jackson was convinced that Lawrence was an assassin in the pay of his political enemies. They, meanwhile, protested their innocence and declared that the president was trying to milk the assassination attempt for sympathy. Meanwhile, the courts declared Richard Lawrence to be of unsound mind. Along with previous inexplicable and bizarre anti-social behaviour, he had believed himself to be the rightful heir to the throne of Britain, and his argument with Jackson stemmed from this belief. The jury had no problem deciding that Lawrence was not responsible for his actions at the time of the shooting. He was indeed mad, and he spent the rest of his life in mental institutions.

The next president to suffer an assassination attempt did not get off quite as lightly as had Andrew Jackson. While President Theodore ('Teddy') Roosevelt (1858–1919) was on the campaign trail in Milwaukee on 14 October 1912 he was shot as he climbed into an open-topped car. The gunman, John Schrank, fired on Roosevelt with a .38 revolver, inflicting a chest wound. As he prepared to fire a second shot, Schrank was wrestled to the ground by the police. Roosevelt insisted on continuing his journey to the Milwaukee Auditorium to give a speech, despite the fact that he was still losing blood. It was later discovered that it had been the thick notes of his speech that had deflected the bullet and thus saved Roosevelt's life that night.

Schrank, like Richard Lawrence, turned out to be an incurable madman. By his own testimony, the ghost of previous President McKinley had come to him and pointed an accusing finger at Theodore Roosevelt. From that moment, Schrank was determined to avenge McKinley, and he pursued the president across America, finally catching up with him in Milwaukee. Schrank was committed to a mental institution, and he died still incarcerated during the Second World War.

The American president who led the nation through the dark wartime days was also the victim of an attempted assassination. He, too, was a Roosevelt. President-elect Franklin Delano Roosevelt (1882–1945) had come ashore from his yacht in Miami and made a short speech to a small public gathering. As he prepared to drive away, the anti-social misfit Guiseppe Zangara stood on a chair and sprayed the president-elect's location with gunfire. The mayor of Chicago (there on vacation) was hit, as were three other men and a woman, all part of the crowd. Chicago's mayor, Anton J. Cermak, was convinced that the Chicago Mob had ordered the assassination and that Zangara had been a contract assassin, a 'torpedo'. However, detailed investigation proved the corrupt politician wrong. Zangara had nursed a bitter grudge against authority for many years and dreamed of striking against the 'capitalist presidents and kings'. He had no extreme political affiliations, yet railed constantly against the system, against capitalism and against society in general. At his trial, Zangara told the court that he had tried to murder Roosevelt in Miami because he happened to be there at the time. If he had seen another prominent politician, he would just as likely have shot at him. With the death of Mayor Cermak three weeks after the shooting, Zangara faced the death sentence for his crime, and at the end of his trial he was convicted and sent to the electric chair.

The oddest assassination attempt in American history took place at Baltimore-Washington International Airport on 22 February 1974. Samuel J. Byck, a disturbed and out-of-work tyre salesman, took a .22 handgun and stormed the Delta Flight 523 for Atlanta. In the cockpit he ordered the flight crew to take off. His plan was simple. Byck would force the pilot to fly the jet airliner over Washington and towards the White House. Then he would shoot the pilot and take the controls himself, guiding the plane in to crash at the last moment straight into the White House. He hoped to kill the incumbent president, Richard Nixon (1913–94), along with the majority of the White House staff, the flight crew, passengers and, of course, himself.

His attempts to get the plane into the air were scotched by basic airport procedure. The plane couldn't get to the runway with the chocks in place, and Byck vented his fury on the pilot and co-pilot, shooting them repeatedly. As he finished firing into the two men, police snipers fired through the cockpit glass, wounding him. Rather than be taken alive, Byck put the gun to his own head and pulled the trigger. Samuel Byck was an inadequate man, who harboured a deep-seated grudge against the establishment. He blamed the 'corrupt' authorities for both his failed career and his disastrous family life. Several years before, Byck had openly threatened the life of Richard Nixon, and the Secret Service had tried to have him prosecuted. It was only the testimony of Byck's psychiatrist at the time that convinced the district attorney to drop the investigation.

In the end, it was Watergate, not an assassin's bullet, that cut short Richard Nixon's administration. His vice-president, Gerald Ford, who presided over the final chaotic months of the Vietnam War, also made history in the field of assassination. Ford has been the only president to have been the victim of an assassination attempt by a woman – twice. On 5 September 1975 the first would-be assassin, twenty-six-year-old

Lynette Alice Fromme, pushed her way to the front of a crowd of spectators outside the California Capitol in Sacramento, the state capital. Ford came within a metre of her, and she brought up her revolver to fire. Luckily for Ford, one of his Secret Service agents spotted the weapon and wrestled it out of her hands. Fromme was unusual. She had been an admirer of the cult leader Charles Manson, who had been imprisoned for his part in the Sharon Tate killings in 1969, and she had continued to carry a torch for the Manson 'family'. Her alleged motive for the attempted assassination was to give Manson a platform to speak in her defence. This did not happen, however, and Fromme was sentenced to life imprisonment for her actions. The court found her sane and guilty.

A copy-cat shooting followed within three weeks of Fromme's attack. This time, a left-wing activist (and on-off informer for the FBI), Sara Jane Moore, actually managed to get a shot off before she was apprehended. The forty-five-year old had sought acceptance among the tightly knit groups of fringe activists and salved her conscience by informing on them to the authorities. As her self-doubt grew and her confidence faded away, Moore took one of her handguns (that day a .38 handgun, her powerful .44 Magnum having recently been confiscated by the police) and sought out the president of the United States. Through this political act Moore may have been seeking some sort of attention and redemption – guilt and isolation overwhelmed her.

She found Gerald Ford outside the St Francis Hotel in San Franciso on 22 September 1975. As he greeted the crowd, Moore pointed her .38 in his direction. She was more than 12 metres (40 feet) away at the time and would have had to be either very skilled or very lucky to have hit the president at that range. At the very moment she pulled the trigger, Moore was grabbed and the shot went wild, wounding a taxi driver. Ford was driven away at high speed and returned to the safety of the White House as quickly as possible. Moore was imprisoned for the attempt on the president's life.

Ford's successor, Jimmy Carter, was thankfully spared the terror and panic of an assassination attempt, but his successor, Ronald Reagan was not. His bloody baptism came on 30 March 1981, early in his term of office. On that day he came under fire from the psychologically disturbed loner John Hinckley, a shooting that has been discussed more fully earlier in this book. It came as a great shock to the nation when Hinckley was found not guilty of attempted murder on the grounds of insanity. It seemed that Hinckley followed in the footsteps of the would-be killers of the past, psychotics such as Richard Lawrence and John Schrank, both judged insane.

It is surely a blessing that there have been relatively few well-organized and politically motivated attempts on a president's life. The psychotic 'madman' has, on the evidence so far available, displayed little tactical sense. This is good news for the president. All have utilized hand-guns in their attempts, weapons not designed to be effective at long ranges (anything over 20 metres/66 feet) or to have reliable killing power. This means that the would-be killers have had to get in close to their targets. Apart from a period of extended 'stalking', none of the disturbed gunmen or women has shown any skill in organizing the assassination and evading subsequent capture. The threat from the lone crank exists. It is a stark reality of high-profile public service, but it is a threat that will always have a low chance of success.

THE ANARCHIST ASSASSINS

Modern terrorism is not quite as modern as most would think. The invisible paramilitary armies of terror that spontaneously erupted out of the political confusions of 1968 were neither the first, nor the most globally orientated. Italy has been rocked by the murderous Red Brigades, Germany has been plagued by the Red Army Faction (RAF), France suffered at the hands of Action Directe, and Japan has the Japanese Red Army. These groups have defined a new method of political struggle, a way of campaigning without votes, elections or a vestige of popular support. The credo is change through terror through murder.

The grandfather of these radical factions was a global movement of terror groups and secret networks that proudly called itself Anarchism, and the Anarchist movement reached almost every industrial nation in the late nineteenth and early twentieth centuries. It was the violent backlash of an educated élite who were trying to wage a war against poverty, oppression and injustice. Much like their modern successors, the Anarchists rarely enjoyed any popular appeal. They fought an undeclared war with dynamite and revolvers to assassinate heads of state and other powerful political figures. These startling actions were supposed to initiate a revolution that would sweep away all forms of oppressive government and liberate the working classes. The flaws in the dogmatic argument of the Anarchist movement need not be analysed here, but it is interesting to note the similarities between the nineteenth-century, dynamite-wielding idealist and the modern European Semtex-carrying terrorist. Idealism and isolation channel the terrorists' energy into sporadic gestures of hate and death. While the Irish Republican Army (IRA) and the Basque separatist group Euzkadi ta Askatasuna (ETA) can claim they are fighting to secure the rights of a minority, the revolutionary groups cannot.

The world had never seen anything like Anarchism when it emerged onto the scene after 1848, the 'year of revolutions'. Revolutionary thinkers like Louis-Auguste Blanqui (1805–81) and Mikhail Bakunin (1814–76), who had disagreed with Karl Marx on the use of violence to achieve their goals, were convinced that the French Revolution of 1789 was only the first of an unending series of social upheavals that would liberate the human race from the tyranny of repressive regimes. Despite a number of stunning Anarchist assassination successes, the movement failed to inspire the chaos and social collapse that it had predicted. The first major success was achieved by Russian Anarchists, who called themselves (ironically) the Will of the People. This violent faction had consumed the words of Bakunin with fervour and in 1879 planned to strike at the pinnacle of power in pre-communist Russia, Tsar Alexander II (r.1855–81).

The group decided to assassinate Alexander as he travelled across Russia in his train. It had discovered that the tsar already lived in fear of his life and that he had cleverly arranged for a decoy train to run ahead of his own train. The tsar reasoned that it would be this decoy that would suffer the effects of any sabotage. Andrei Zhelyabov, a charming and talented leader within the Will of the People, led a daring band of saboteurs that prepared a devastating explosive charge along the railway. If this murder attempt should fail, a second team, led by Zhelyabov's lover Sophia Perovskaya, was prepared to set a second charge a day's ride further along the track. Zhelyabov's charge failed to go off. Now it was up to Perovskaya's team to carry out the assassination. As the first train approached the location of the dynamite, the assassins readied themselves. They allowed the first train to pass over the booby trap, and as the second train rumbled unwittingly over it, they detonated the charge, blowing the rails apart and derailing the train. On closer inspection, however, Perovskaya and her terrorists realized that they had been the victims of a clever double-bluff. The first 'decoy' train had been the one carrying the tsar.

Will of the People was not daunted by this spectacular failure and the next year planted a bomb in the banqueting hall of the tsar's Winter Palace. It caused extensive damage, but the tsar and his family had not yet arrived and they escaped death or injury. The final attempt was made on 1 March 1881. On this day the tsar had planned to review his troops, and Will of the People had been able to find out which route he would take. Accordingly, Zhelyabov arranged to open a basement cheese shop along the route to act as a 'front' for a carefully prepared booby trap. From the basement, the group tunnelled under the street and planted a powerful bomb that would be detonated the instant Alexander's carriage passed overhead. Out of the blue, Zhelyabov was captured and the plan was put in jeopardy. On the day of the parade the tsar's guards altered the route of the carriage, bypassing the carefully prepared bomb. The group had been thorough, however, and had stationed two assassins with hand-held bombs further along the route.

The first activist, Rysakov, pushed forward out of the crowds and threw his bomb at the tsar's carriage. Although it inflicted severe damage, killing several people and damaging the carriage, the tsar was unharmed. Alexander then made the fateful decision to step out of his carriage and supervise the care of the wounded. It was then that the second anarchist, Grinevitsky, rushed forward with a phial of nitro-glycerine. He hurled it at the tsar's feet. This second explosion was even more devastating than the first, killing twenty men outright and wounding many more. Among those mortally wounded were both Alexander and the assassin, Grinevitsky. Alexander had lost his legs and one of his eyes in the terrific blast and he died within the hour.

Despite this success, the Will of the People could not survive the terrible backlash unleashed by Alexander's harsh successor, Alexander III (r.1881–94). Russian radicals, including Perovskaya, were rounded up and arrested, and most, including both Zhelyabov and Perovskaya, were executed. All resistance to the regime vanished under the savage repression that followed. Alexander III distanced himself from the people he ruled and was in many ways a far worse alternative to Alexander II. A year on, despite the great volume of blood that had been spilt to kill the tsar, nothing had changed for the better.

Anarchists in other countries waged a similar war against the political establishment. Some of their successes were breath-taking. On 24 June 1894 a fervent Italian activist, Santo Caserio, approached the open-topped coach of the president of France, Marie-François-Sadi Carnot (1837–94). Hidden within a rolled-up newspaper Caserio held a dagger, and as he came within reach of the president he drew it out and stabbed Carnot, inflicting a fatal wound. Only six years later the king of Italy, Umberto I (r.1878–1900) was shot and killed by a revolver-wielding Anarchist called Gaetano Bresci. Umberto was not popular, and Bresci travelled from the United States specifically to commit this crime. After receiving life imprisonment, Bresci committed suicide.

Even the United States could not escape the international Anarchist revolution. Leon Czolgosz (1973–1901), an unbalanced individual and loyal Anarchist, had been greatly impressed by Bresci's act and by the praise that he had received in Anarchist publications worldwide. In 1901 he tried to get more involved in the American Anarchist movement, but his anti-social behaviour marked him out as a dangerous 'loose cannon'. This rejection by a group that rejected 'normal' society drove Czolgosz over the edge. Perhaps to prove his devotion to the cause, Czolgosz travelled to Buffalo in New York state and attended the Pan American exposition. There, on 6 September, he waited patiently in line with a crowd of well-wishers to shake hands with President William McKinley. As he stepped up to the president, he pulled out a revolver from a false bandage and shot him in the stomach. McKinley died eight days later, following abortive surgery. Czolgosz was convicted and sentenced to the electric chair on 29 October.

The Anarchists laboured under the same false assumption as had the medieval Assassins. They did not understand that murdering an individual member of a country's government or its royal family did not bring about the end of the post they held, and that this, with all its powers and responsibilities, survived intact. There would always be officials ready to step into the victim's shoes. Without a complimentary strategy of revolution, matching ruthless violence with clever political manoeuvring, these desperate and bloody attempts to cut off the head of the nation-state were doomed to failure.

One assassination carried out only a decade later had a tremendous impact. The carefully planned murder of the Austrian Archduke Franz Ferdinand on 28 June 1914 proved to be the spark that lit the touchpaper to war. His death provoked an immediate reaction from several European nations, and by August the continent had erupted into war. The uneasy settlement of the First World War led to the rise of Adolf Hitler and the emergence of Nazism. Historians accept that the Second World War was the result of the war of 1914–18. No other assassination in human history has been the cause of so much chaos, bloodshed and destruction. And yet the Anarchists who had been praying for such global catastrophe did not have a hand in this tragic murder.

The Archduke was visiting Sarajevo, the capital of Bosnia, with his wife Sophie. He was a powerful man and heir to the throne of the Austro-Hungarian Empire. This vast, imperial super-state overshadowed the politics of Eastern and Central Europe. However, a shadowy Serbian terror group, the Black Hand, had for several years waged a secret assassination campaign against the empire. It had tried (and failed) to assassinate the emperor himself in 1911. The leader of this murder cult was known to his operatives as 'Apis', but he was in reality Colonel Dragutin Dmitrievich. He specialized in recruiting youths to carry out the murders, and he looked out for boys who were suffering from tuberculosis. Since they were destined for an early grave, Apis convinced them that it was better to die in a blaze of glory, and each one swore an oath to the Black Hand.

As the archduke toured Sarajevo in his open-topped car, Apis had arranged for seven young assassins to be on the streets that day. Each carried a cyanide capsule to swallow if he was captured, in addition to pistols and hand grenades. The crowds lining the archduke's route were large enough to allow the Black Hand agents to mingle freely and find suitable places from which to launch an ambush, but a heavy police presence deterred several of the conspirators from attempting an attack. One of the boys took his chance and threw a grenade at the car, but it bounced off the bonnet and exploded on the road, wounding a soldier named Colonel Merizzi. Gavrilo Princip, one of the assassins further along the route, heard the explosion and assumed the Black Hand murder had succeeded. He found a nearby café and relaxed. Meanwhile the archduke decided to continue with his itinerary. He made his speech as arranged and then insisted on visiting the wounded Merizzi in hospital. As the car negotiated the streets of Sarajevo it was spotted by Princip outside the café. Immediately the boy drew his pistol and strode forward. He got off two well-aimed shots before he was captured. Ferdinand was badly wounded in the neck and he lived just long enough to watch his beloved wife, Sophie, die in his lap. She had taken the second deadly bullet. Despite swallowing his cyanide capsule as arranged, Gavrilo Princip survived the poison and eventually died in prison during the world war he had helped to start.

MURDER AND MODERN TERROR

Anarchism lost much of its impetus in the years following the First World War. Yet the tactics of terror would not be forgotten. The modern era has seen the shocking assassination of several powerful political personalities. Three major types of terrorist killer can be identified. There are the left-wing revolutionary terrorist groups, the Islamic paramilitary factions and a plethora of nationalist or separatist terrorist groups.

In 1978 the Italian Red Brigades illustrated just how ruthless and well organized the modern assassin could be. On 16 March they first kidnapped and then murdered the prominent Italian politician (and five-times premier) Aldo Moro (1916–78). Moro was a landmark in the nation's turbulent political landscape, the leader of the Christian Democrat Party and the most highly favoured of the candidates for the Italian presidency. His successful attempts to unite various warring political parties seemed destined to usher in a new era of left-wing accommodation, but his crucial compromise agreement with the Communist Party signalled to the uncompromising terror groups, the Red Brigades, that they could expect no sympathy from any quarter. For this work, Aldo Moro was to be targeted for assassination.

The Red Brigades had originally been formed in the early 1970s in the bloody wake of the first attacks by the Red Army Faction (also known as the Baader-Meinhof gang). Unlike the RAF, the Red Brigades lacked both central control and unity of purpose. What they lacked in sophisticated organization, however, they made up for in violent abandon. At the end of the 1970s around 2000 Red Brigade attacks were being made every year, with politicians and judges forming the bulk of the brigades' victims.

Moro was sitting in the back seat of his chauffeur-driven car on 16 March when the killers struck. With him were two armed bodyguards. A follow-up car containing three more bodyguards followed closely behind. At an intersection, the two cars were forced to come to a stop by another car emerging suddenly from a side street. They were boxed in. A large number of terrorists (perhaps a dozen or more) ran towards the trapped cars. Many opened fire with automatic weapons and quickly shot dead the five outnumbered and out-gunned bodyguards. Moro was captured alive, dragged from the car and hauled off at speed to a secret prison. A great deal of planning had gone into the successful operation. Once a suitable ambush site was selected, one possible obstacle, a van parked outside the owner's shop, had to be eliminated. To this end the terrorists located the van's night-time parking place; they then slashed all four of its tyres the night before the raid. Moro now became a pawn in the political game played so fanatically by the brigades. They believed that the commitment of the Communist Party to the multi-party agreement would falter under such pressure. The brigades miscalculated.

By the start of May the security forces had still been unable to track down Moro or his kidnappers. The Red Brigades had meanwhile released pictures of their prisoner in captivity as well as letters from Moro that called for the authorities to recognize the demands of the terrorists. They demanded the immediate release of several Red Brigade prisoners from Italian jails. On 18 April the terrorists provided proof that their captive was still alive (by photographing him with the daily newspaper) and warned the government that Moro had only forty-eight hours to live. The government refused to accede to their demands, and further attempts to negotiate Moro's release ended in failure. On 5 May the terrorists again warned that Moro was to be killed, and four days later the world was shocked to learn that the terror group had actually carried out the murder. The body of the politician was found stuffed into the boot of an car that had been abandoned halfway between the Communist and Christian Democrat Party offices. He had been shot repeatedly.

Several years later the gunman who was suspected of pulling the trigger on Aldo Moro was captured and convicted. His name was Prospero Gallinari. More than thirty other Red Brigade terrorists were convicted for their part in the murder, some of them women. The repercussions of the Aldo Moro killing were not those foreseen by the Red Brigades. Although political turmoil did ensue, the terror group was no nearer to inciting revolution than it had been in the mid-1970s. Although the experience should have taught the left-wing terrorists a lesson in the futility of political assassination, it did not, and the immense weight of public opinion turned against the movement. By the mid-1980s the Red Brigades had been all but smashed.

Revolutionary assassinations were being attempted all over Europe. Among many other victims, the RAF murdered the industrialist Hans-Martin Schleyer in October 1977 and Günter von Drenkmann, president of the supreme court, in November 1974. The international revolutionary terrorist, Carlos ('The Jackal') Marighella, tried to murder Joseph 'Teddy' Sieff on New Year's Eve 1973. Sieff was the wealthy and influential president of Marks & Spencer. Action Directe assassinated the

French general René Audran in 1985 and Georges Besse, the chairman of Renault, the following year. The Greek terror group, November 17, has murdered a number of VIPs, including Richard Welch, the CIA station chief in Athens, and Pavlos Bakoyannis, a prominent member of the Greek parliament. In Spain, the First of October Anti-Fascist Group (GRAPO), has selectively assassinated several military commanders, as well as the head of the Spanish prison service. Despite the murderous roll-call, none of the much vaunted objectives of these ultra-left-wing terror groups have ever been realized. As a mark of violent protest, the murder of prominent figures has successfully thrust these organizations into the media spotlight. As a method of overthrowing Western capitalist society, however, the murders have proved tragically pointless.

The practice of assassination has not been confined to the continent of Europe, of course. Many political murders have taken place in the Middle East, the home of the original Nizari Ismaili. One of the most savage insurrections of the 1990s has taken place in Algeria. There, a catalogue of government and terrorist atrocity has been punctuated by a shocking series of high-profile murders. The assassinations continue to the present day, with the West seemingly indifferent to the killings. Other struggles in the Middle East, some more complex, others much longer running, have been a catalyst for innumerable bouts of directed violence – many times directed at a mistrusted leadership.

In recent decades a number of Arab leaders have been targeted by their own people for coming to some agreement with the government of Israel. To some Muslim hardliners this is tantamount to forging a pact with the devil. Anwar Sadat, president of Egypt since 1970, earned the warm praise of the international community for his efforts during the Camp David Accords, and for the part he played during the negotiations, Sadat was able to share the 1978 Nobel Peace Prize with the Israeli prime minister, Menachem Begin. This peaceful accommodation with the Israelis did not please everyone, however. A hard core of Islamic fundamentalists within Egypt's armed forces were vehemently opposed to the new order, and they were determined to make their displeasure known. Sadat understood the danger he faced. He told his wife on one occasion: 'No one will kill me, Jehan, unless it is the fundamentalists.'

They struck on 6 October 1981. The event chosen as the venue for the assassination was a military parade taking place in Cairo on that day. Security around the parade was tight, and Sadat felt secure from any threat. When it came, the attack proved highly unexpected. With jets roaring overhead and long columns of army vehicles streaming past, there was no one who expected that the parade itself would conceal an assassination team. A truck came to a sudden halt opposite the podium on which sat President Sadat and a large contingent of Egyptian dignitaries. Out of it came an army officer, Lieutenant Khaled el-Islambouly, and three soldiers, all armed. Sadat stood up, ready to salute the officer in what he considered to be a part of the official proceedings, but one of the team lobbed a couple of grenades towards the stand. One exploded short of the president, the other proved to be a dud. The shocked audience was not to be spared, however. The soldiers opened up on the crowd with automatic weapons. More than thirty people were badly wounded, and eleven were killed instantly or died later from their wounds. President Anwar Sadat was one of those eleven. Despite emergency surgery carried out by some of Cairo's top specialists, Sadat died only two hours after the shooting.

The assassins had made their point, but they were apprehended and sentenced to death. As many as 800 other people were implicated in the conspiracy to murder Sadat. The inquiry, led by President Mubarak (Sadat's successor), seemed to be in danger of becoming a purge. Despite a swift and thorough investigation, which laid the blame for the murders at the feet of a sect called the Takfir Wal-Hajira, Egyptian fundamentalism survived. The attempt of the killers (according to Mubarak) had been to assassinate the entire Egyptian cabinet and replace it with an Iranian-style Islamic state. Without the popular support that so few terrorist groups enjoyed, the assassination (in isolation) meant nothing. There could be no revolution without an uprising and so the fundamentalist state so earnestly fought for by Takfir Wal-Hajira would always remain an unattainable goal. The 1990s saw a resurgence in fundamentalist terror attacks, directed not against the Egyptian government but against the economy. Indiscriminate attacks on tourists have taken place infrequently, culminating with the terrible slaughter of more than sixty tourists at the Temple of Queen Hatshepsut in late 1997.

For the British people political assassination has often been associated with the Irish republican movement. Queen Victoria felt the sting of Irish politics in 1849, and since 1969 the conflict in Northern Ireland has left an indelible mark on British history. Northern Ireland (known also, though inaccurately, as Ulster) is an integral part of the United Kingdom, with a population split between Protestant 'unionists' and Catholic 'nationalists'. Where politics and violence meet, the paramilitary terror groups thrive, and pre-eminent among them are the unionist Ulster Defence Association (UDA) and the nationalist Irish Republican Army (IRA). Both groups have maimed, tortured and murdered through three decades of unrelenting and unresolved struggle. The IRA quickly brought their campaign of terror to the British mainland in a crude effort to force the hand of the government at Westminster, but bombs and mortar attacks have done little to sway either public or political opinion. If anything, British resolve has been hardened by these attacks. This has even been the case when individual political figures have been targeted by the IRA or other, equally violent, republican factions.

On 30 March 1979 a Conservative Member of Parliament, Airey Neave, was killed in a sophisticated car bomb explosion as he left the House of Commons. Neave supported Margaret Thatcher in her bid to become Britain's first female prime minister. As her principal adviser on Irish matters, Neave recommended a hardline military approach to the Northern Ireland problem, a stance that inevitably attracted the attention of the IRA. If, and when, Thatcher won the election, many experts predicted that Neave would be installed as secretary of state for Northern Ireland. The twisted wreckage of his car was removed from the ramp leading out of the underground car park of the Palace of Westminster. Investigators discovered that the explosives packed under the car had been detonated by a mercury tilt-switch, carefully calibrated to respond to the ramp of the car park.

It was soon clear, however, that the IRA had not planted the bomb that killed Neave. The blame fell on a radical splinter group calling itself the Irish National Liberation Army (INLA). The assassination had been a successful bid to beat the IRA to a prime target and an attempt to usurp some of the gruesome notoriety normally acquired by the IRA.

Not to be outdone, the IRA planned its own high-profile assassination. They upped the stakes and struck directly at Britain's oldest and most revered institution, the royal family. Earl Mountbatten was the cousin of the queen, and he had served with great distinction in the Far East during the Second World War. The earl spent every summer at a quiet retreat at Cassiebawn Castle in Ireland, and although he was offered protection he never considered himself a terrorist target. The retired earl spent his days sailing and fishing, and on 27 August 1979, only five months after the spectacular murder of Airey Neave, Mountbatten's yacht *Shadow V* was blown to smithereens by an IRA bomb hidden away in the vessel's engine room. The bomb-makers were honing their craft – the detonation had been activated by a radio signal transmitted by an IRA terrorist on the cliffs across the bay.

Seventy-nine-year old Earl Mountbatten died instantly, along with his grandson and a young boat boy. In addition, four of his party were badly wounded, one dying in hospital the next day. The assassination hit headlines around the world and horrified the British public. So what was the point, in view of the subsequent bad publicity? Mountbatten had long since retired and had made no statements about Irish politics, yet as a target he seemed to have everything the killers needed. Connected by blood to the monarch, he was virtually a piece of British history, having personally managed the negotiations that resulted in Indian independence. Above all, however, he was vulnerable. Several people were arrested in connection with the murder, including Thomas McMahon, a known member of the IRA. Forensic evidence connected him indisputably to the bombing of the *Shadow V* and he was imprisoned for life.

It seemed that bombs were the way forward for the IRA, and the prime minister, Margaret Thatcher, who assumed office in May 1979, was only too aware of this threat. With the murder of Airey Neave she had lost a close friend, and the dangers of complacency had been hammered home in no uncertain terms. On entering office Margaret Thatcher immediately procured two armoured limousines for Downing Street use. She expanded the Special Branch detachment assigned to guard important MPs from around a dozen officers (during the Wilson era) to over a hundred. Iron gates were installed at the vulnerable end of Downing Street to limit access to the prime minister's front door. A metal detector also appeared behind the door of Number 10 to scan individuals as they entered the prime minister's residence. Armed policewomen were introduced into the close protection entourage of both the queen and the prime minister. A core of Special Branch detectives assigned to the protection of political VIPs was trained in (and armed with) the concealable Heckler and Koch MP5K machine pistol. The Army's élite Special Air Service (SAS) Regiment began to train selected police officers in their role as bodyguards for 'high risk' politicians and members of the royal family. Bag searches, body searches, metal detectors and X-ray machines would, in the Thatcher era, become sensible precautions adopted during the visits of foreign leaders and at political conferences. Despite these extensive precautions (some taken after 1984), however, the IRA made a shocking attempt to wipe out the entire Conservative cabinet with the detonation of a single bomb.

The Brighton bomb became a pivotal point in Margaret Thatcher's years in office. Her image as the Iron Lady achieved a ready lustre when the military gamble to retake the Falkland Islands in 1982 paid off, and as a survivor of the 1984 Brighton hotel bomb, the Iron Lady seemed armour-plated. A number of other Conservative politicians were not so lucky. The seaside town of Brighton serves as the traditional venue for the party's annual conference, and in 1984 many of the delegates and members of the cabinet were staying at the Grand Hotel. In the early hours of 12 October, as some guests slept and as others socialized in the hotel's bar, an IRA 'sleeper' bomb exploded several stories up, ripping out the guts of the building and causing several floors to collapse. More than thirty people were injured; four were killed. Margaret Thatcher was lucky to escape serious injury or death after she walked out of the bathroom which, seconds later, was crushed by the floors collapsing above.

The bomb had actually been hidden inside room 629 three weeks before the conference was due to begin. According to one estimate, it had been specifically set to explode 24 days, 6 hours and 36 minutes after being primed. This would result in the bomb exploding at 2:45 a.m. on the last night of the Conservative conference. The device, 14 kilograms (more than 30 pounds) of Irish Frangex high explosive, had been wrapped in cling-film before being hidden. This may have prevented sniffer dogs from detecting its distinctive odour. Other methods of bomb detection were not employed, and could have included chemical detection (to pick up traces of the Frangex), radio detection and even battery pulse detection (used to locate the low-level emissions of timer batteries).

Eight months later, Patrick Magee and three accomplices were arrested in Glasgow and charged with the bombing of the Grand Hotel. They were captured along with 60 kilograms (more than 130 pounds) of plastic explosive and detailed plans for an audacious bombing campaign that would have devastated a number of seaside resorts around Britain. This, however, seemed to be only the feint for an assassination plot to murder SAS-veteran (and later Gulf War commander) Major-General Sir Peter de la Billière as well as a number of other high profile individuals. One of these individuals was the Queen Mother, who was to have been assassinated with an Armalite AR-150 assault rifle as she walked in the grounds of Balmoral Castle. Peter Sherry, an IRA killer known as the 'Armalite Kid', was to have carried out this grisly murder.

The use of assassination as a tool of politics – as a weapon – is indiscriminate. One might think that the carefully planned murder of a specific individual should be anything but indiscriminate. The reality is that the aftermath of a political assassination is always unpredictable and dangerous. Anyone trying to change political or public opinion through the use of deadly violence is desperate indeed – but this should hardly come as a surprise. A number of odd assassination outcomes have proved revealing about the direct and the indirect effects of this particular crime. Governor George Wallace was shot and paralysed by loner Arthur Bremer in 1972, and the experience transformed Wallace's personal outlook. From being a fierce supporter of segregation, Wallace mellowed, and later won the governorship of Alabama with the help of the Black vote. Even a successful murder might have the opposite effect to that intended. The Anarchist murder of Tsar Alexander II in 1881 did not achieve any material or political benefit for the downtrodden Russian peasantry. Rather it paved the way for the dour Alexander III, who blocked any proposal for reform and virtually annihilated the revolutionary groups that were attempting to overthrow the monarchy.

Like a stone tossed into a pond, each assassination sends shock waves out into the society in which it takes place. What happens after the murder depends on a number of factors, ranging from success (was the victim wounded or killed?), public opinion, international sentiment, the quality of any official post-assassination investigation and the policies of the victim's successor. The affiliations and intentions of the killer further complicate the matter. It is no wonder then that despite the thousands of people who would wish to see a prominent political figure dead, only a tiny minority of unbalanced and lonely people pick up a gun and make an attempt. For terrorist groups, the pitfalls of assassination are identical, yet these desperate organizations have continued to shoot and bomb their way across the political spectrum. This unique type of warfare began many years ago, yet in all that time not a single urban revolution has ever succeeded.

Can the assassin alter events? Can he – or she – change history? The British prime minister Benjamin Disraeli was convinced that he could not, and several assassinations seem to back up this theory. In the immediate aftermath of President Kennedy's death his policies were faithfully continued by the new president, Lyndon Johnson. The Muslim Assassins of Persia carried out a number of political murders, none of which brought about the end of the Ottoman Empire, their intended goal. The murder of Julius Caesar did not banish the threat of tyranny but merely kept it at bay for a further twenty years. And in the nineteenth century the assassination of Abraham Lincoln had no other effect than the creation of the presidential secret service.

But then there are assassinations that provoke powerful reactions, which have, quite literally, changed the course of history. If Philip II of Macedon had not been murdered, would his son Alexander the Great have marched the Macedonian army across the known world? The calculated murder of Archduke Franz Ferdinand certainly altered world history, initiating one of the bloodiest wars in human history. Some historians trace the rise of Japanese militarism in the 1930s to the murder of prime minister Tsuyoshi Inukai Ki.

The powerful effect that a single assassination can have has been witnessed with alarming regularity in the political cauldrons of Israel and Northern Ireland. With peace negotiations making headway and with necessary compromises following in their wake, any aggrieved individual can take a gun and 'make a statement' through murder. Passions on both sides are inflamed, and the process of peace seems doomed. Fortunately, despite numerous bombings and the spectacular assassination of prime minister Yitzhak Rabin in 1995 by a discontented Israeli fanatic, both Irish and Israeli peace initiatives have weathered the attempts at destabilization. As peace takes one step forwards, the assassin tries to force it back by another two steps. Assassination can change history, and every assassin believes that he or she is in control.

Conclusion

That which does not kill us, makes us stronger

Friedrich Wilhelm Nietzsche

The cult of assassination has a long pedigree, with its origins in the remote and unrecorded past. Its victims have included men of peace, men of war, innocents, tyrants and intellectuals. Surely, with such a terrifying litany of death and despair over the centuries, some lesson has at last been learned. What do the lessons of history teach us if not the folly of ignoring what has gone before? From our perspective, standing tall on 5000 years of history, we can certainly recognize four key features, which every potential victim of assassination should bear in mind. These four features are certainty, predictability, warning and security.

CERTAINTY

It is certain that fame will increase a victim's chances of being assassinated. Being in the public eye marks that individual out as someone special, as someone important — a celebrity or a VIP. One way to try to avoid assassination is to shun such status. There have been many people who have become (or have narrowly avoided becoming) victims because of their fame. Gianni Versace, the Italian fashion designer, was murdered outside the gates of his mansion in 1997 by a disturbed serial killer. Versace was a successful businessman, a multi-millionaire, a celebrity and an icon. He was murdered not because of his views or his policies, but because of his fame. In the following year, film director Steven Spielberg revealed that he had been working with the police to protect himself and his family from the threats of a stalker. This psychotic individual had threatened to abduct Spielberg and then sexually assault him. The Hollywood film-maker feared for the lives of his wife and children and was forced to turn his mansion into a fortress, recruiting an army of security specialists and bodyguards.

Of course, there is little that these two men could have done to avoid the attentions of these unbalanced men. The writer Salman Rushdie, however, whom we briefly discussed in Chapter 5, became the target for Muslim assassination because of what he had written. His novel *Satanic Verses* takes a cutting and satirical look at some aspects of the Muslim religion. There are those who argue that, as a former practising Muslim, Rushdie brought down the *fatwa* upon himself. This, of course, presupposes that Rushdie could have anticipated the extreme reaction to his words. Many writers have received a painful reminder in the aftermath of the *Satanic Verses* affair: it does not do to offend the sensibilities of a powerful international group capable of terrorist assassination. But for many writers and journalists the belief in freedom of speech far outweighs the threat of assassination.

It should be noted that journalists in Britain have often come under attack from groups based in this country. Anti-fascist journalists such as Nik Toczek, courageously committing their views to print, have been targeted by neo-Nazis groups, led, until recently, by Combat 18. In several instances hit lists of anti-fascist writers have appeared in Combat 18's magazine *Stormer*. These lists carried their names, telephone numbers and addresses. Alongside was the ominous message: 'Redwatch. You have the Addresses. Now get the Scum.'

Accepting a position of authority can also draw fire from antagonists of that position. The office of the secretary of state for Northern Ireland, for example, carries with it a formidable security presence, irrespective of which individual is holding the post. Often, when an increasing amount of power is invested in one particular position, a backlash can occur. Jealousy, hatred, ambition and frustration can all provoke a potential assassin. Tyrants, those who hold all the reins of power, rarely sleep peacefully at night. Caesar, Hitler, Trujillo and any one of the many Japanese feudal lords lived in the shadow of imminent assassination.

For the cautious and the wise, this lesson is easily appreciated. Caesar's successor, Augustus, worked over a period of years to carry on from where his mentor Julius Caesar had left off. He made every effort to disguise his moves, ensuring that his dictatorship was marked by a freedom and power-sharing that the Roman people could more easily stomach. That his ploy succeeded can perhaps be judged by the record of attempts on his life over the forty-one years of his reign. There were none.

PREDICTABILITY

Any potential victim can minimize the success of an attack by making his movements as unpredictable as possible. Hitler survived several attempts because of his sudden changes of plan. The assassin needs to select an opportunity carefully, and if no opportunity arises the assassination has already been foiled. Those would-be victims who follow set routines make the killer's task easy; those who travel along set routes without adequate security are providing the assassin with the perfect opportunity. Only by changing the route of his procession at the last minute did Tsar Alexander II avoid a large bomb that had previously been planted under the road. Carrero Blanco, the Spanish prime minister who was destined to succeed General Franco as head of state, fell victim to the very same murder technique in 1973. The prime minister visited the same Roman Catholic church in Madrid, the San Francisco de Borja, every morning. Accordingly, his assassins, members of the Basque terror group ETA, had months to plan and organize the killing. They rented a basement close to the church and dug a tunnel out beneath the road. Every morning, after mass, Carrero Blanco's car passed overhead. After a sizeable amount of explosive had been smuggled into the cellar, the bomb was planted beneath the road and primed ready for detonation. On 20 December 1973 the bomb exploded, blowing a huge crater in the street, throwing parts of the scrapped car high over the roofs and killing the prime minister, his driver and bodyguard.

The terrorist leader Ali Hassan Salameh died in similar circumstances. His use of the same route by car through the war-torn streets of Beirut gave Israel's security forces the perfect opportunity to finally kill him. Believed to have been the mastermind behind the 1972 Munich Olympic massacre, Salameh had eluded the Israeli secret service for seven years. Once located, however, the Israeli agents planted a powerful car bomb in the street used by Salameh on a regular basis. As he drove past, the bomb was command detonated by one of the team-members, killing Salameh outright.

Lee Harvey Oswald could not have wished for more advance warning of President Kennedy's Dallas itinerary. The president's planned route through the city and into Dealey Plaza was detailed in the Dallas newspapers three days earlier. Today such advance notification of routes to be travelled would never be allowed. Any close protection agency that takes its job seriously tries to release as little information as possible to as few people as possible.

WARNING

Those assassins who are committed to murdering their intended target for a clearly defined purpose may often give some prior indication of their attack. Sometimes it may be no more than a hate campaign that a leader ignores at his peril. Other times it might actually be a failed assassination attempt. Rather than make rapid changes to either itinerary or security, many would-be victims count their lucky stars and get on with life. The assassins then try again and this time do not botch the job. Malcolm X must have wondered about the safety of attending Harlem's Audubon Ballroom in 1965 to address a crowd of supporters, when only seven days earlier he and his family had been lucky to survive a fire-bomb attack. 'It doesn't frighten me,' he said simply. 'It doesn't quieten me down in any way or shut me up.' John Wilkes Booth made no secret of his intentions to kidnap President Lincoln. Booth could often be found drinking around town, and as the alcohol removed his inhibitions he would loudly tell anyone who would listen what he thought of Lincoln and what he wanted to do to him.

Julius Caesar had several warnings about his impending doom (and not all from soothsayers), and John F. Kennedy knew full well the risks he was taking by visiting Texas in 1963. Advisers had warned him that the right-wing, gun-toting state would not give the president much of a warm welcome during his November visit. Despite such warnings, many victims have preferred to trust to fate rather than their own common sense. Queen Victoria was the victim of several failed attempts, but at no time were her security procedures (such as they were) reviewed or improved. She had even spotted the same face in the crowd on separate occasions. This was unusual, she knew, yet she failed to take precautionary measures. Her Majesty was head of state and head of the Church, and put her faith (and her life) in God's hands.

The common philosophy of the threatened VIP is a shrug of the shoulders and a defeatist 'if it happens, it happens' approach. Lord Mountbatten was just as fatalistic, asking those who wanted him to maintain some protection against the IRA, 'What would they want with an old man like me?' Even level-headed and politically aware Robert Kennedy had no words of wisdom on this subject. Considering the terrible fate that had befallen his brother, the senator seems to have had no interest in his personal safety. 'If anyone wants to kill me, it won't be difficult,' he once said. Yoko Ono, asked to comment about the murder of John Lennon, said 'There can be one crank anywhere,' almost as if assassination itself was some indiscriminate angel of death.

But assassins are never indiscriminate – this is what defines them as such – they are human beings, men and women, carrying knives, guns or detonators. They want to kill an individual and will try their utmost to achieve that goal.

SECURITY

One of the most crucial lessons to be learned by the potential victim is that security is paramount. But security often has to be balanced with other considerations. In Western democracies, the political necessity to get out and meet the people clashes head-on with the duty of the close protection officer, who, along with his colleagues, must ensure that no opportunity presents itself for a would-be assassin to strike. While the enthusiastic politician shakes hands, waves and chats with a crowd of well-wishers, the bodyguard is furiously scanning the crowd, watching the hands, looking for familiar faces, for guns, for strange behaviour.

Despots and crime lords rarely balk at surrounding themselves with armed guards. They have no public sensibilities to offend. Those political heavy-weights who *do* require them sometimes ignore the advice of their advisers and refuse to be surrounded by soldiers, bodyguards or detectives. President Lincoln despised his military bodyguard, which he said made him feel like a European emperor, and he used regularly to ask his coachman to try and outrun the escorting cavalry troopers. His assassination led directly to the establishment of the US Secret Service.

Bodyguards have often been seen as just another trapping of office, along with the perception that the greater the number of guards, the greater the ego of the personality being protected. In previous eras this has forced many VIPs to forgo the kind of close protection needed. Some individuals revel in the size of their entourage. Certain notorious pop stars regularly hit the headlines when the antics of their security team ruffles feathers. Even heads of state have been known to go over the top: the Libyan dictator Colonel Gaddafi once attended an Arab conference in the company of a bodyguard made up wholly of female soldiers. With an ever vigilant and ever critical media machine poised for scandal, the boorish behaviour of a fanatical close protection team can inflict serious harm to a VIP's image. Image is everything. Better to look accessible, friendly and open, than guarded, suspicious and frightened. And as Lincoln once commented: 'If I wore a shirt of mail and kept myself surrounded by a bodyguard, it would all be the same.' Many politicians would agree with Lincoln.

Today, the power of the media is universally recognized, but so is the power of the assassin. Modern close protection teams attempt to mate subtlety with security. Bodyguards wear suits and often try to appear as advisers or other officials. Women are used more often, and the bodyguards take up a position both in front of and behind the 'principle' (as professional bodyguards refer to the potential assassination victim). The modern close protection team tries to stay one step ahead of any assassin, searching buildings for bombs, keeping itineraries secret, using backup or decoy cars, cutting short potentially dangerous 'walkabouts' if need be and taking photographs of the crowds (to be compared with photographs of other crowds at other events in order to locate recurring, and therefore suspicious, faces).

It should also be noted that it is sometimes one's own bodyguards who make the most efficient assassins. Who else can get in so close to carry out the murder? Who else has complete access to – and can sometimes even control – the principle's itinerary? President Sadat was ambushed by his own troops during a military parade. India's prime minister, Indira Ghandi, was murdered on 31 October 1984 by one of her own Sikh bodyguards. India was in turmoil following an army raid on the most holy temple of the Sikh religion, the Golden Temple at Amritsar. Sikh opposition to the government turned violent, and yet Indira Ghandi refused to have a number of Sikhs within her personal bodyguard removed. This decision cost the prime minister her life.

A great many Roman emperors became victims of the Praetorian Guard, that body of hand-picked troops with the sole purpose of protecting the emperor and his family. Following the death of Caligula, it was actually the Praetorian Guard who discovered the feeble and frightened Claudius cowering in a wing of the imperial palace and who placed him on the throne. This started a precedent. Over the course of two centuries the Praetorian Guard had the opportunity to make and unmake emperors, murdering those of whom it grew weary. The emperor Pertinax was put onto the throne by the Praetorian Guard after its commander-in-chief had murdered emperor Commodus. When Pertinax showed signs of being an able ruler who wanted to make reductions to Rome's military forces, the Guard turned on him and paraded his head around the streets of Rome. According to tradition, the Praetorians then held up the empire of Rome for auction, finally handing it over to Didius Julianus in AD 193.

Certainty, predictability, warning and security — four lessons taught with blood over three millennia. Despite the lessons, assassinations and assassination attempts continue to make the news. The human hunger for power, in all its forms, pushes the desperate to take that ultimate step — to use murder as a step on the ladder to success.

Select Bibliography

Andrew, Christopher, and Gordievsky, Oleg, *KGB*, Hodder & Stoughton, London, 1990

Balsamo, W., and Carpozi Jr, George, *The Mafia*, Virgin Books, London, 1997

Balsiger, David, and Sellier Jr, Charles E., *The Lincoln Conspiracy*, Schick Sunn Classic Books, Los Angeles, 1977

Becker, J., *Hitler's Children: The Story of the Baader-Meinhof Gang*, Granada, London, 1977

Blakey, G. Robert, and Billings, Richard N., *Fatal Hour: The Assassination of President Kennedy by Organized Crime*, Berkley Books, New York, 1981

Braschlev, William, *The Don: The Life and Death of Sam Giancana*, Harper & Row, New York, 1977

Breitman, George, Porter, Herman and Smith, Baxter, *The Assassination of Malcolm X*, Pathfinder, New York, 1991

Bresler, Fenton, *Who Killed John Lennon?*, St Martin's Press, New York, 1989

Brogan, Patrick, *World Conflicts*, Bloomsbury, London, 1989

Bruce, Paul, *The Nemesis File*, Blake, London, 1995

Cassels, Lavender, *The Archduke and the Assassin*, Stein & Day, New York, 1984

Clarke, James W., *American Assassins: The Darker Side of Politics*, Princeton University Press, Princeton, New Jersey, 1982

Clarke, James W., *On Being Mad or Merely Angry: John Hinkley Jr, and Other Dangerous People*, Princeton University Press, Princeton, New Jersey, 1990

SELECT BIBLIOGRAPHY

Conquest, Robert, *The Great Terror: Stalin's Purges of the Thirties*, Macmillan, London, 1968

Conquest, Robert, *Stalin and the Kirov Murder*, Oxford University Press, Oxford, 1989

Courtney, Nicholas, *Princess Anne*, Weidenfeld & Nicolson, London, 1986

Davis, John H., *Mafia Kingfish — Carlos Marcello and the Assassination of John F. Kennedy*, McGraw Hill, New York, 1989

Downard, Shelby, *Sorcery, Sex, Assassination* (ed. Adam Parfrey), Apocalypse Culture, Amok Press, New York, 1993

Edington, Harry, *The Borgias*, Hamlyn, London, 1981

Elliott, Paul, *Warrior Cults*, Cassell, London, 1995

Elliott, Paul, *Brotherhoods of Fear*, Cassell, London, 1998

Garzetti, A., *From Tiberius to the Antonines*, Methuen, London, 1974

Geraghty, Tony, *The Bullet-Catchers*, Grafton, London, 1988

Gibbon, Edward, *The History of the Decline and Fall of the Roman Empire*, Dell Publishing Co., New York, 1963

Herman, Edward S., and Brodhead, Frank, *The Rise and Fall of the Bulgarian Connection*, Sheridan Square Publications, New York, 1986

Kaiser, Robert Blair, *'R.F.K. Must Die!'*, E.P. Dutton, New York, 1970

Kedward, Roderick, *The Anarchists,* Macdonald, London, 1971

Lane, Mark, and Gregory, Dick, *Murder in Memphis: The FBI and the Assassination of Martin Luther King*, Thunder's Mouth Press, New York, 1993

Lewis, B., *The Assassins: A Radical Sect in Islam*, Weidenfeld & Nicolson, London, 1967

Maclear, Michael, *Vietnam: The Ten Thousand Day War*, Eyre Methuen, London, 1981

Mallett, Michael, *The Borgias*, Barnes & Noble, New York, 1969

Marks, John, *The Search for the 'Manchurian Candidate'*, Allen Lane, London, 1979

Marrs, Jim, *Crossfire: The Plot That Killed Kennedy*, Carroll & Graf, New York, 1989

Meier, Christian, *Caesar*, HarperCollins, London, 1995

Menninger, Bonar, *Mortal Error: The Shot that Killed JFK*, Sidgwick & Jackson, London, 1992

Moss, R., *Urban Guerrillas: The New Face of Political Violence*, Temple Smith, London, 1972

Nash, Jay Robert, *World Encyclopedia of Organized Crime*, Headline Book Publishing, London, 1993

O'Brien, Joseph F. and Kurins, Andris, *Boss of Bosses*, Simon & Schuster, New York, 1991

Pasley, F.D., *Al Capone,* Faber & Faber, London, 1966

Payne, Robert, *The Life and Death of Trotsky*, McGraw-Hill, New York, 1977

Powers, Thomas, *The Man Who Kept the Secrets: Richard Helms and the CIA*, Pocket Books, New York, 1979

Rodriquez, Felix I., and Wiseman, John, *Shadow Warrior*, Graf, New York, 1992

Roscoe, Theodore, *The Web of Conspiracy: The Complete Story of the Men who Murdered Abraham Lincoln*, Prentice Hall, Englewood Cliffs, New Jersey, 1960

Ruthven, Malise, *A Satanic Affair*, Chatto & Windus, London, 1990

Scullard, H.H., *From the Gracchi to Nero. A History of Rome 133 BC to AD 68*, Routledge, London, 1982 (5th edn)

Segaller, Stephen, *Invisible Armies: Terrorism into the 1990s*, Sphere Books, London, 1987

Seth, Ronald, *Encyclopedia of Espionage*, Book Club Associates, London, 1974

Shirer, William L., *The Rise and Fall of the Third Reich*, Secker & Warburg, London, 1960

Short, Martin, *Crime Inc: The Story of Organized Crime*, London, 1984

Sifakis, Carl, *Encyclopedia of Assassinations*, Headline, London, 1993

Speriglio, Milo, *The Marilyn Conspiracy*, Pocket Books, New York, 1986

Suetonius, *The Twelve Caesars* (trans. R. Graves, revised M. Grant), Penguin Books, Harmondsworth, Middlesex, 1989

SELECT BIBLIOGRAPHY

Summers, Anthony, *Goddess: The Secret Lives of Marilyn Monroe*, Victor Gollancz, London, 1985

Summers, Anthony, *The Kennedy Conspiracy*, Paragon House, New York, 1989

Turnbull, Stephen, *Ninja: The True Story of Japan's Secret Warrior Cult*, Firebird Books, Poole, 1991

Turner, William, and Christian, Jonn, *The Assassination of Robert F. Kennedy: The Conspiracy and Coverup*, Thunder's Mouth Press, New York, 1993

Wilson, Colin, and Seaman, Donald, *Encyclopedia of Modern Murder 1962–1982*, Arthur Baker, London, 1983

Woodward, Bob, *Veil: The Secret Wars of the CIA 1981–1987*, Pocket Books, New York, 1987

Index